FAMILIAR FAVORITES

45 Timeless Stan

Arranged by Richard

Richard Bradley is one of the world's best-known and best-selling arrangers of piano music for print. His success can be attributed to years of experience as a teacher and his understanding of students' and players' needs. His innovative piano methods for adults (*Bradley's How to Play Piano* – Adult Books 1, 2, and 3) and kids (*Bradley for Kids* – Red, Blue, and Green Series) not only teach the instrument, but they also teach musicanship each step of the way.

Originally from the Chicago area, Richard completed his undergraduate and graduate work at the Chicago Conservatory of Music and Roosevelt University. After college, Richard became a print arranger for Hansen Publications and later became music director of Columbia Pictures Publications. In 1977, he co-founded his own publishing company, Bradley Publications, which is now exclusively distributed worldwide by Warner Bros. Publications.

Richard is equally well known for his piano workshops, clinics, and teacher training seminars. He was a panelist for the first and second Keyboard Teachers' National Video Conferences, which were attended by more than 20,000 piano teachers throughout the United States.

The home video version of his adult teaching method, *How to Play Piano With Richard Bradley*, was nominated for an American Video Award as Best Music Instruction Video, and, with sales climbing each year since its release, it has brought thousands of adults to—or back to—piano lessons. Still, Richard advises, "The video can only get an adult started and show them what they can do. As they advance, all students need direct input from an accomplished teacher."

Additional Richard Bradley videos aimed at other than the beginning pianist include *How to Play Blues Piano* and *How to Play Jazz Piano*. As a frequent television talk show guest on the subject of music education, Richard's many appearances include "Hour Magazine" with Gary Collins, "The Today Show," and "Mother's Day" with former "Good Morning America" host Joan Lunden, as well as dozens of local shows.

Project Manager: Tony Esposito

Contents

Over the Rainbow

From the Motion Picture *The Wizard of Oz*

Lyric by E.Y. HARBURG
Music by HAROLD ARLEN
Arranged by Richard Bradley

1.
C
2.
C
by.
true.
Some - day I'll wish up - on a star and
1
3
5
3
5

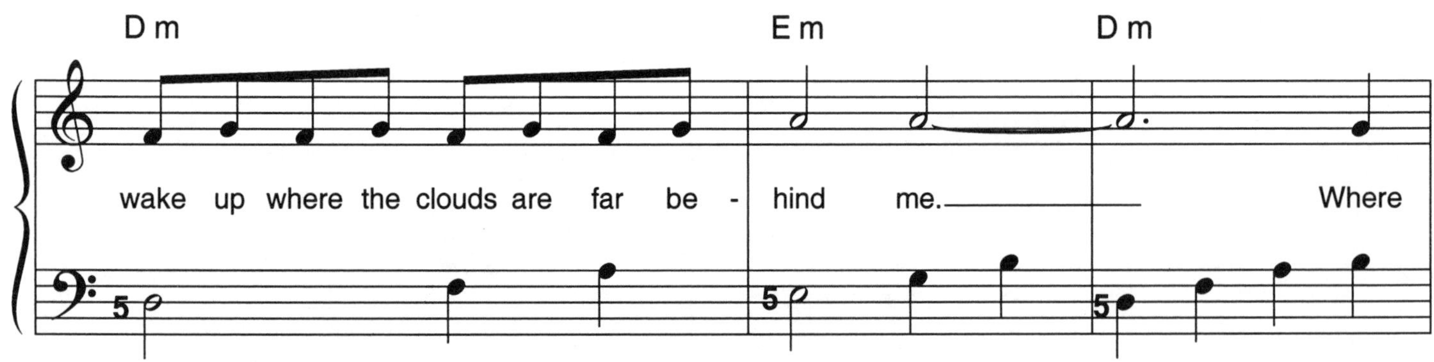
D m
E m
D m
wake up where the clouds are far be - hind me. Where
5
5
5

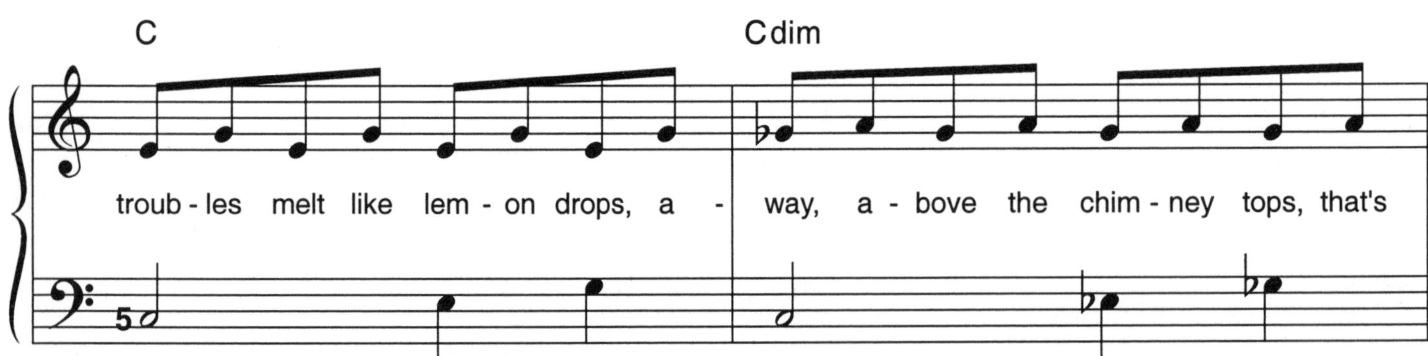
C
Cdim
troub - les melt like lem - on drops, a - way, a - bove the chim - ney tops, that's
5

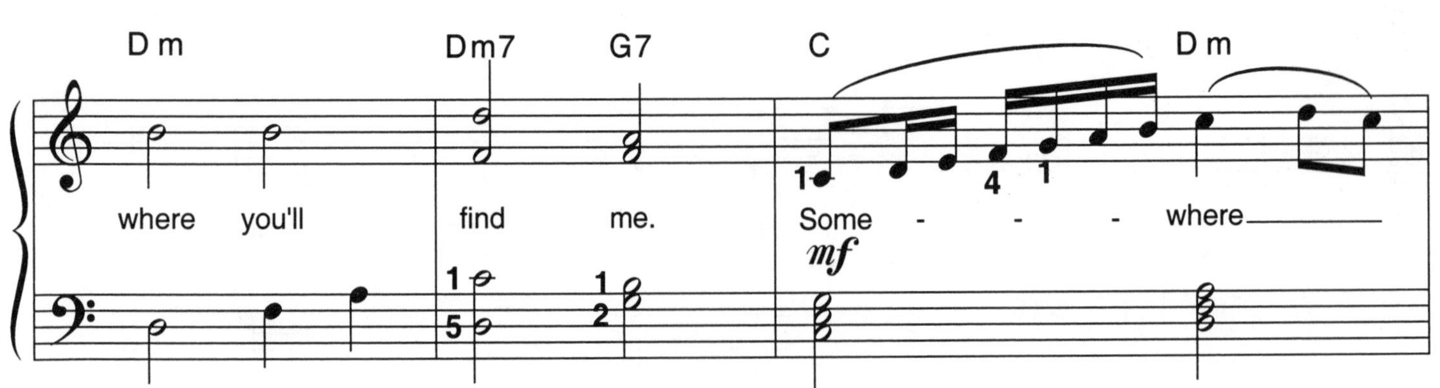
D m
Dm7
G7
C
D m
where you'll find me.
Some - - - where
mf
1
4
1
1
5
1
2

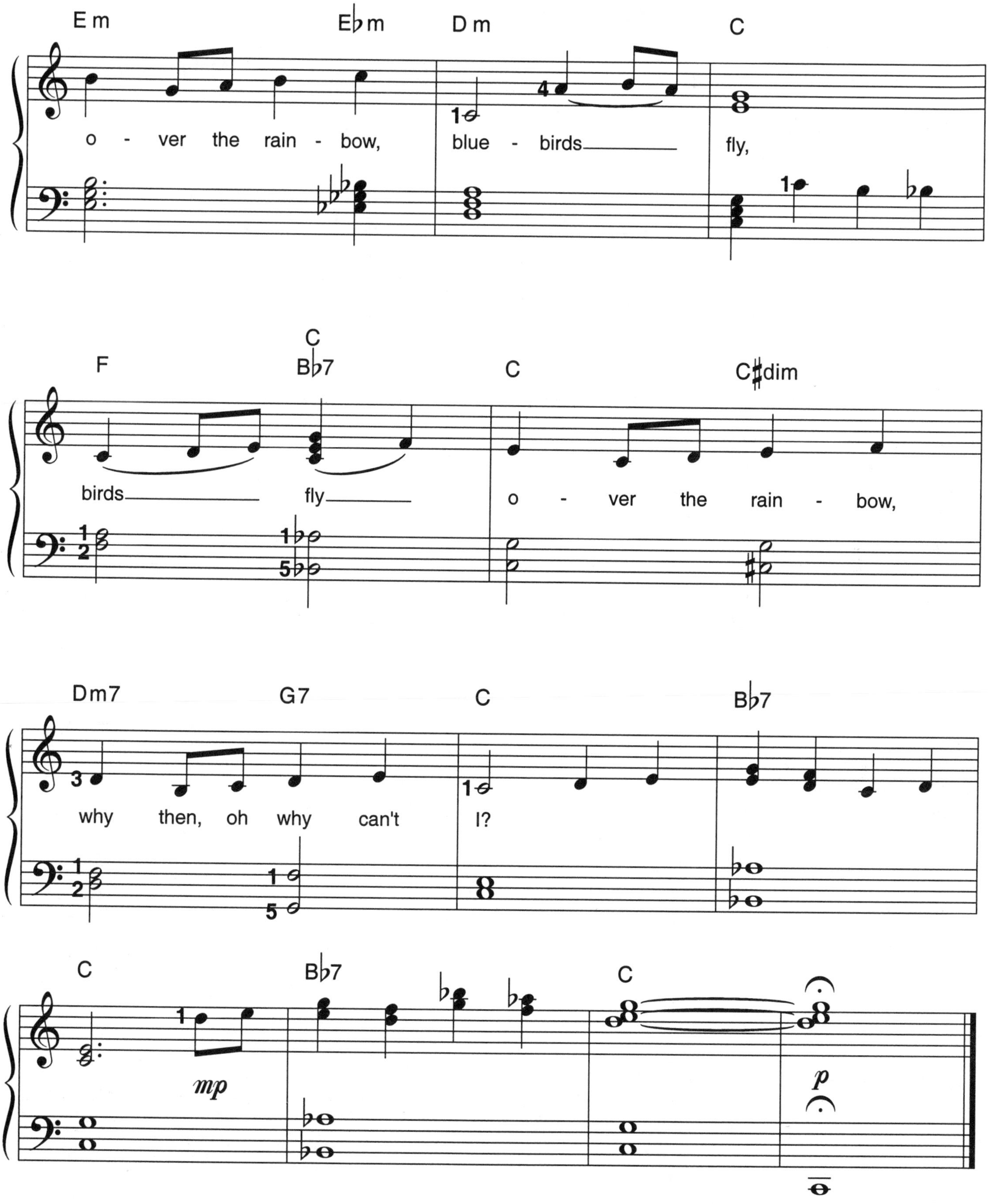

Em
E♭m
Dm
C
o - ver the rain - bow,
blue - birds
fly,
F
C
B♭7
C
C♯dim
birds
fly
o - ver the rain - bow,
Dm7
G7
C
B♭7
why then, oh why can't
I?
C
B♭7
C
mp
p

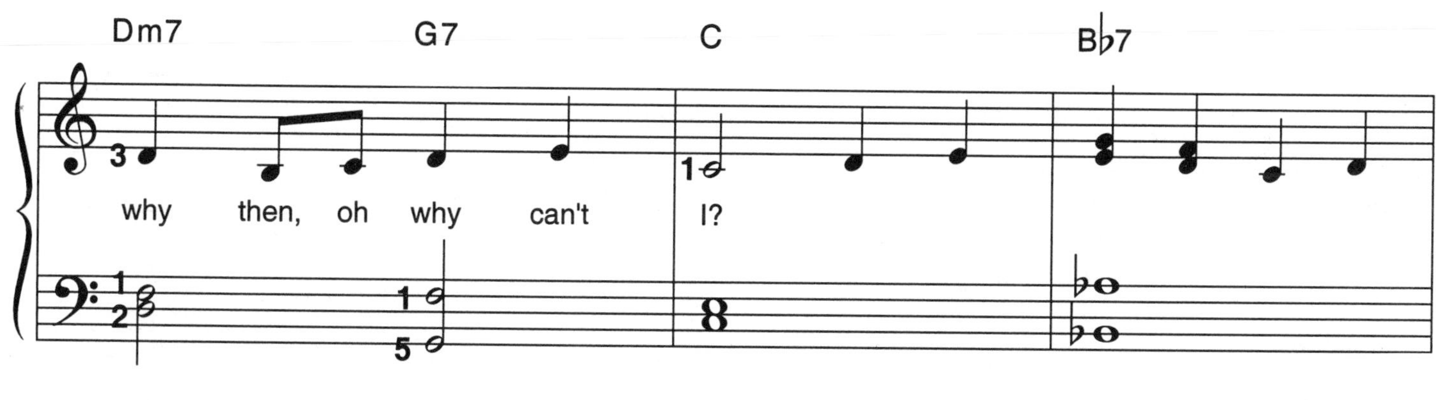

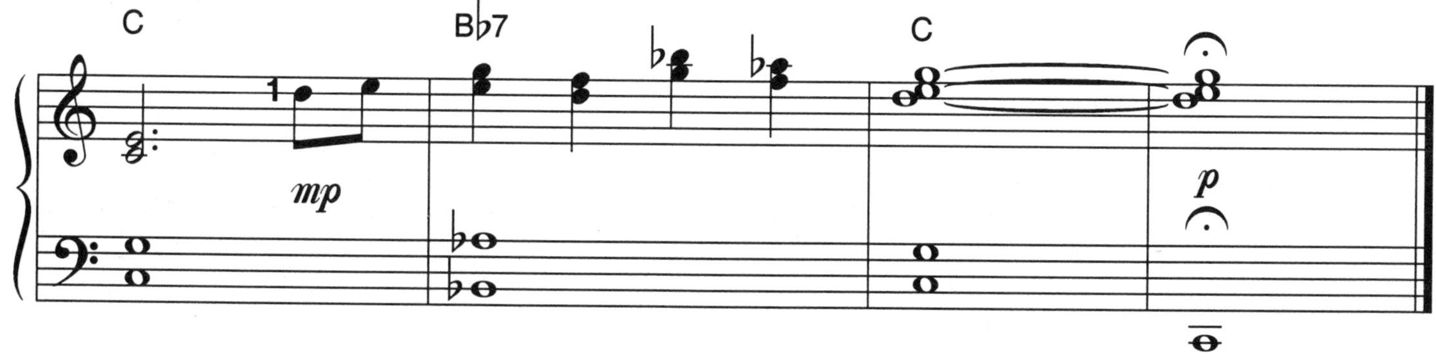

As Time Goes By

From the Motion Picture *Casablanca*

Words and Music by
HERMAN HUPFELD
Arranged by Richard Bradley

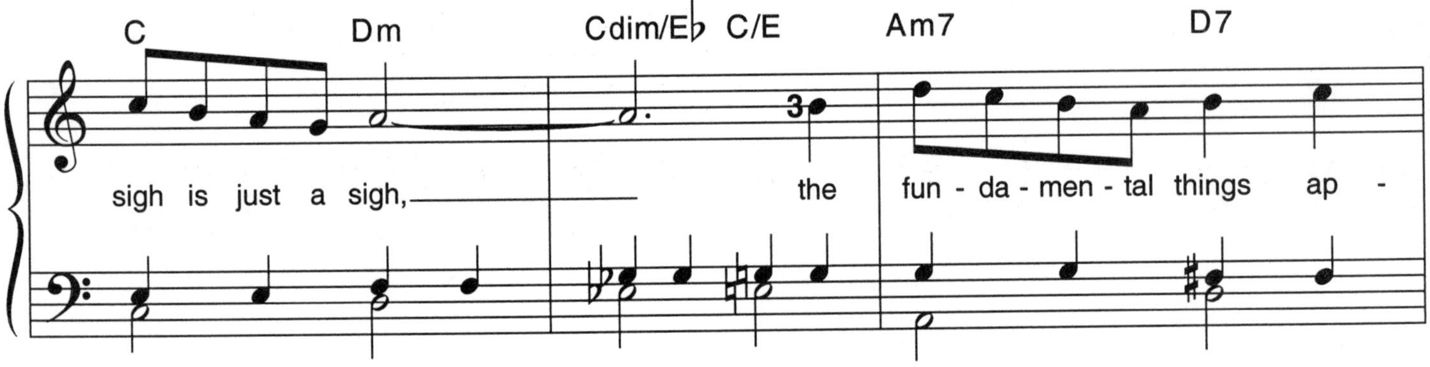

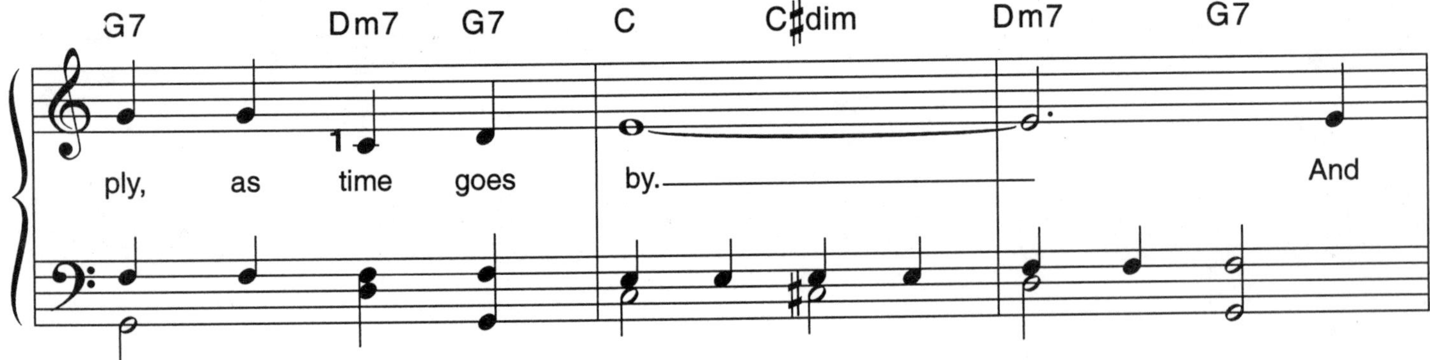

C
Dm
Cdim/E♭C/E
Am7
D7
that you can re - ly;
No
mat - ter what the fu - ture

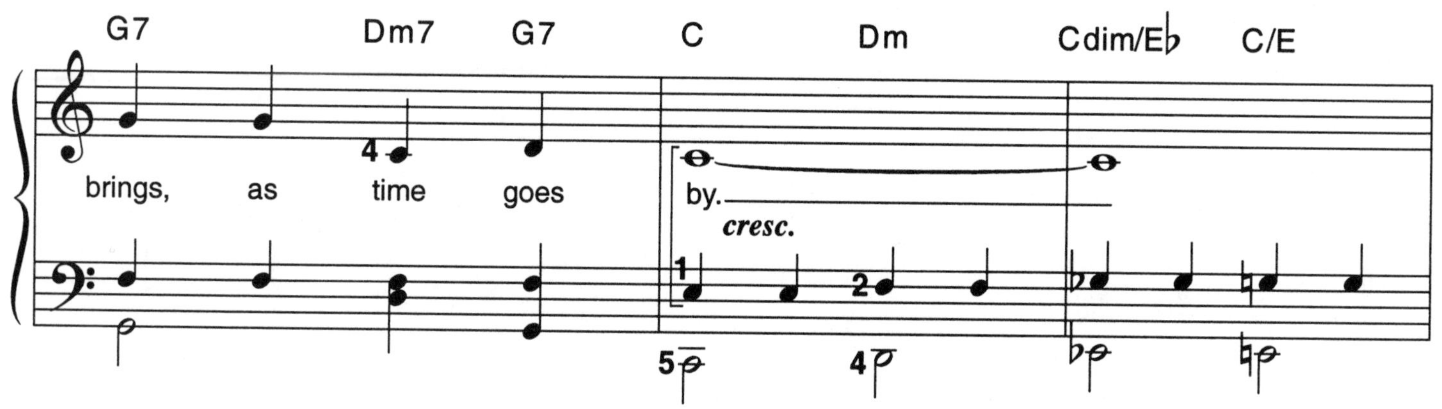
G7
Dm7
G7
C
Dm
Cdim/E♭
C/E
brings, as time goes
by.
cresc.

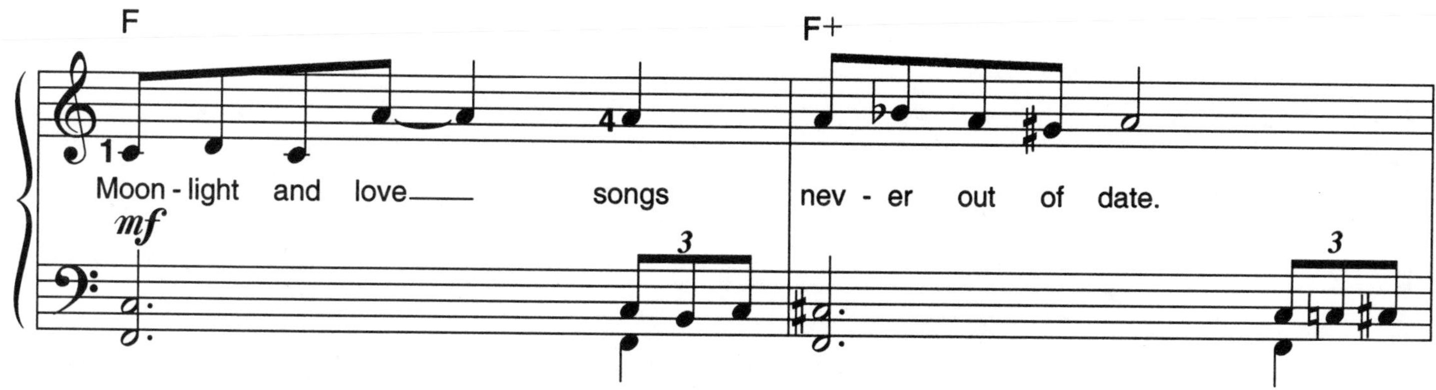
F
F+
Moon - light and love
songs
nev - er out of date.
mf

F6
F♯dim
Hearts full of pas - sion,
jeal - ous - y and hate;

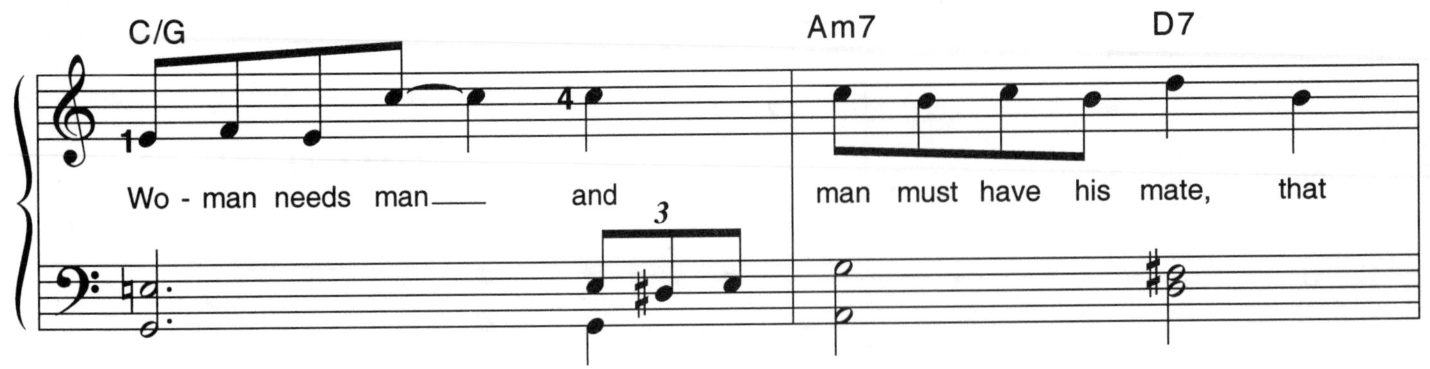
C/G
Am7
D7
Wo - man needs man___ and
man must have his mate, that

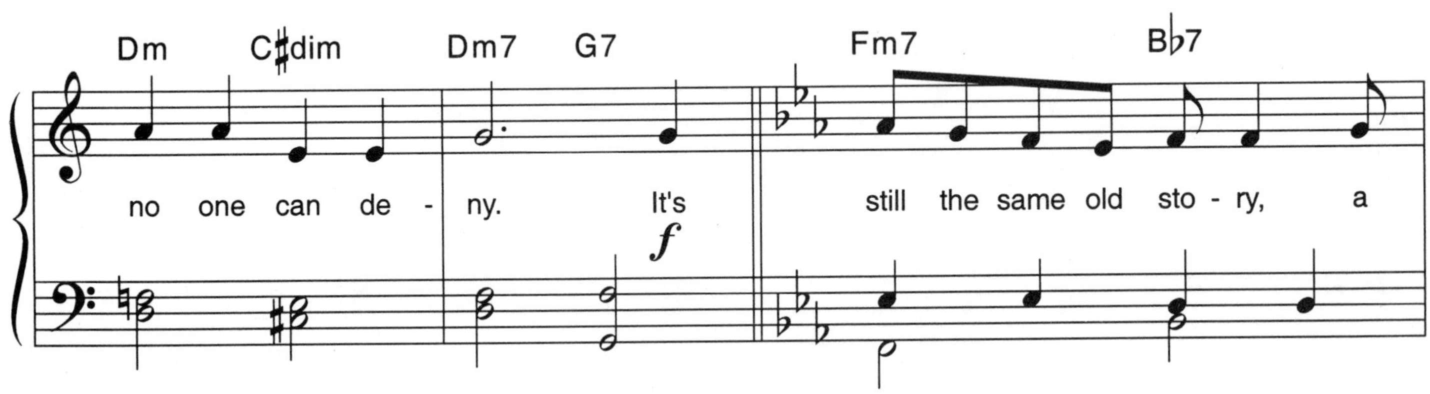
Dm
C♯dim
Dm7
G7
Fm7
B♭7
no one can de - ny. It's
still the same old sto - ry, a

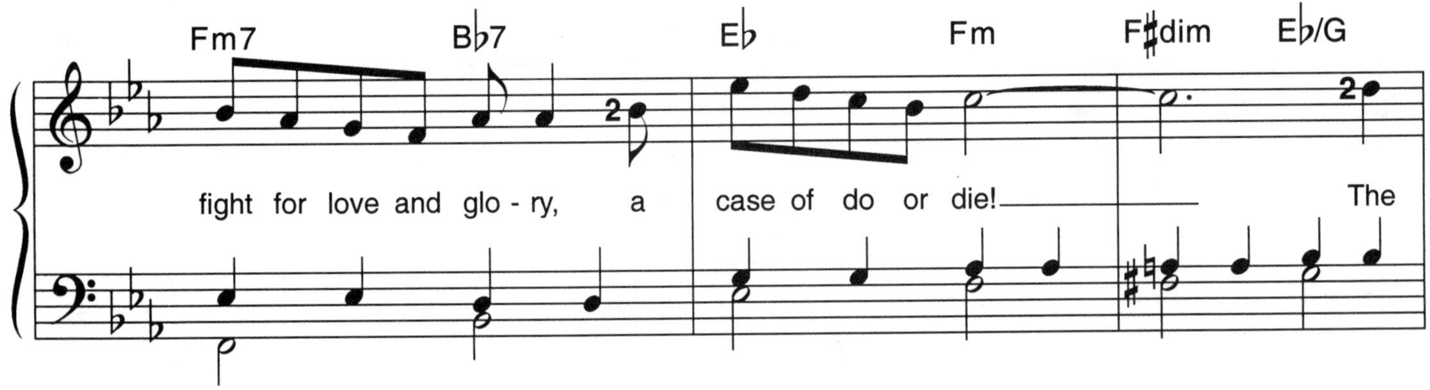
Fm7
B♭7
E♭
Fm
F♯dim
E♭/G
fight for love and glo - ry, a
case of do or die!___ The

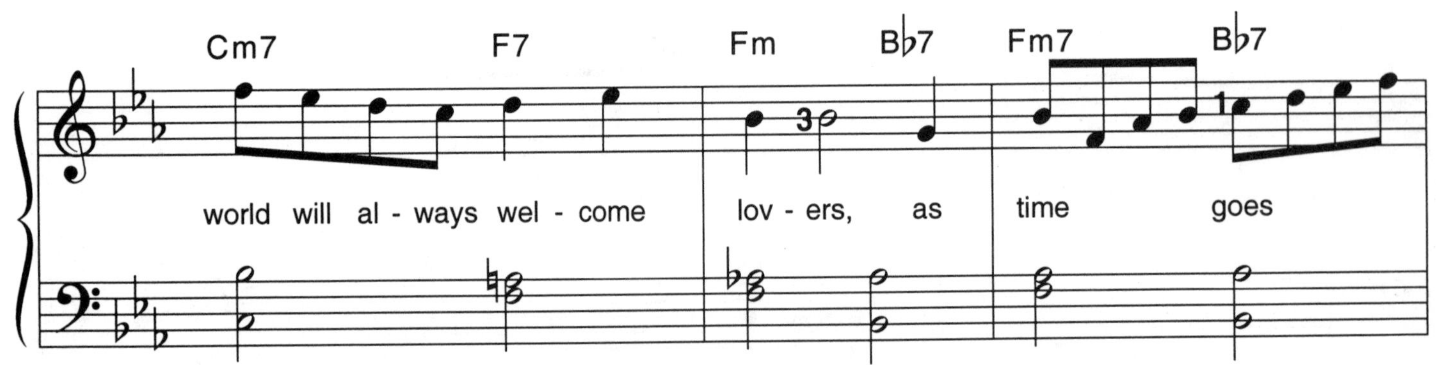
Cm7
F7
Fm
B♭7
Fm7
B♭7
world will al - ways wel - come
lov - ers, as
time goes

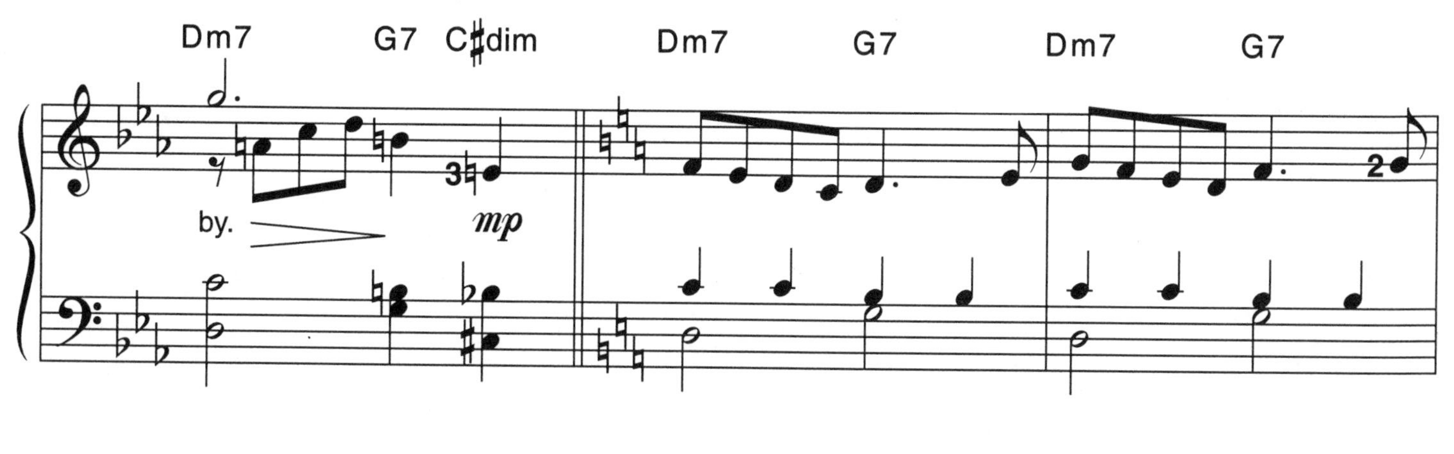
Dm7
G7
C♯dim
Dm7
G7
Dm7
G7
by.
mp

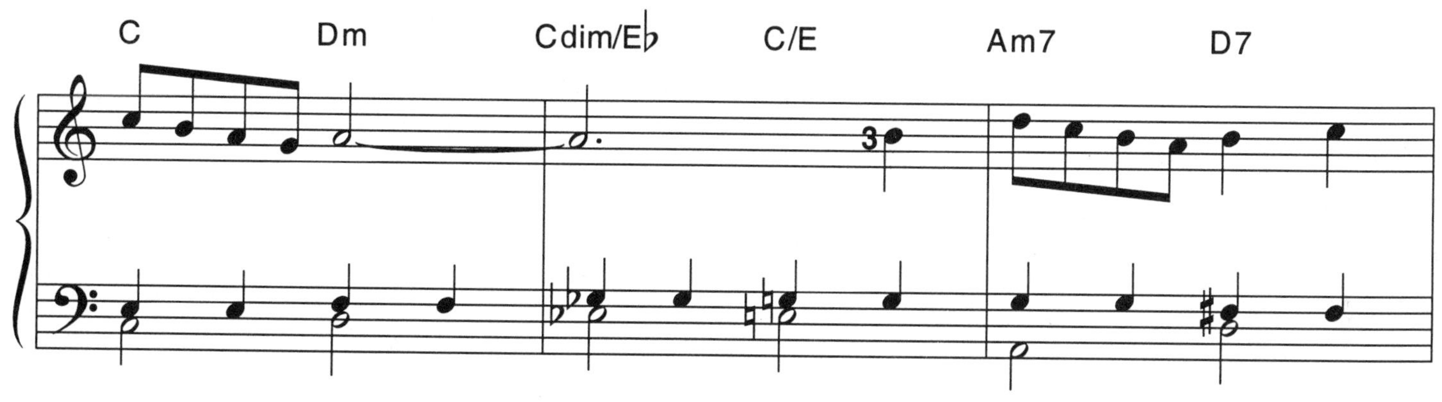
C
Dm
Cdim/E♭
C/E
Am7
D7

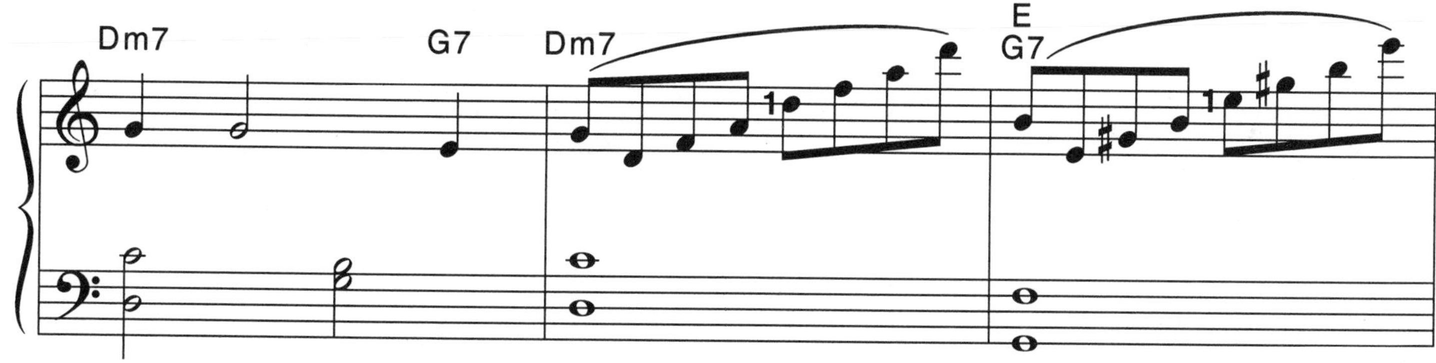
Dm7
G7
Dm7
E
G7

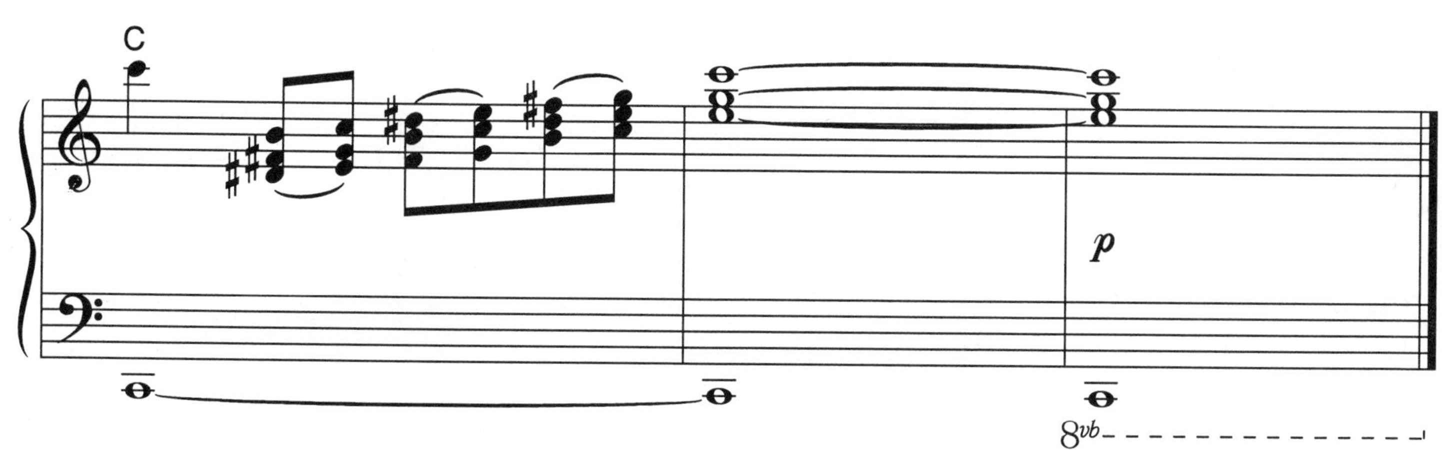
C
p
8vb

Summertime

From the Folk Opera *Porgy and Bess*

Music by GEORGE GERSHWIN
Lyric by IRA GERSHWIN,
DU BOIS and DOROTHY HEYWARD
Arranged by Richard Bradley

Moderate, with expression ♩ = 82

mf *p*

with pedal

8va

mp

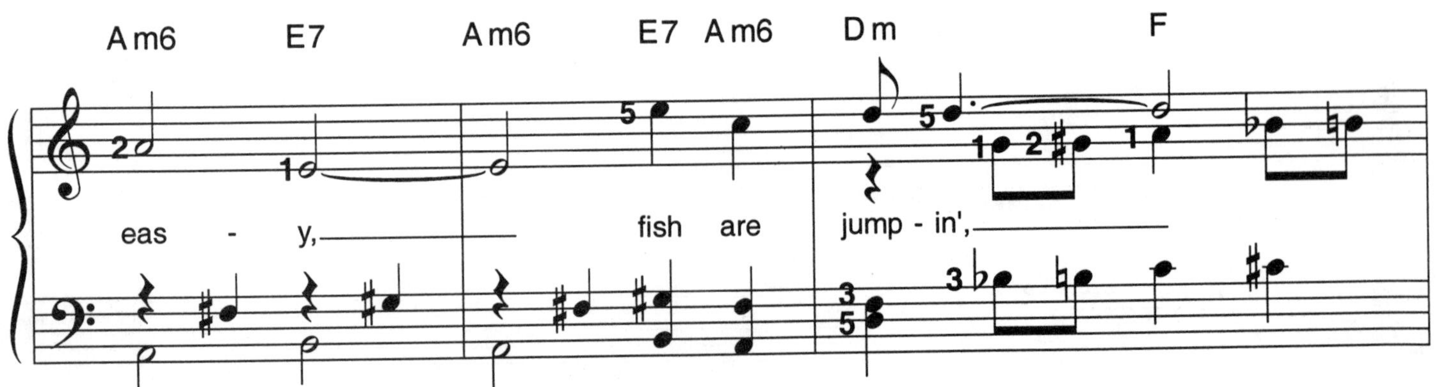

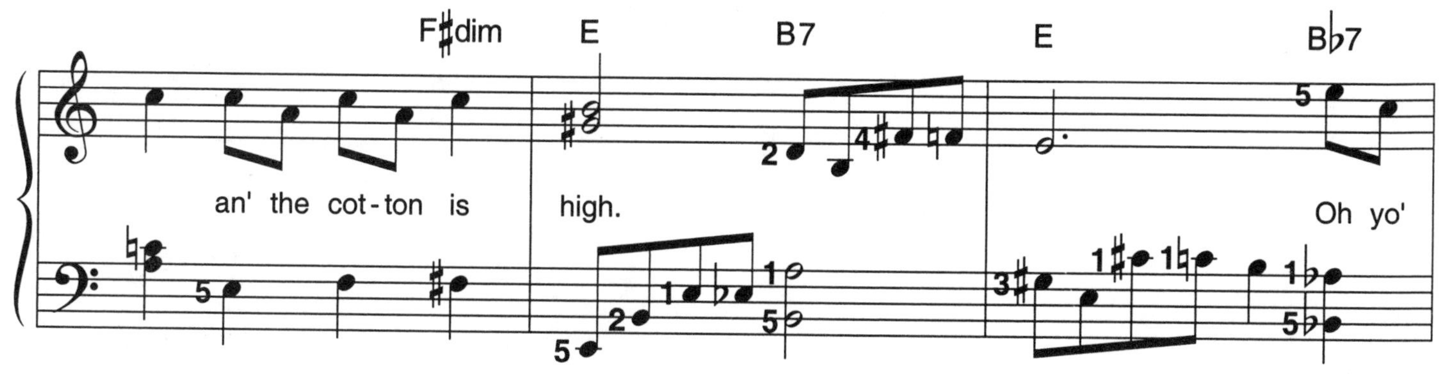
F♯dim
E
B7
E
B♭7
an' the cot-ton is
high.
Oh yo'

Am6
E7
Am6
E7
Am6
E7
dad - dy's rich,
an' yo' ma is good - look - in',

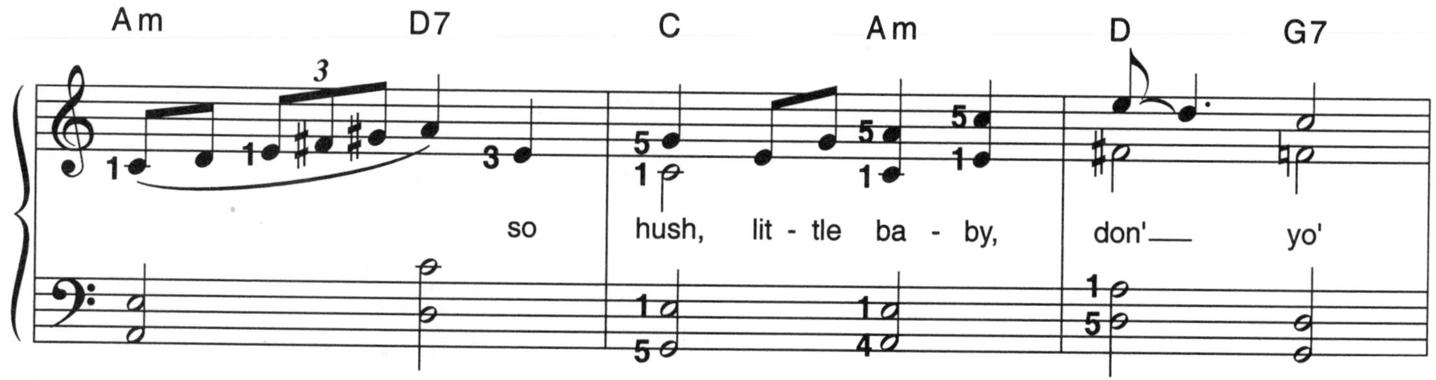
Am
D7
C
Am
D
G7
so
hush, lit - tle ba - by,
don' yo'

Am
Am6
E7
8va
cry.

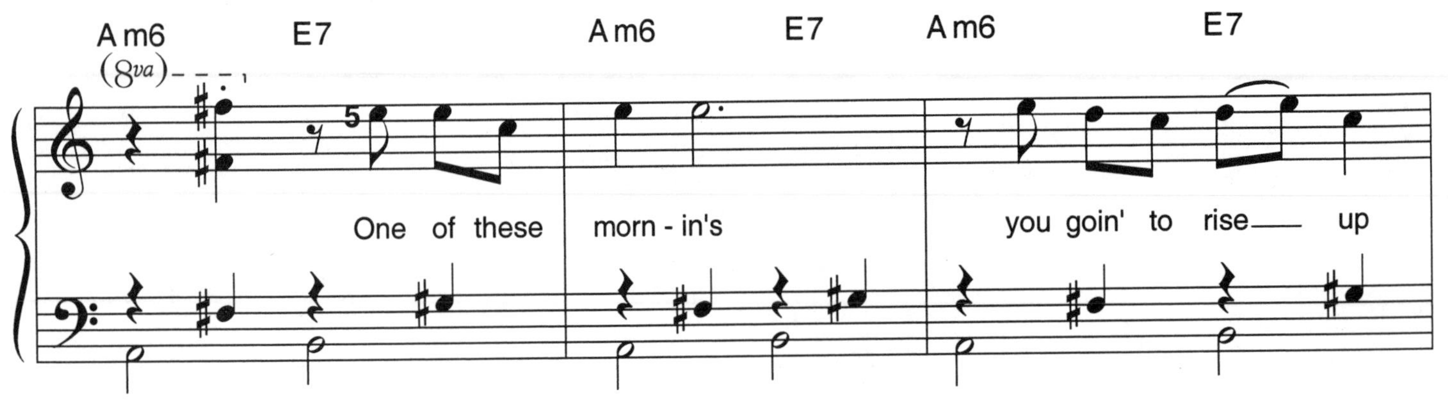
Am6
E7
Am6
E7
Am6
E7
(8va)
One of these
morn - in's
you goin' to rise up

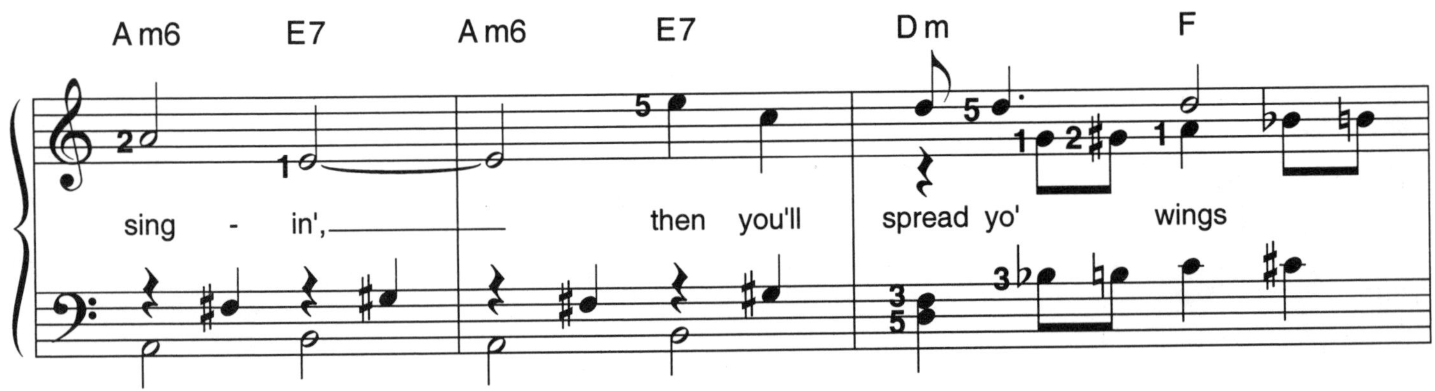
Am6
E7
Am6
E7
Dm
F
sing - in',
then you'll
spread yo' wings

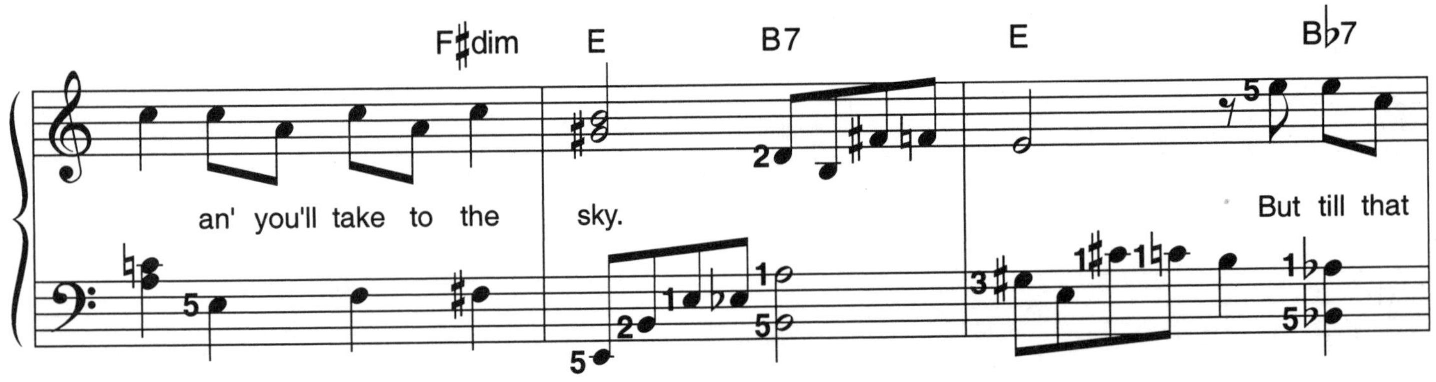
F♯dim
E
B7
E
B♭7
an' you'll take to the
sky.
But till that

Am6
E7
Am6
E7
Am6
E7
morn - in;
there's a noth - in' can
harm you

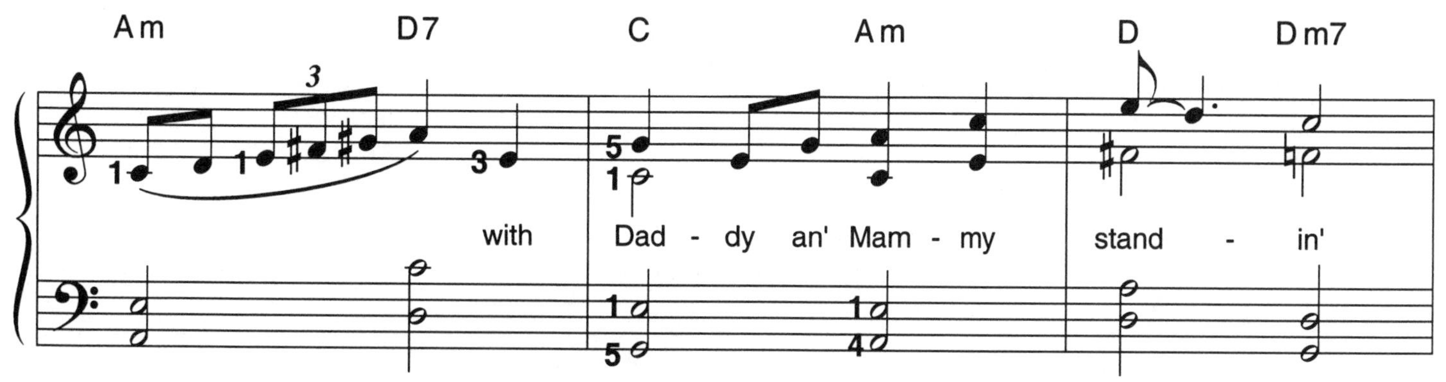
Am
D7
C
Am
D
Dm7
with
Dad - dy an' Mam - my
stand - in'

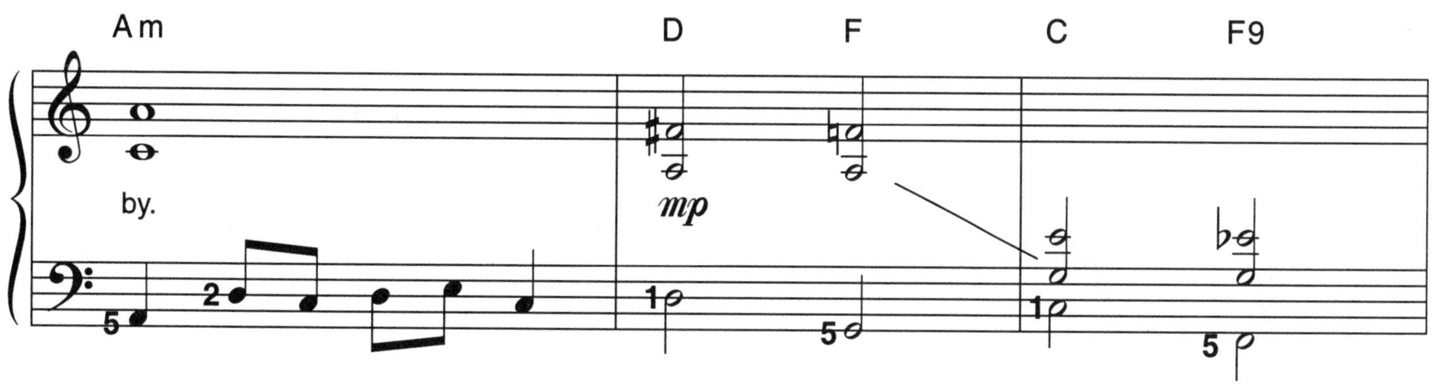
Am
D
F
C
F9
by.

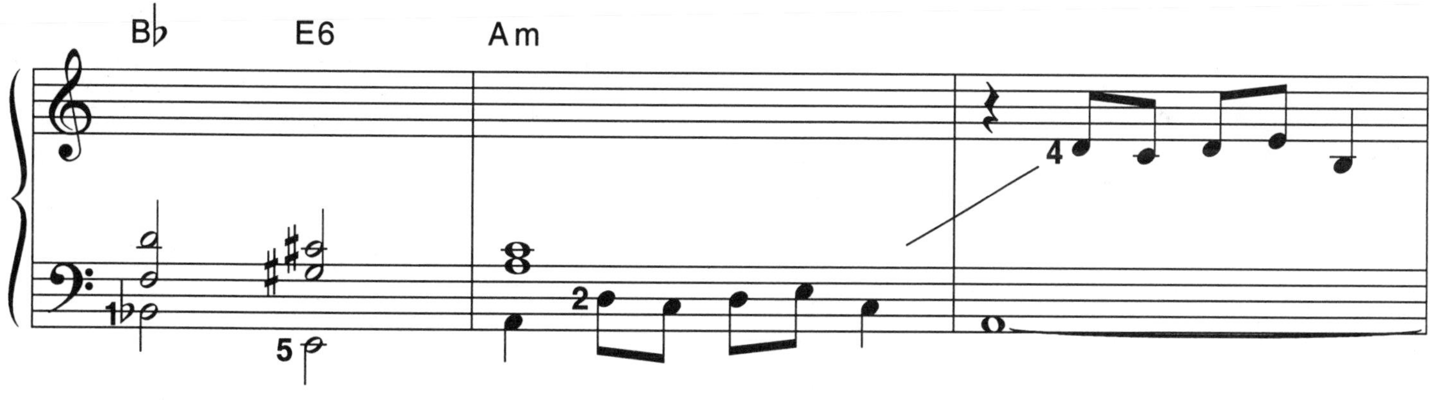
B♭
E6
Am

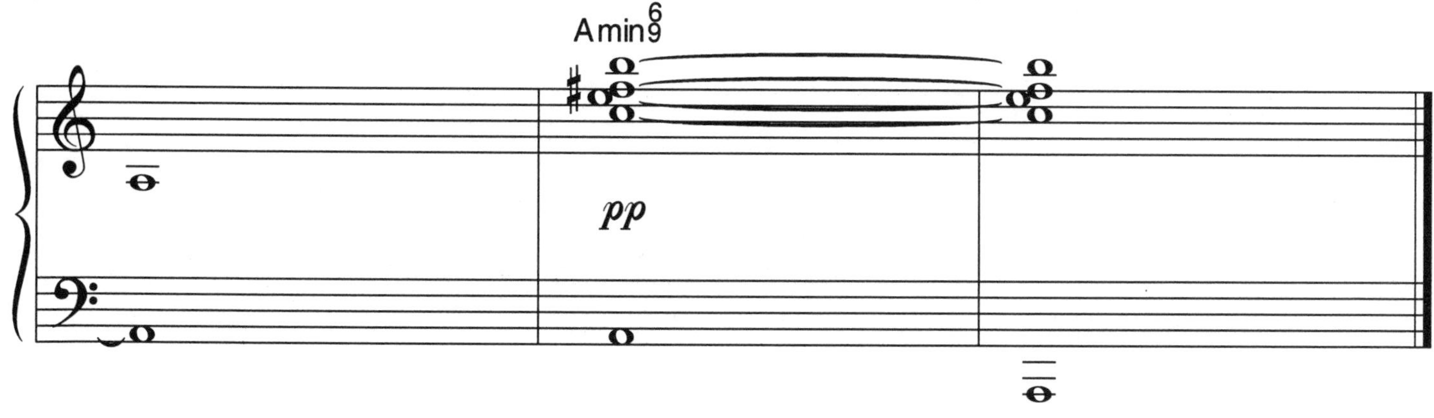
Amin 6/9

Where or When

From the Broadway Musical *Babes in Arms*

Words by LORENZ HART
Music by RICHARD RODGERS
Arranged by Richard Bradley

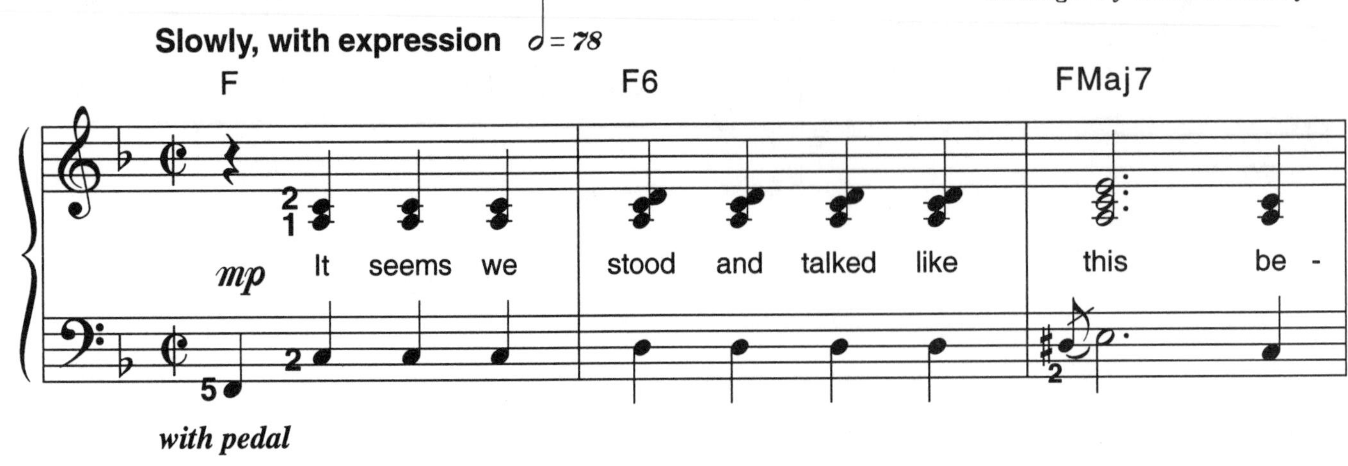

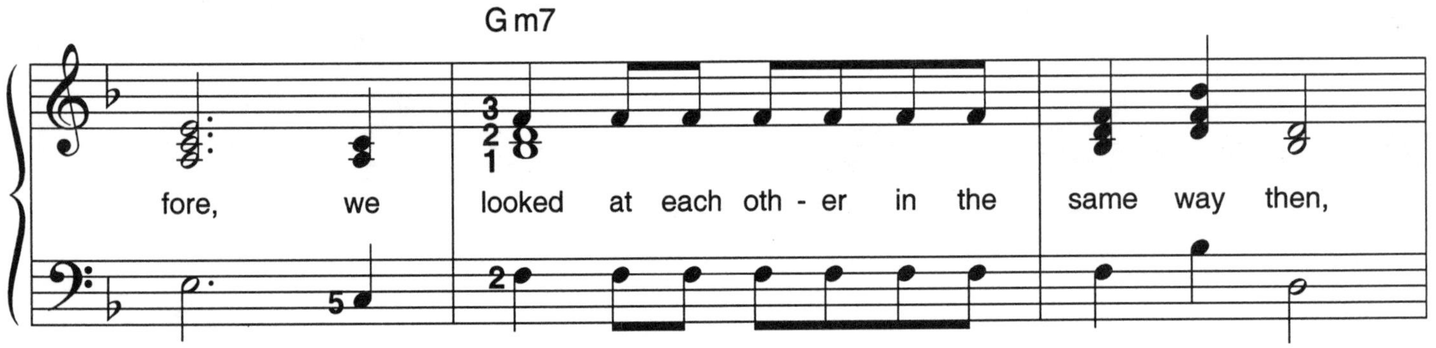

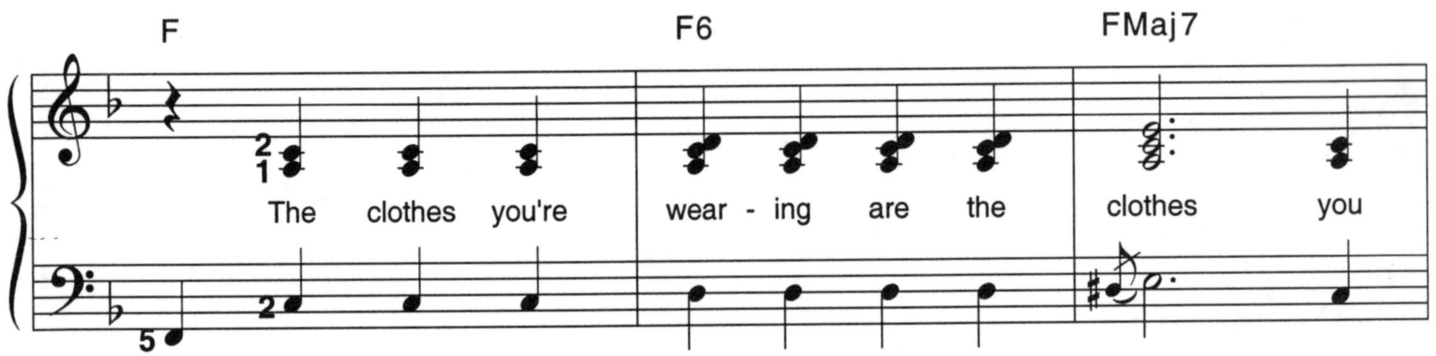

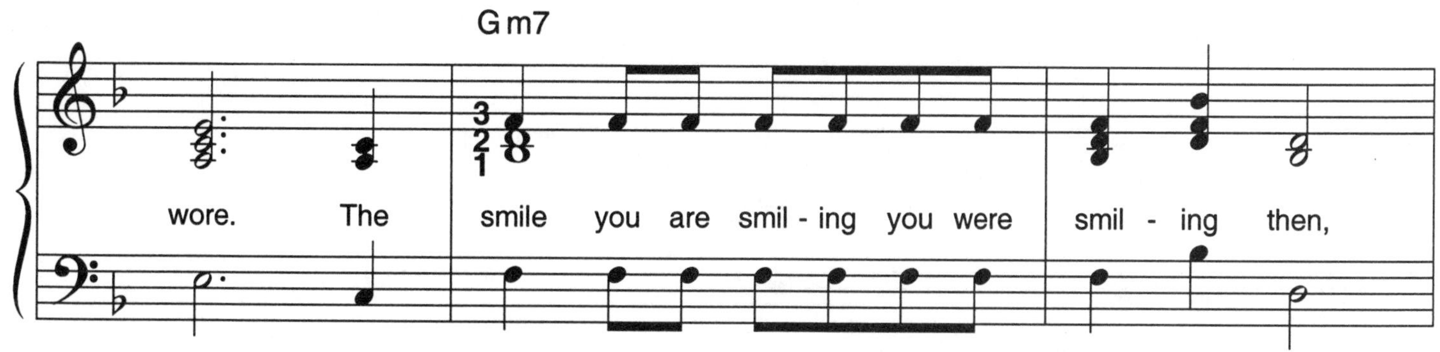
Gm7
wore. The
smile you are smil - ing you were
smil - ing then,

FMaj7
F6
Gm7
C7
but I can't re-mem - ber
where or
when.

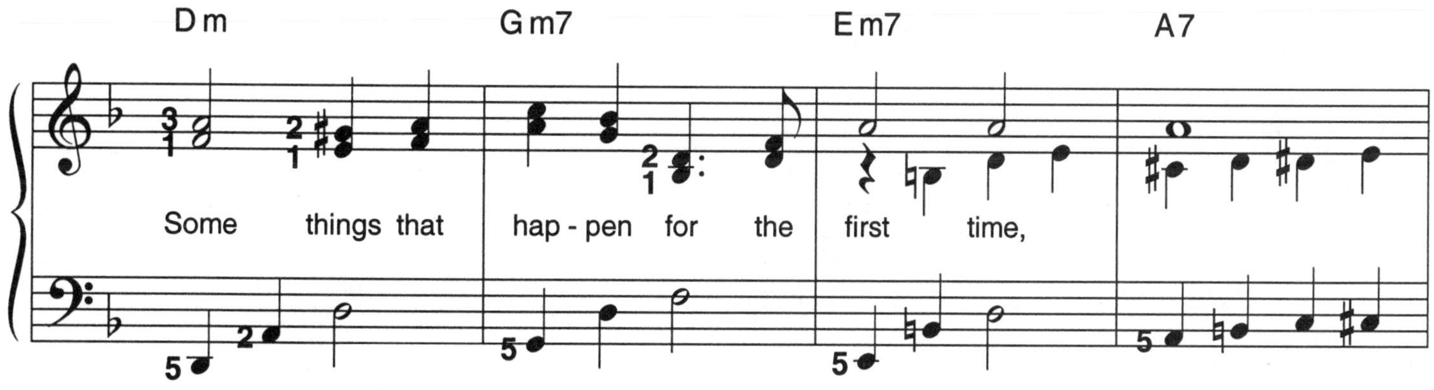
Dm
Gm7
Em7
A7
Some things that
hap - pen for the
first time,

Dm
Gm7
Dm7
G7
C9
C7(♭9)
seem to be
hap - pen - ing a -
gain.

F
F6
FMaj7
And so it seems that we have met be -

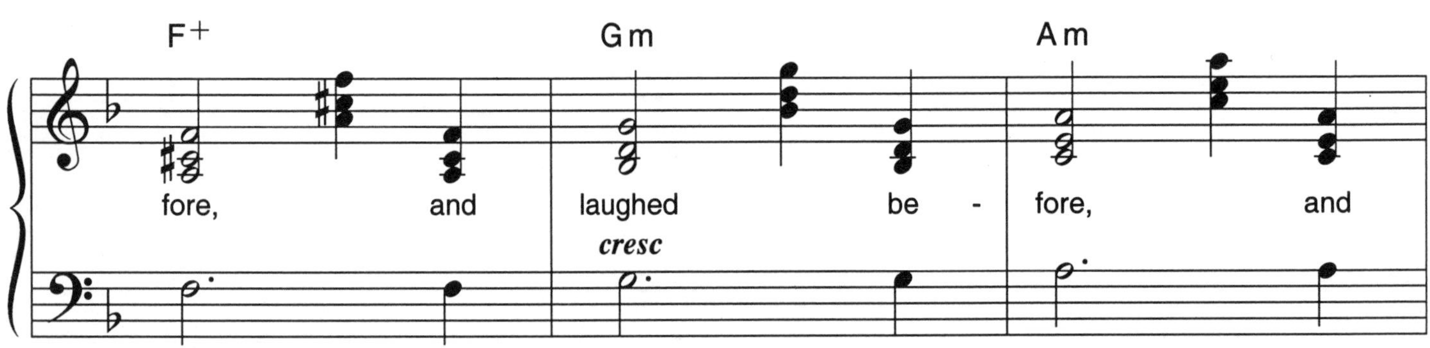
F+
Gm
Am
fore, and laughed be - fore, and
cresc

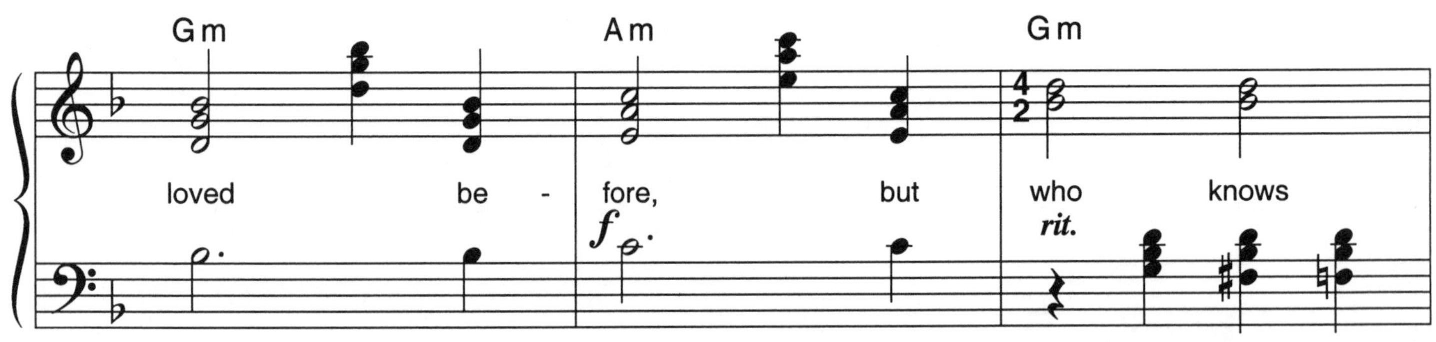
Gm
Am
Gm
loved be - fore, but who knows
rit.

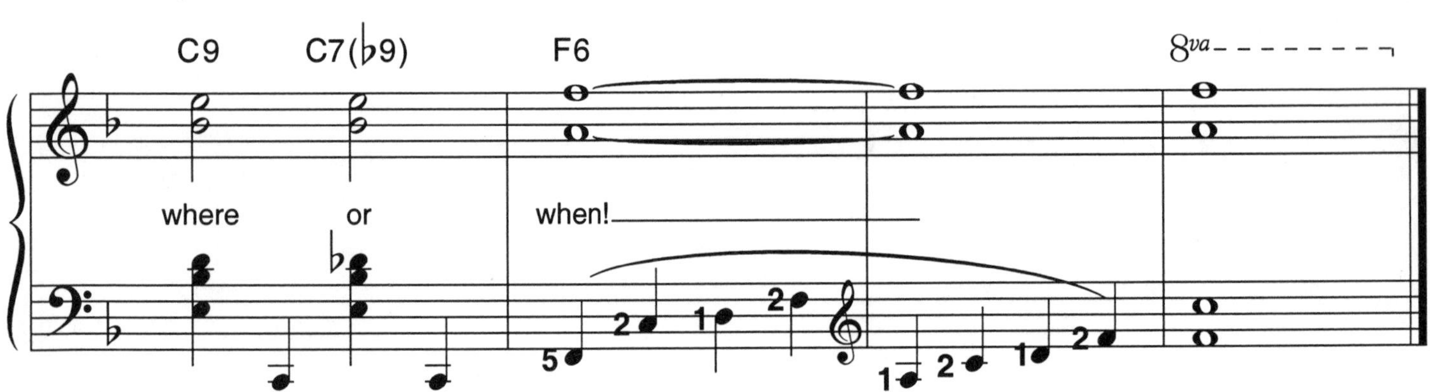
C9
C7(♭9)
F6
8va
where or when!

Misty

Lyric by
JOHNNY BURKE

Music by
ERROLL GARNER
Arranged by Richard Bradley

F♯7
FMaj7
Cm7
F7/E♭
way, and a thou - sand vi - o - lins be - gin to
B♭Maj7
B♭6
B♭m/G
F
E♭
play, or it might be the sound of your hel - lo, that
F
Dm
Gm
C7
To Coda
mu - sic I hear, I get mist - y the mo - ment you're
F
A♭
G
G♭
F
N.C.
near. You can say that you're
Cm7
Cm7/G
F
F/C
lead - ing me on, but it's just what I

Verse 3:
On my own, would I wander through this wonderland alone,
Never knowing my right foot from my left,
My hat from my glove, I'm too misty and too much in love.

How Long Has This Been Going On?

Words by
IRA GERSHWIN

Music by
GEORGE GERSHWIN
Arranged by Richard Bradley

G/B
E♭7
D7/A
C7
E♭7
D7
Lis - ten sweet, —
I re - peat: —
How
long has this been go - ing

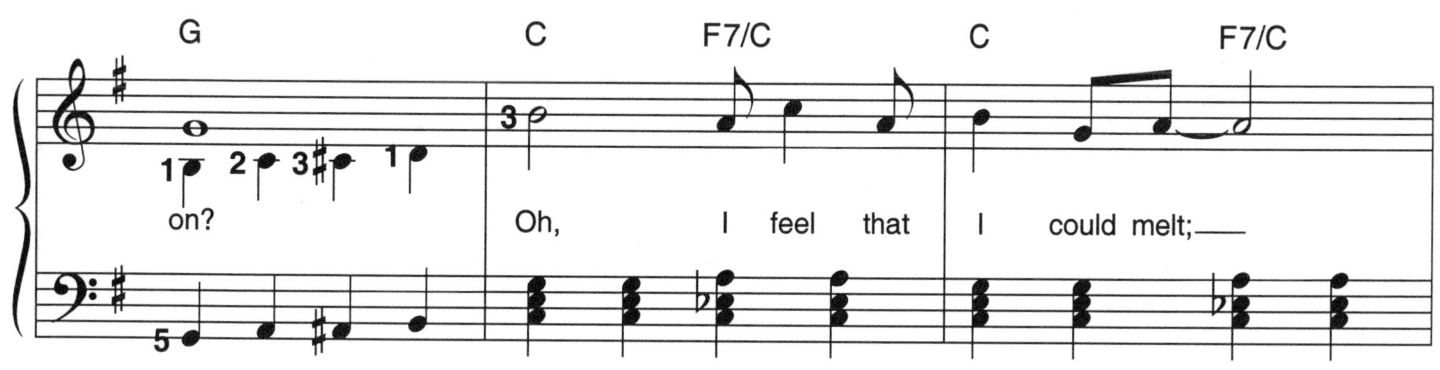
G
C
F7/C
C
F7/C
on?
Oh,
I feel that
I could melt; —

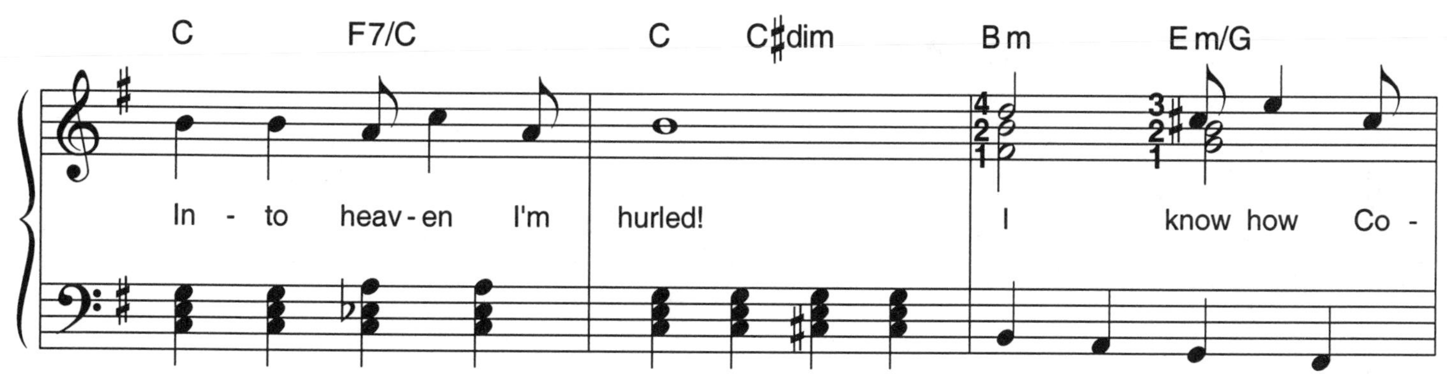
C
F7/C
C
C♯dim
Bm
Em/G
In - to heav - en I'm
hurled!
I know how Co -

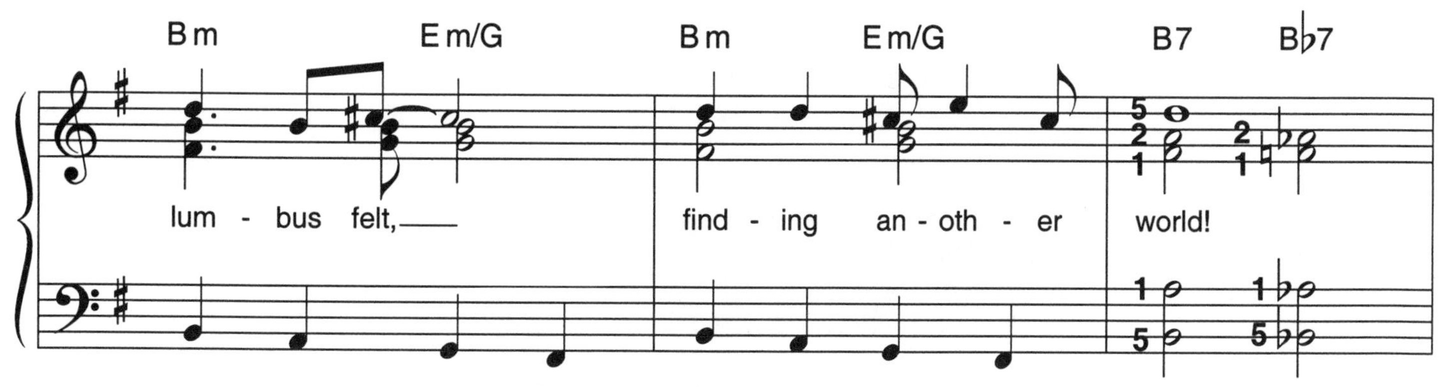
Bm
Em/G
Bm
Em/G
B7
B♭7
lum - bus felt, —
find - ing an - oth - er
world!

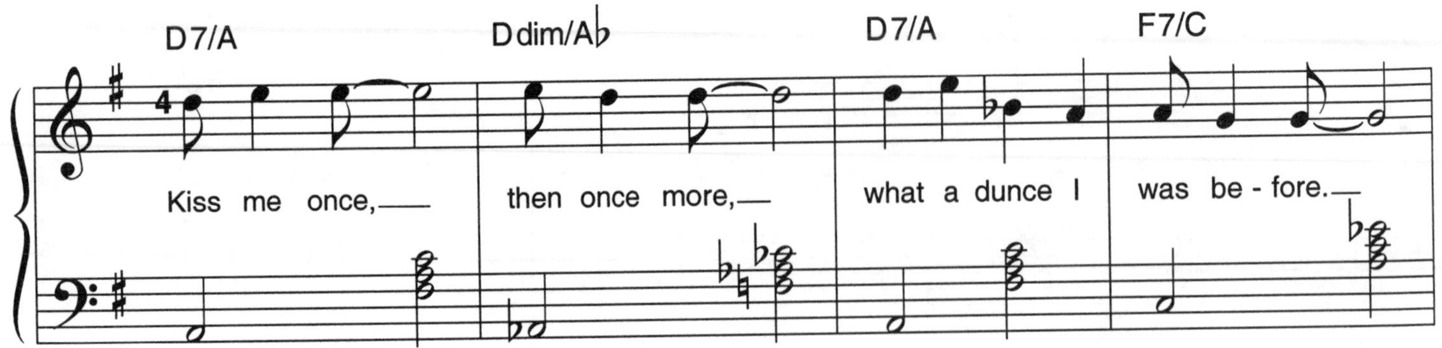

Verse 2:
I could cry salty tears;
Where have I been all these years?
Listen, you, tell me do,
How long has this been going on?
What a kick! How I buzz!
Boy, you click as no one does!
Hear me sweet, I repeat:
How long has this been going on?
Dear, when in your arms I creep,
That divine rendezvous,
Don't wake me, if I'm asleep,
Let me dream that it's true.
Kiss me twice, then once more,
That makes thrice, let's make it four!
What a break! For Heaven's sake!
How long has this been going on?

Blue Moon

Lyrics by
LORENZ HART

Music by
RICHARD RODGERS
Arranged by Richard Bradley

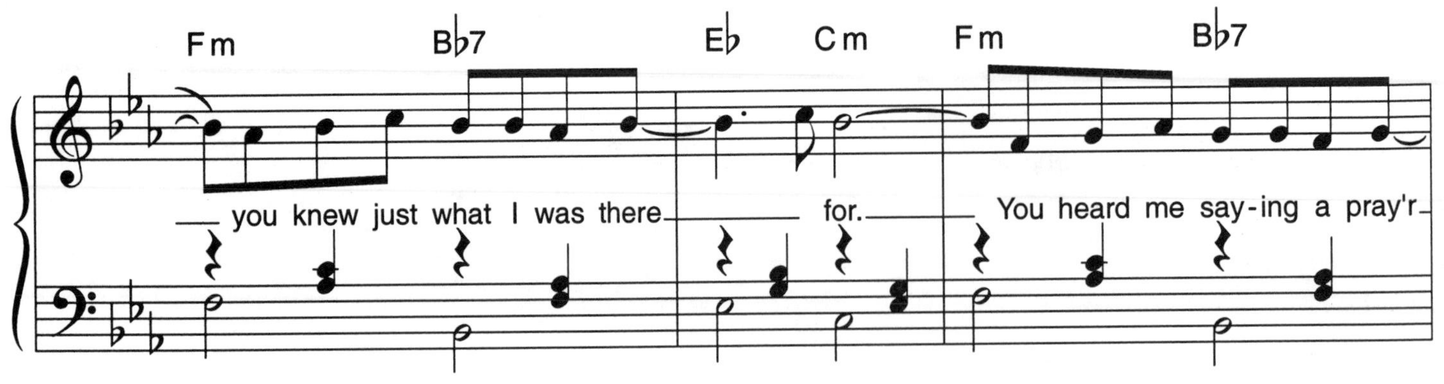
Fm
B♭7
E♭
Cm
Fm
B♭7
you knew just what I was there for. You heard me say-ing a pray'r

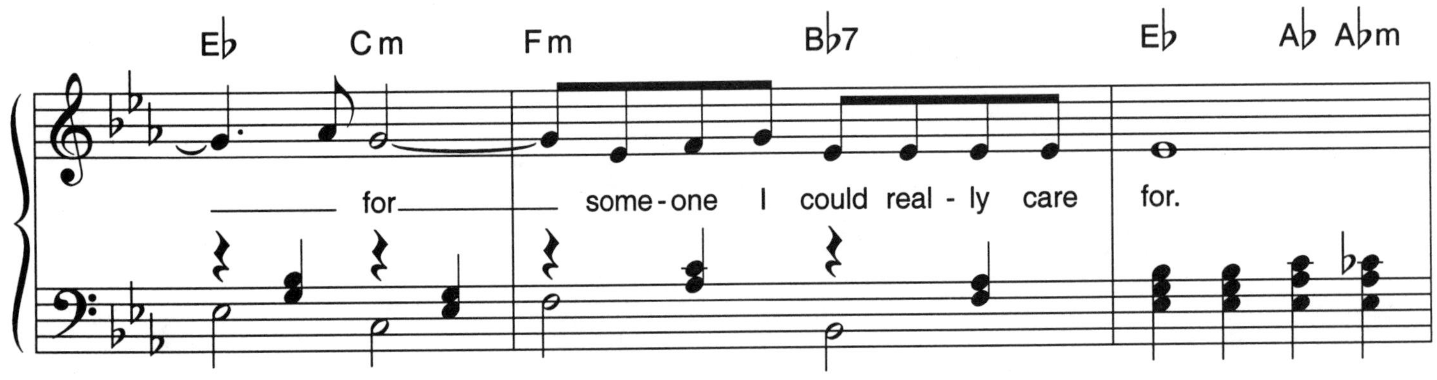
E♭
Cm
Fm
B♭7
E♭
A♭
A♭m
for some-one I could real - ly care for.

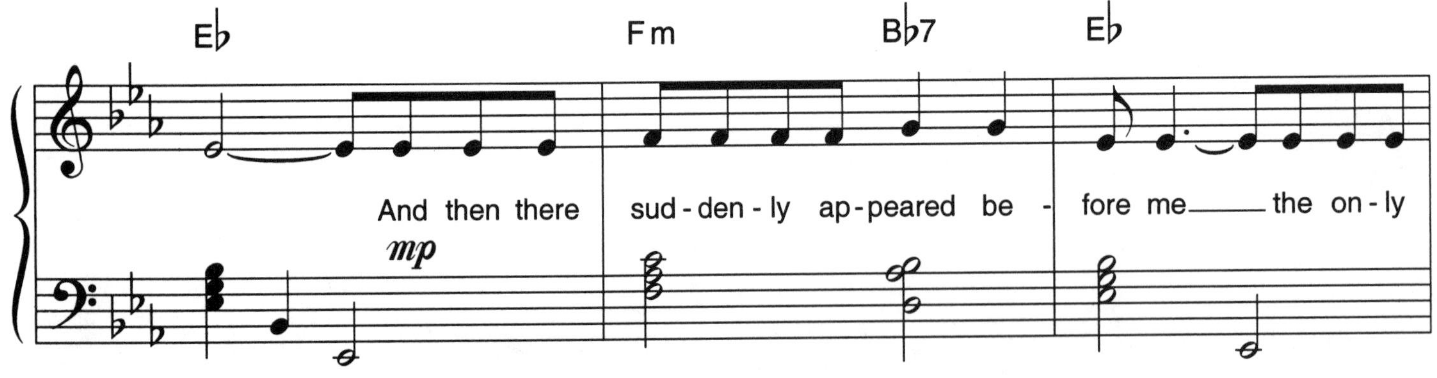
E♭
Fm
B♭7
E♭
And then there sud - den - ly ap-peared be - fore me the on - ly
mp

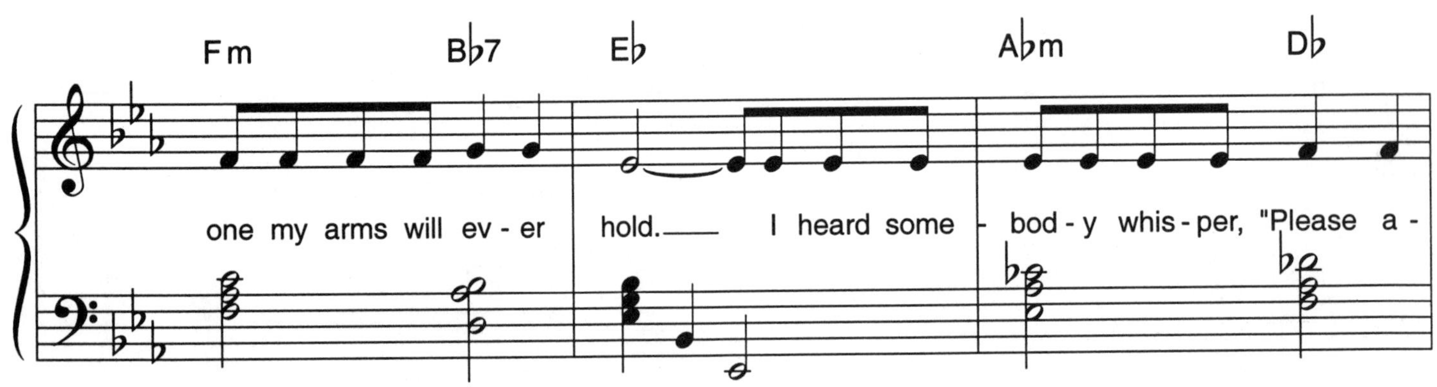
Fm
B♭7
E♭
A♭m
D♭
one my arms will ev - er hold. I heard some - bod - y whis - per, "Please a -

G♭
B♭6
F7
B♭7
B7
C7
dore me." And when I
looked, the moon had turned to
gold!
Blue
mf

F
Dm
Gm
C7
F
Dm
moon
now I'm no - long - er a - lone.

Gm
C7
F
Dm
Gm
C7
with - out a dream in my heart,
with - out a love of my

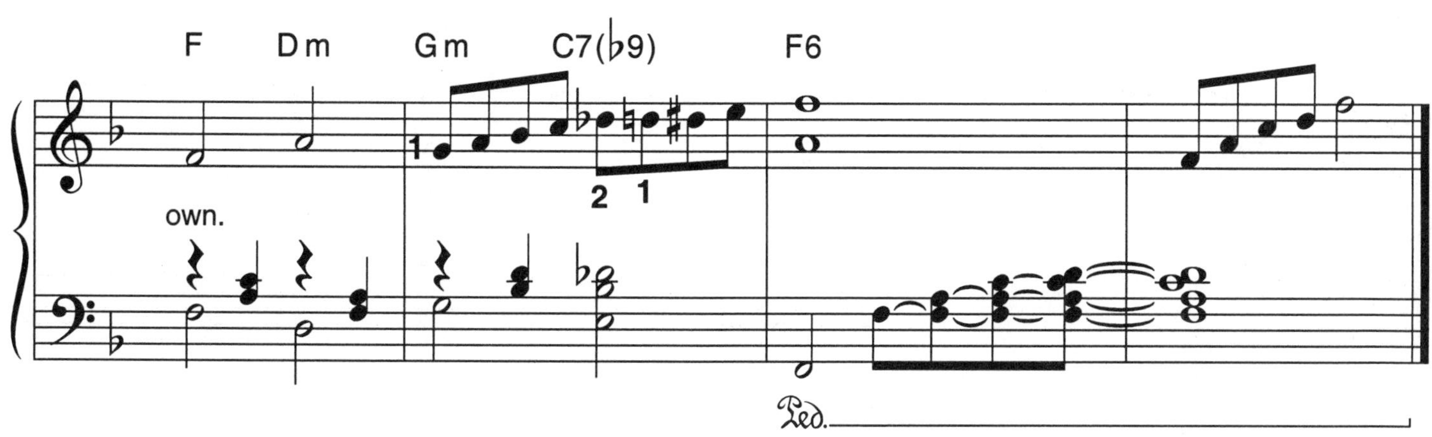
F
Dm
Gm
C7(♭9)
F6
own.
Ped.

What Are You Doing the Rest of Your Life?

From the Motion Picture *The Happy Ending*

Lyric by ALAN and MARILYN BERGMAN
Music by MICHEL LEGRAND
Arranged by Richard Bradley

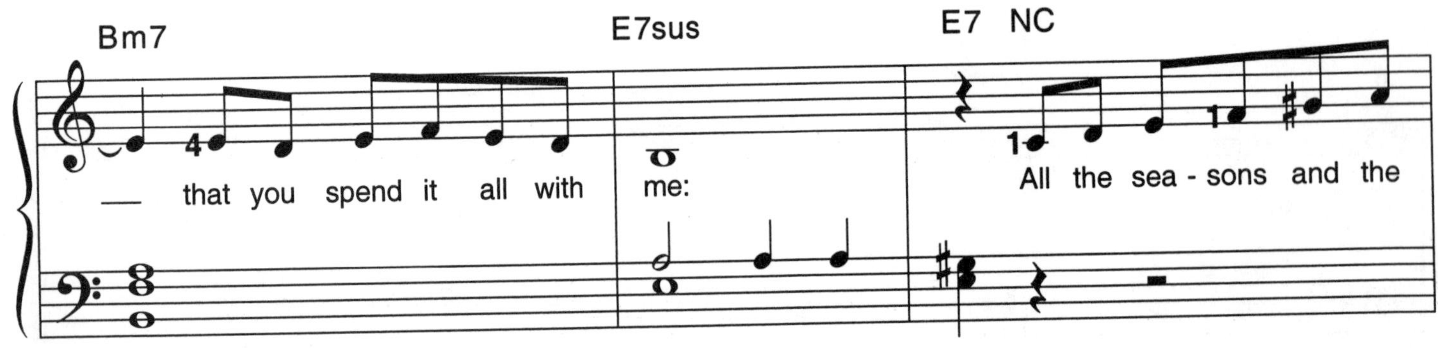

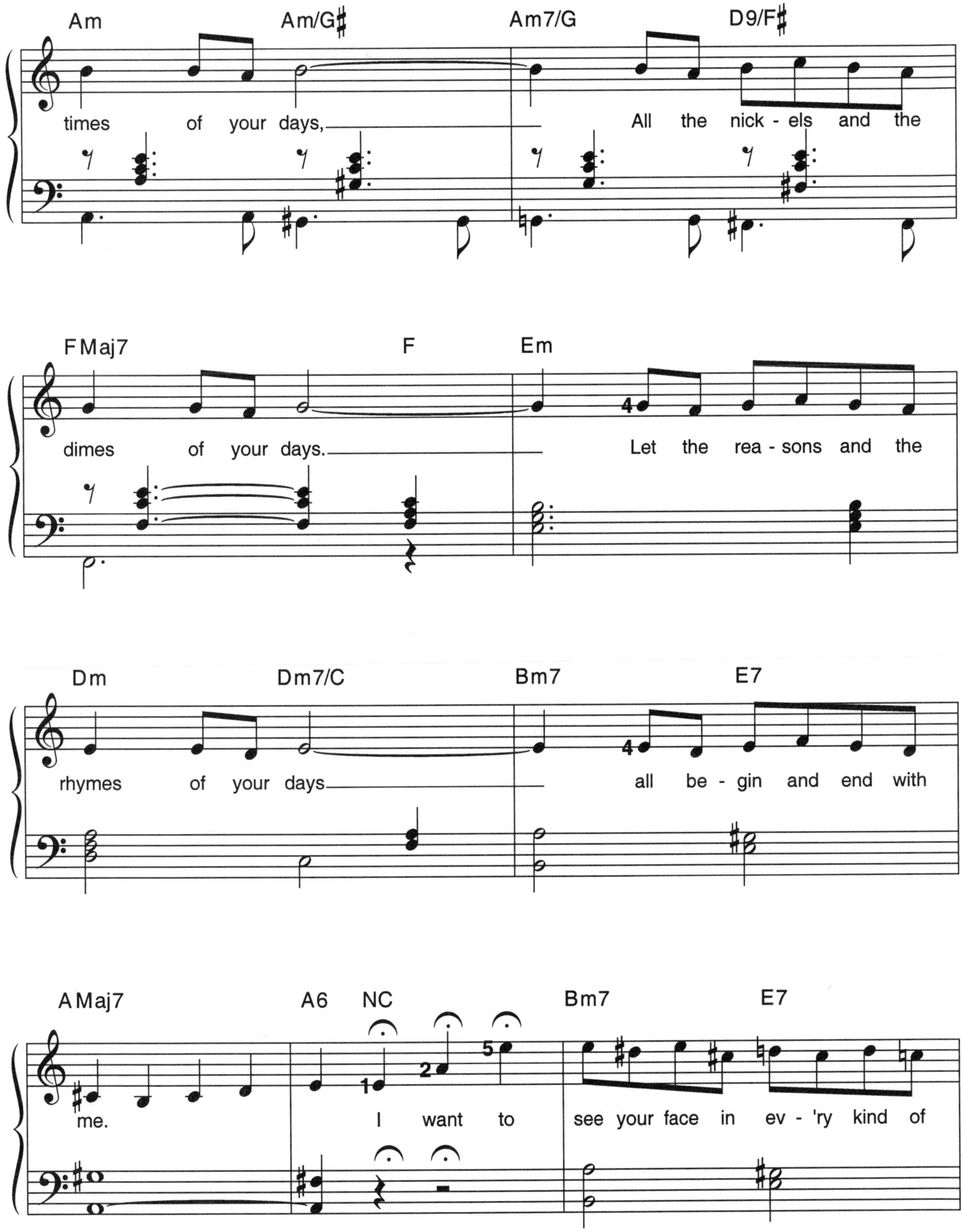

Am Am/G♯ Am7/G D9/F♯

times of your days, All the nick - els and the

FMaj7 F Em

dimes of your days. Let the rea - sons and the

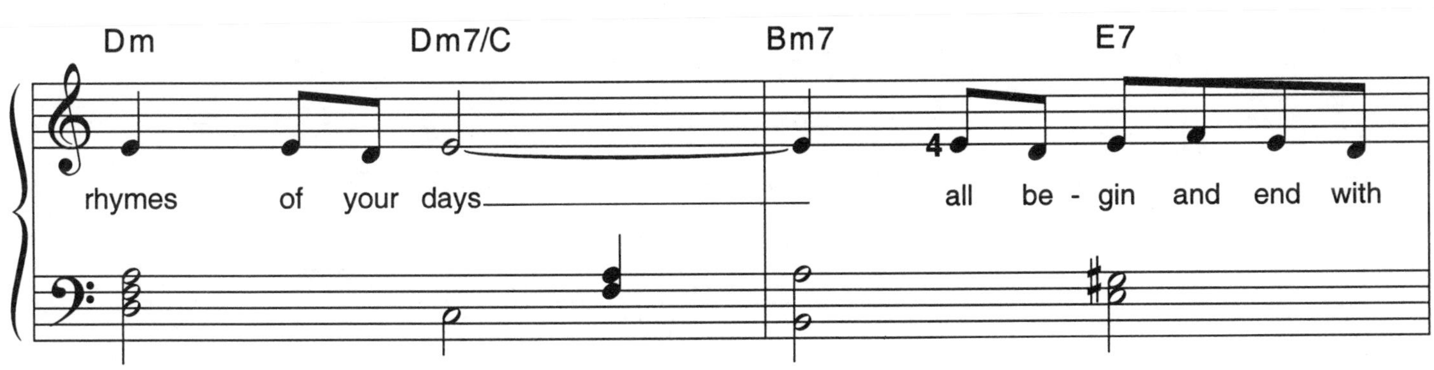

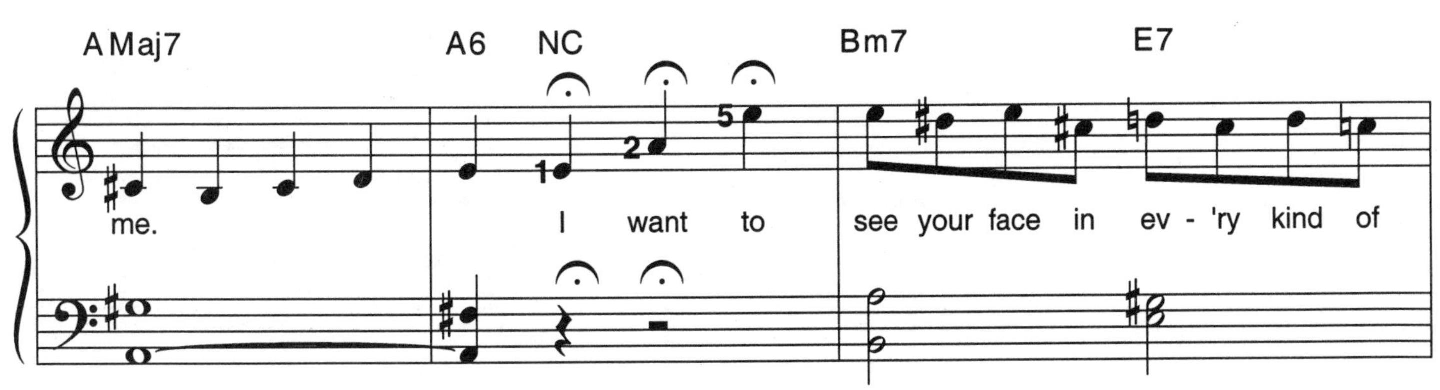

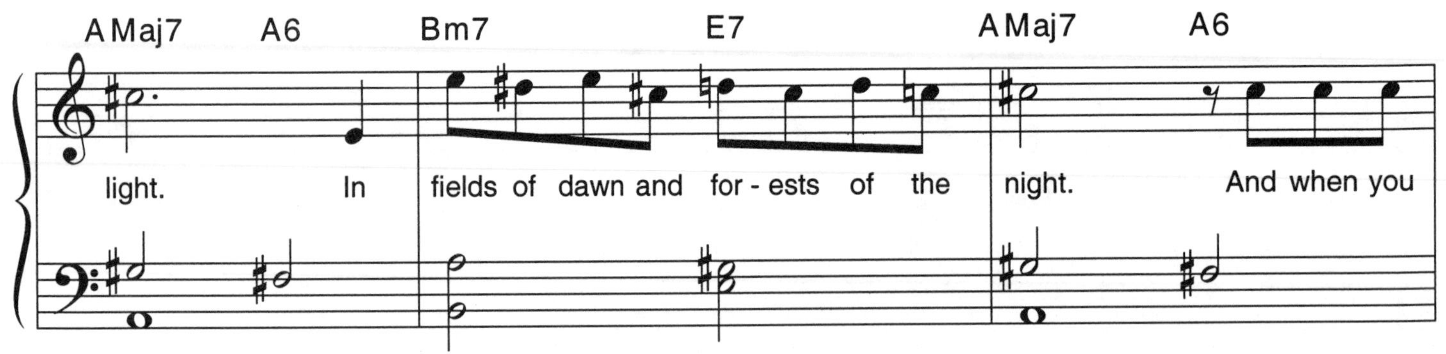
AMaj7
A6
Bm7
E7
AMaj7
A6
light. In fields of dawn and for - ests of the night. And when you

A♭Maj7
D♭7
G♭Maj7
NC
stand be - fore the can - dles on a cake, Oh, let me be the

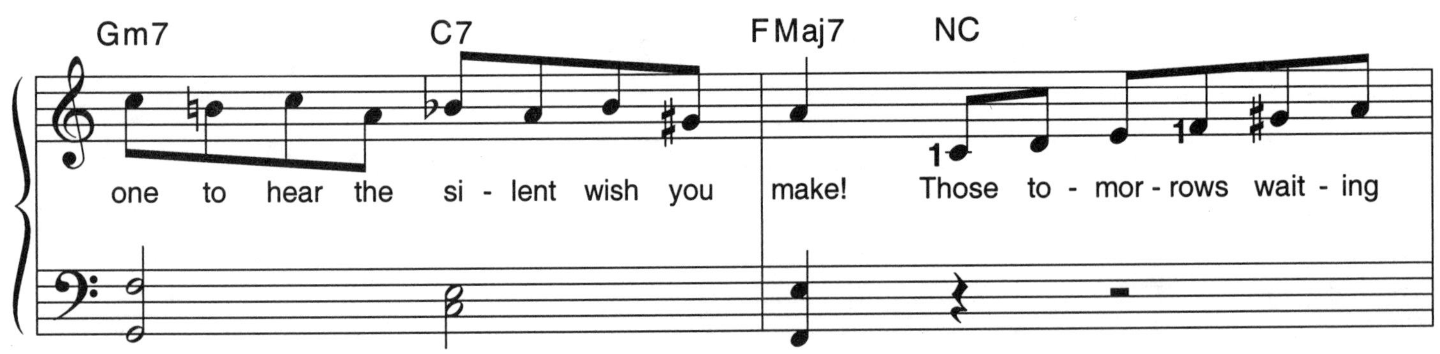
Gm7
C7
FMaj7
NC
one to hear the si - lent wish you make! Those to - mor - rows wait - ing

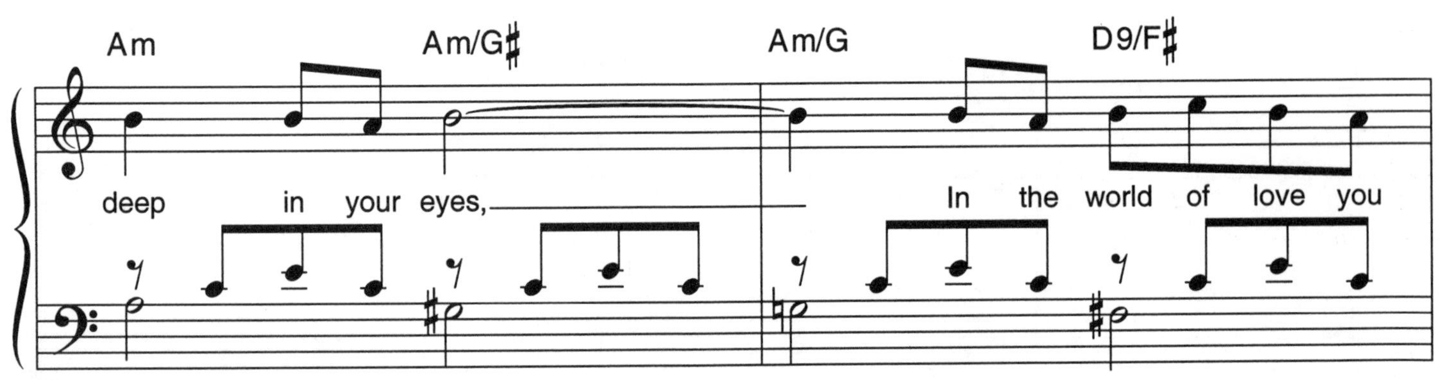
Am
Am/G♯
Am/G
D9/F♯
deep in your eyes, In the world of love you

FMaj7
F
Em
keep in your eyes,
I'll a - wak - en what's a -
Dm
Dm7/C
Bm7
E7sus
sleep in your eyes.
It may take a kiss or
two!
E7
F
Em Dm
Bm7
E7
Thru
all of my life,
sum - mer, win - ter, spring and
FMaj7
F7♭5
Am/E
fall of my life,
All I ev - er will re - call of my life is
Bm7
E7
Am
all of my life with
you!

Singin' in the Rain

From the Motion Picture *Singin' in the Rain*

Lyric by ARTHUR FREED
Music by NACIO HERB BROWN
Arranged by Richard Bradley

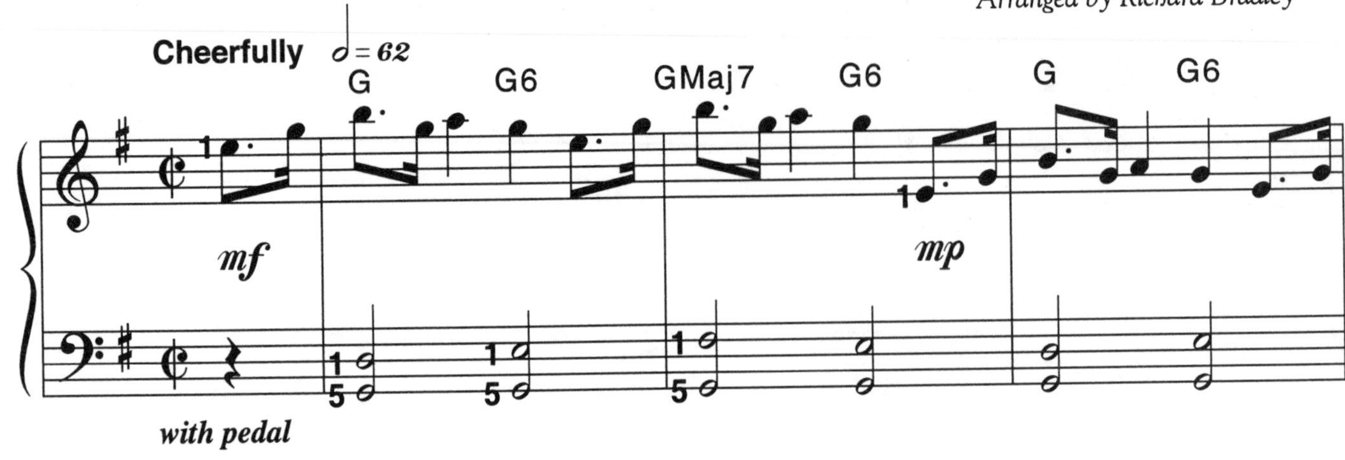

laugh - ing at
clouds so
dark up a -

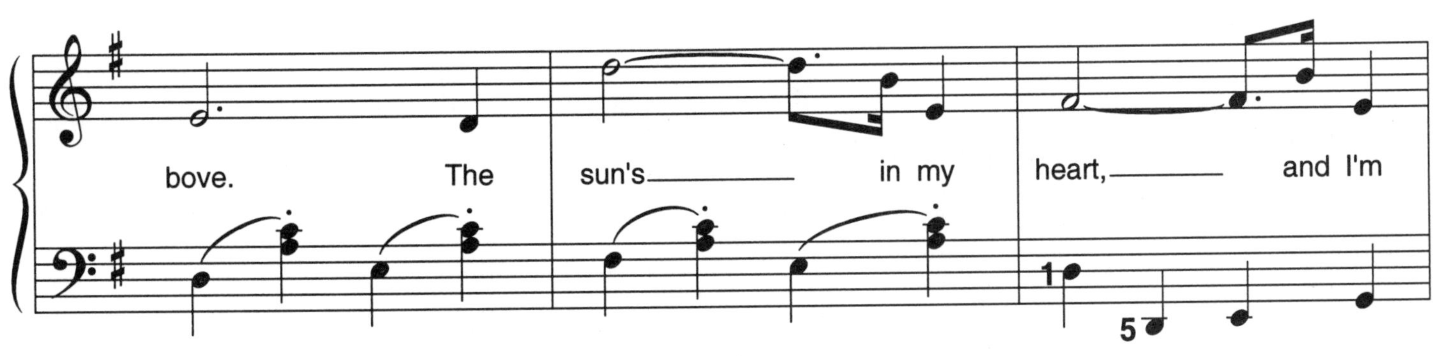
bove. The
sun's in my
heart, and I'm
1
5

G
read - y for
love. Let the
storm - y clouds
1
2
1
2
1

chase ev - 'ry - one from the
place. Come

Fdim
D7
2
on with the rain, I've a smile on my
face. I'll walk down the lane with a
hap - py re - frain, and sing - in' just
G
1
sing - in' in the rain.
1
5
G6
GMaj7
G6
G

Anything Goes

From the Broadway Musical *Anything Goes*

Words and Music by
COLE PORTER
Arranged by Richard Bradley

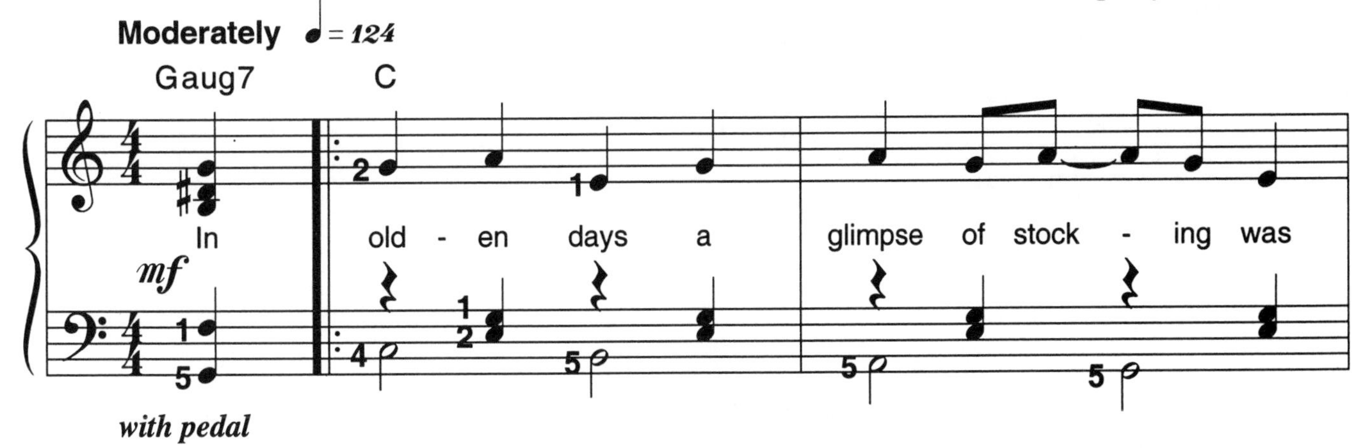

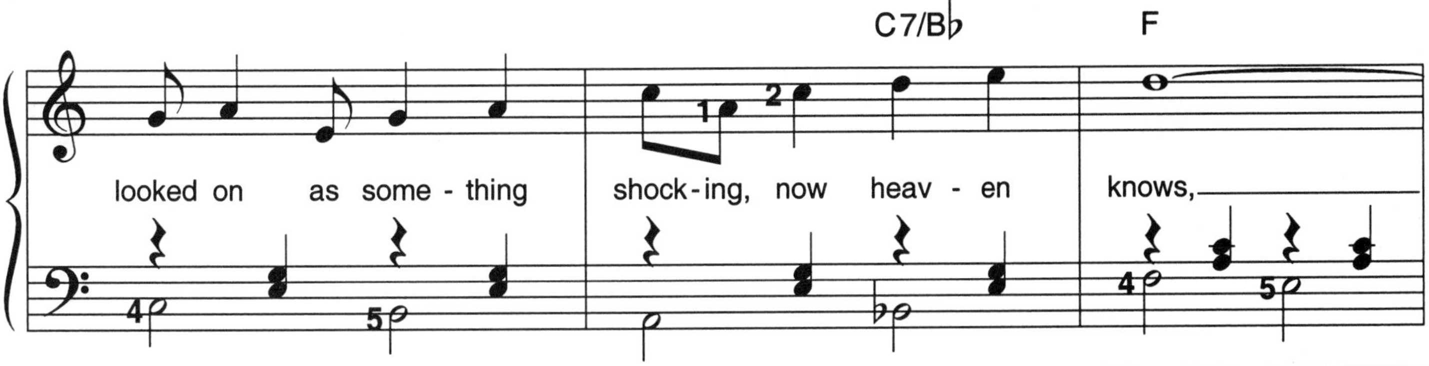

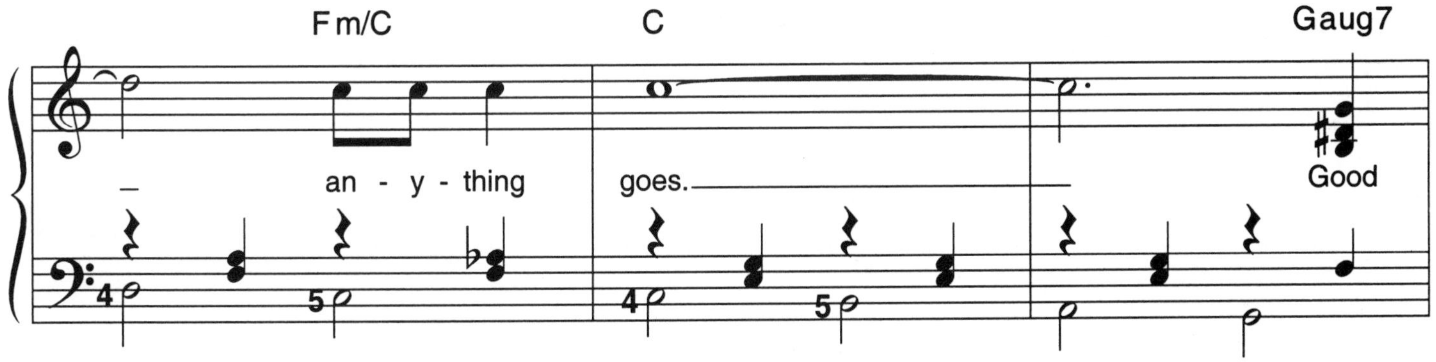

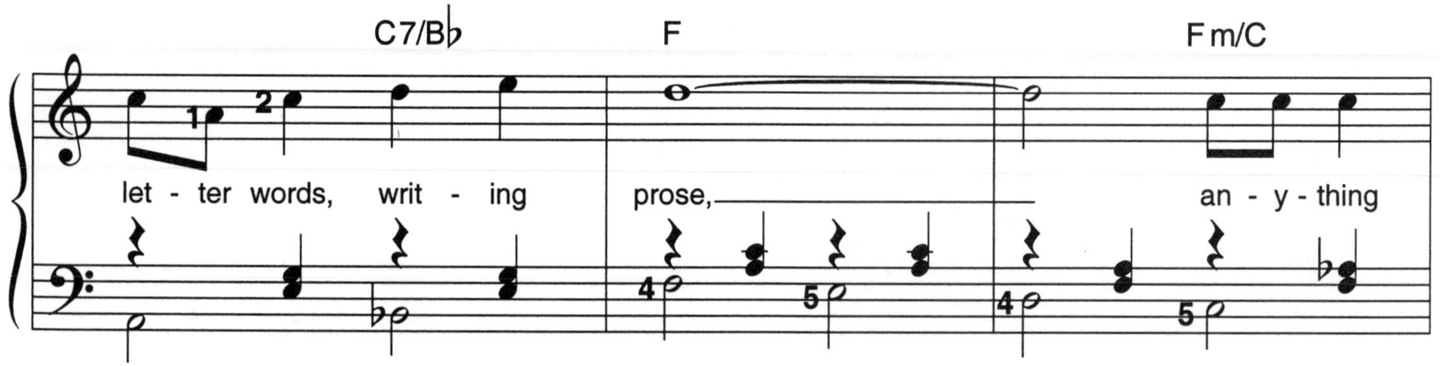
C7/B♭
F
Fm/C
let - ter words, writ - ing
prose,
an - y - thing

C
B7
E
goes.
The world has gone
mad to - day and good's

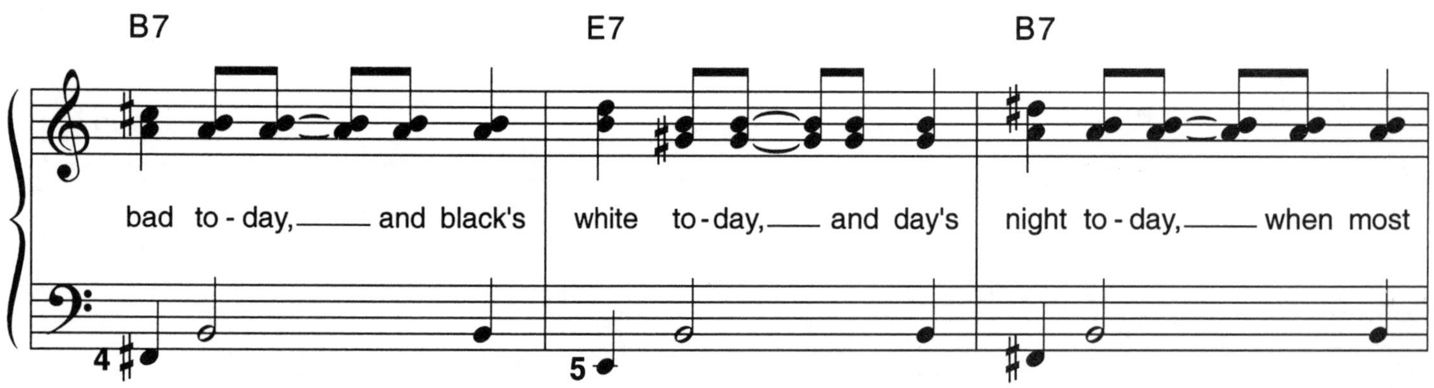
B7
E7
B7
bad to - day, and black's
white to - day, and day's
night to - day, when most

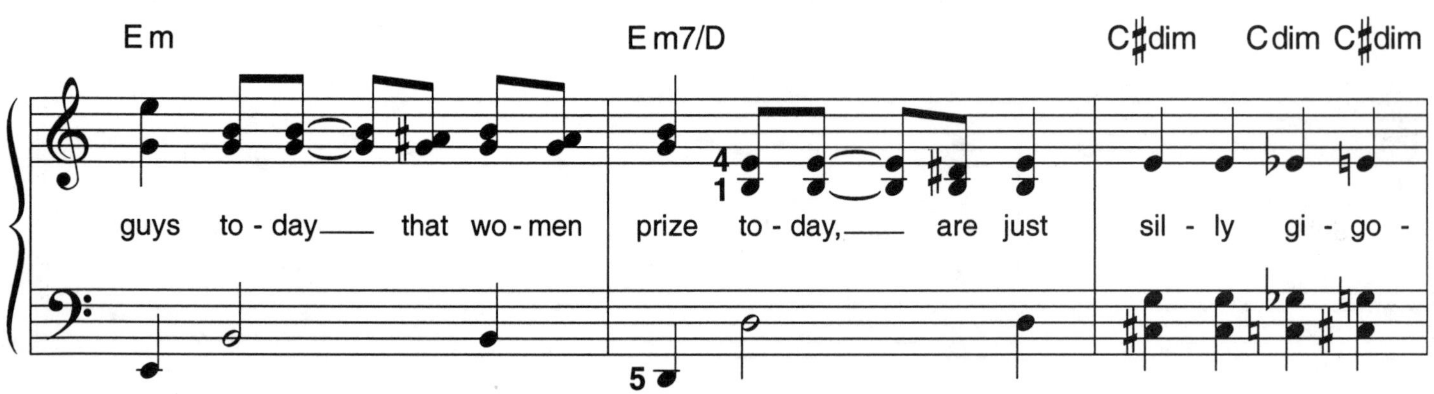
Em
Em7/D
C♯dim Cdim C♯dim
guys to - day that wo - men
prize to - day, are just
sil - ly gi - go -

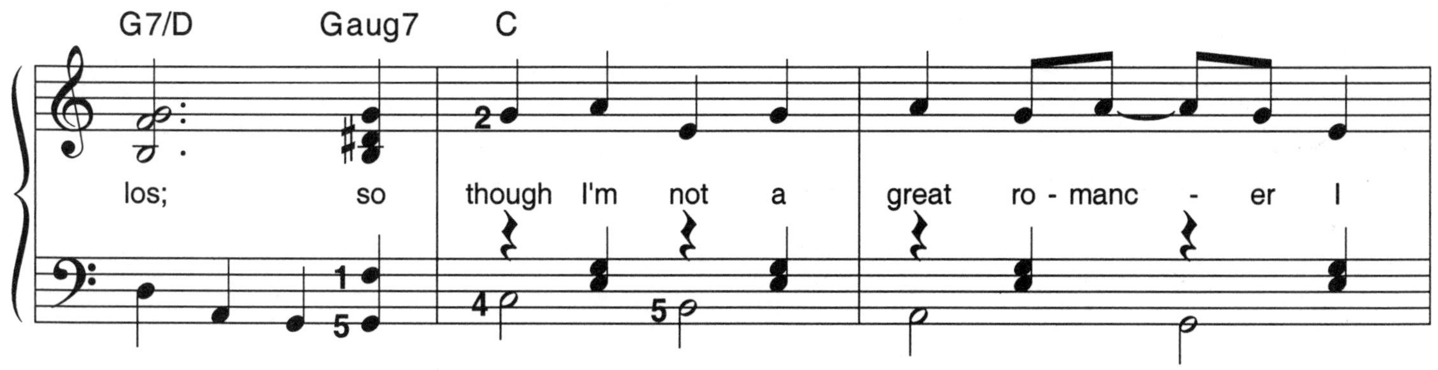
G7/D
Gaug7
C
los; so though I'm not a great ro - manc - er I

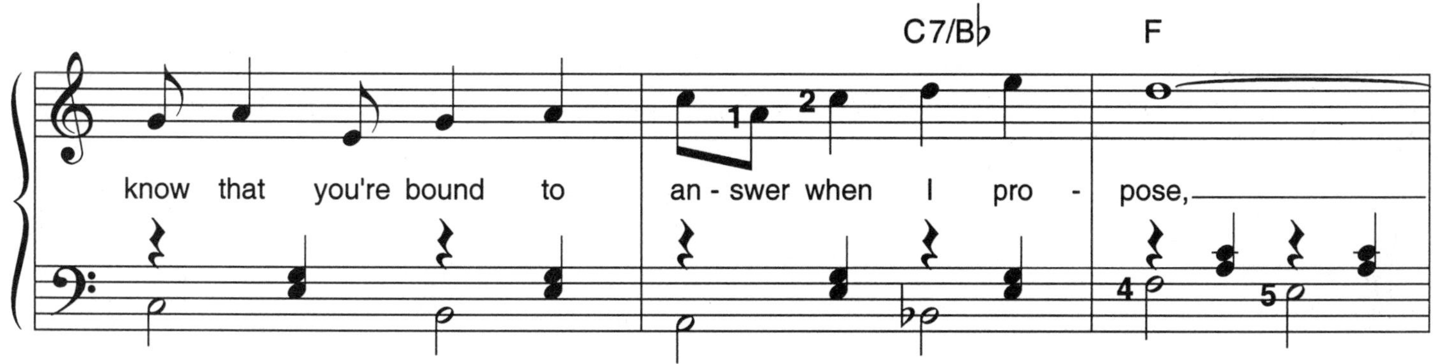
C7/B♭
F
know that you're bound to an - swer when I pro - pose,

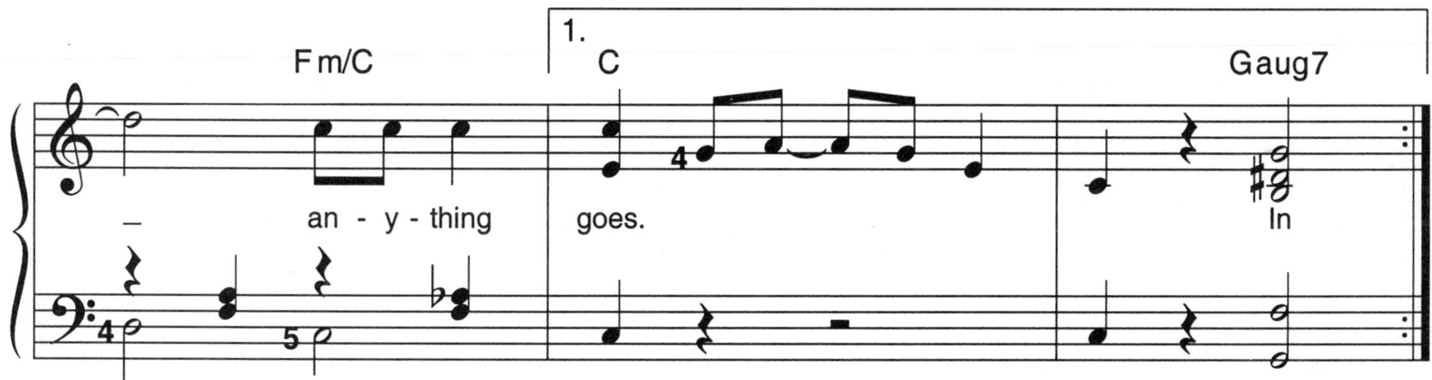
Fm/C
1.
C
Gaug7
— an - y - thing goes. In

2.
C
goes.

Just You, Just Me

Lyric by
RAYMOND KLAGES

Music by
JESSE GREER
Arranged by Richard Bradley

C
Cdim
Dm
G7
F
you.
Oh,
gee!
What are your
Fm
C
G♯dim
Am
D7
charms for?
What are my arms for?
Use your im -
G7
C
Em7(♭5)
A7
Dm
Dm7(♭5)
ag - i - na - tion!
Just
you,
Just
G
C
F
Fm
C
D7
G7
me,
I'll tie a
lov - ers knot
'round won - der - ful
C
F
Fm
C
D7
G7
C
you.

My Funny Valentine

From the Broadway Musical *Babes in Arms*
and the Motion Picture *Pal Joey*

Words by LORENZ HART
Music by RICHARD RODGERS
Arranged by Richard Bradley

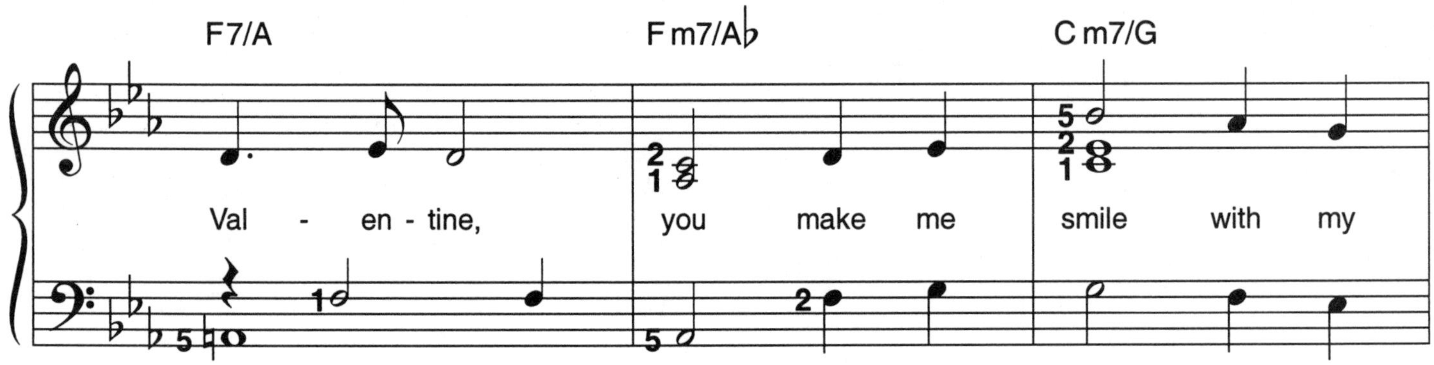

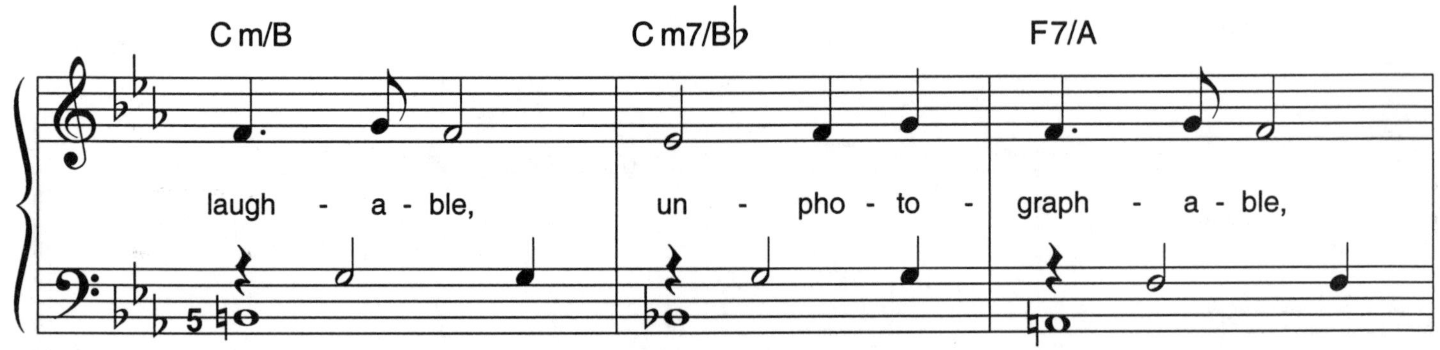

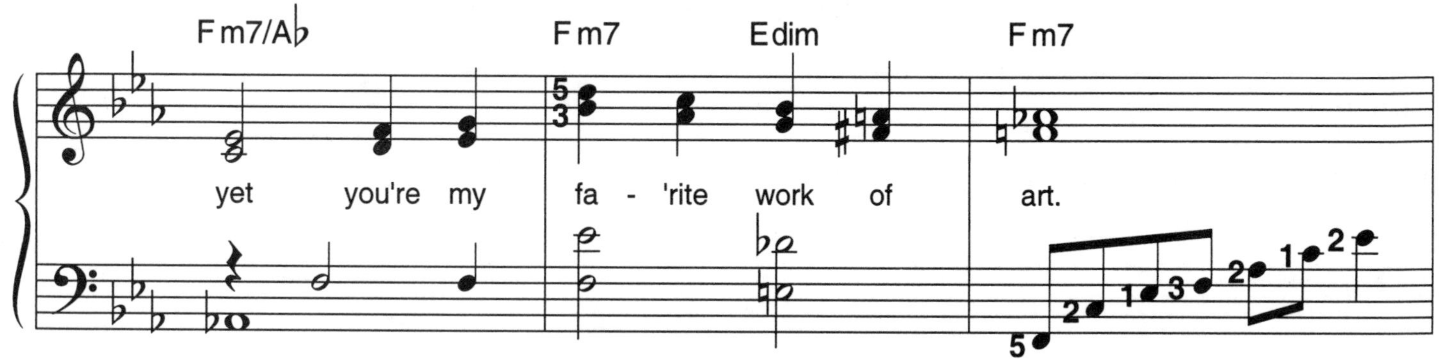
Fm7/A♭
Fm7
Edim
Fm7
yet you're my fa - 'rite work of art.

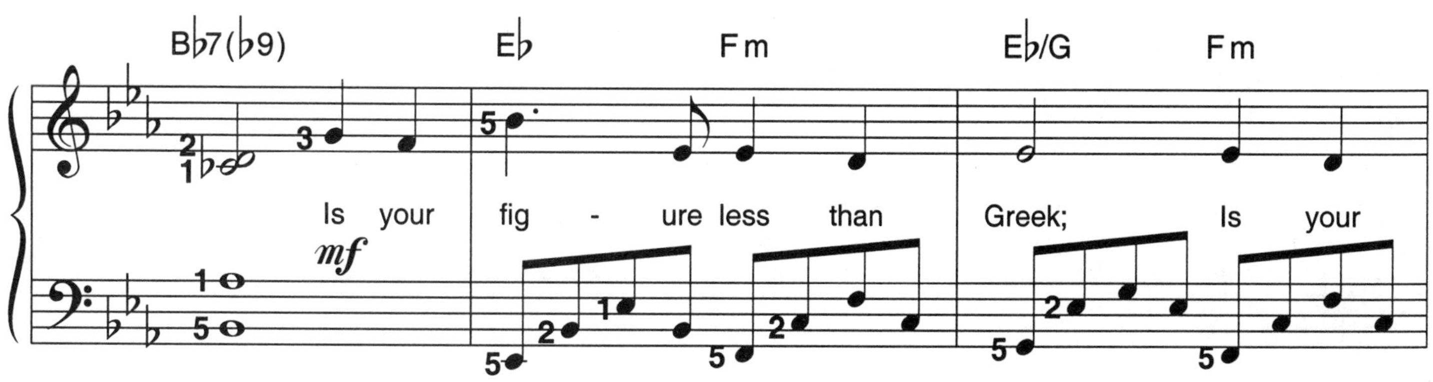
B♭7(♭9)
E♭
Fm
E♭/G
Fm
Is your fig - ure less than Greek; Is your
mf

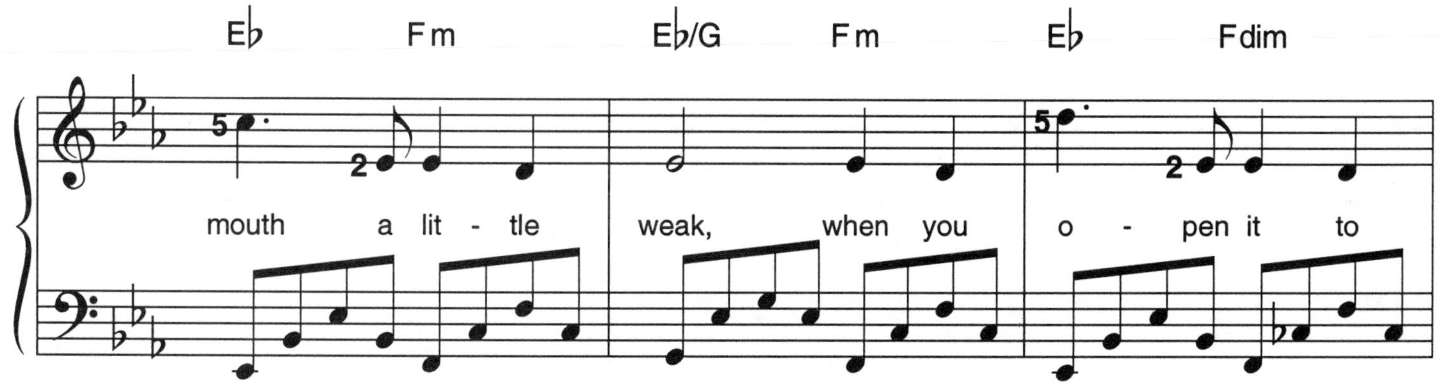
E♭
Fm
E♭/G
Fm
E♭
Fdim
mouth a lit - tle weak, when you o - pen it to

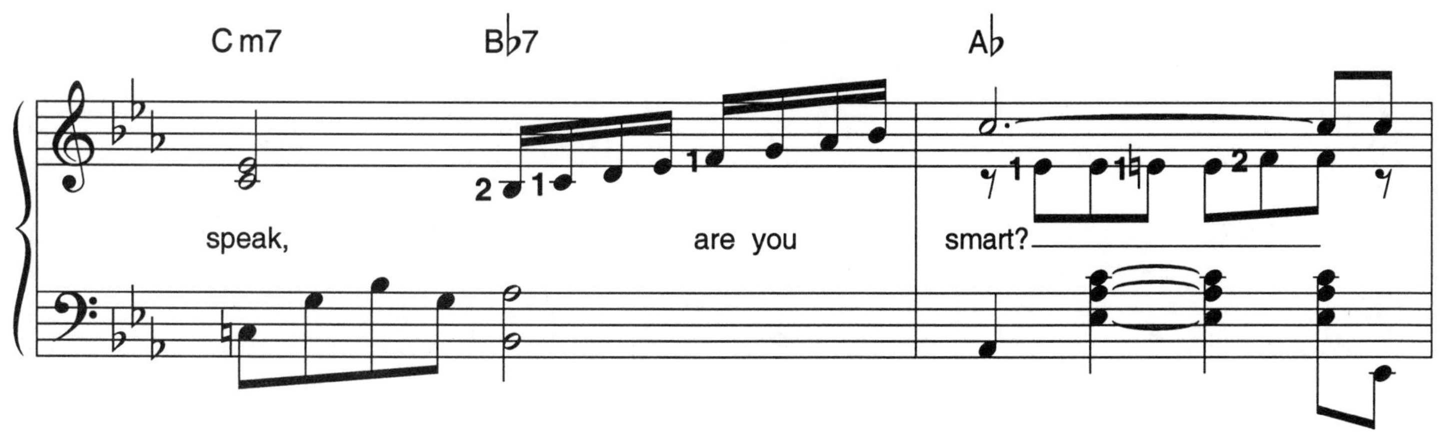
Cm7
B♭7
A♭
speak, are you smart?

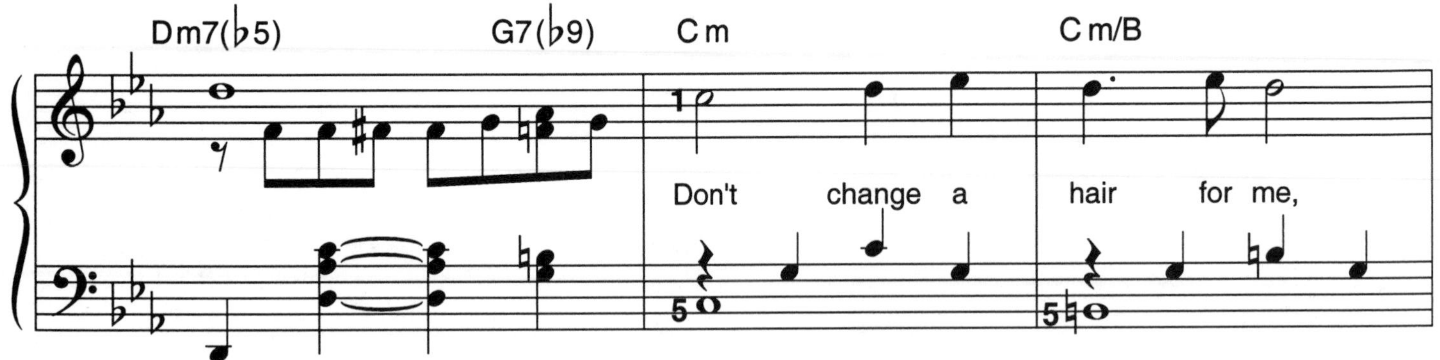
Dm7(♭5)
G7(♭9)
Cm
Cm/B
Don't change a hair for me,

Cm7/B♭
F7/A
Fm7/A♭
D7/A
G7/B
not if you care for me, stay, lit - tle Val - en - tine,

Cm
B♭m7
E♭7
A♭Maj7
Fm
B♭7
stay!
Each day is Val - en - tine's

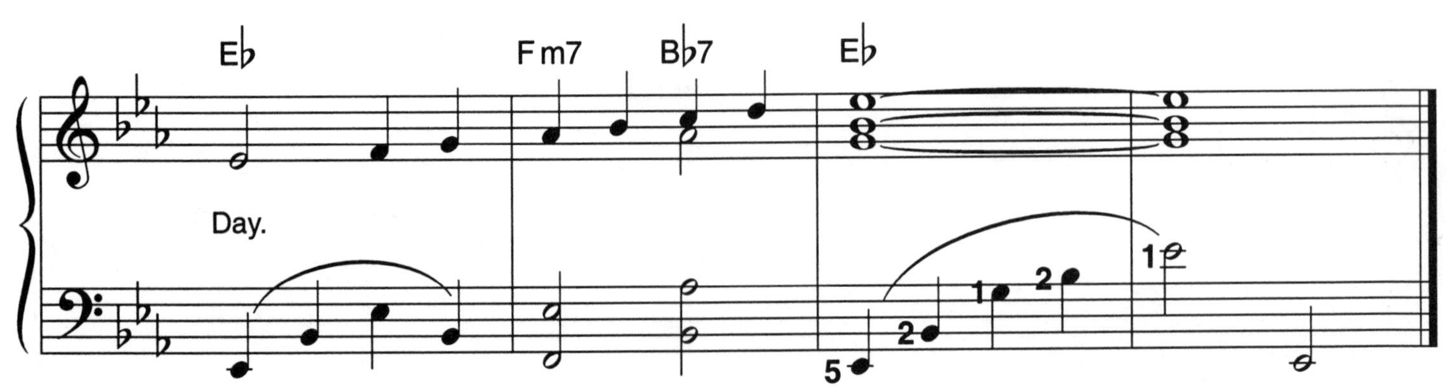
E♭
Fm7
B♭7
E♭
Day.

'S Wonderful

From the Broadway Musical *Funny Face*

Words by IRA GERSHWIN
Music by GEORGE GERSHWIN
Arranged by Richard Bradley

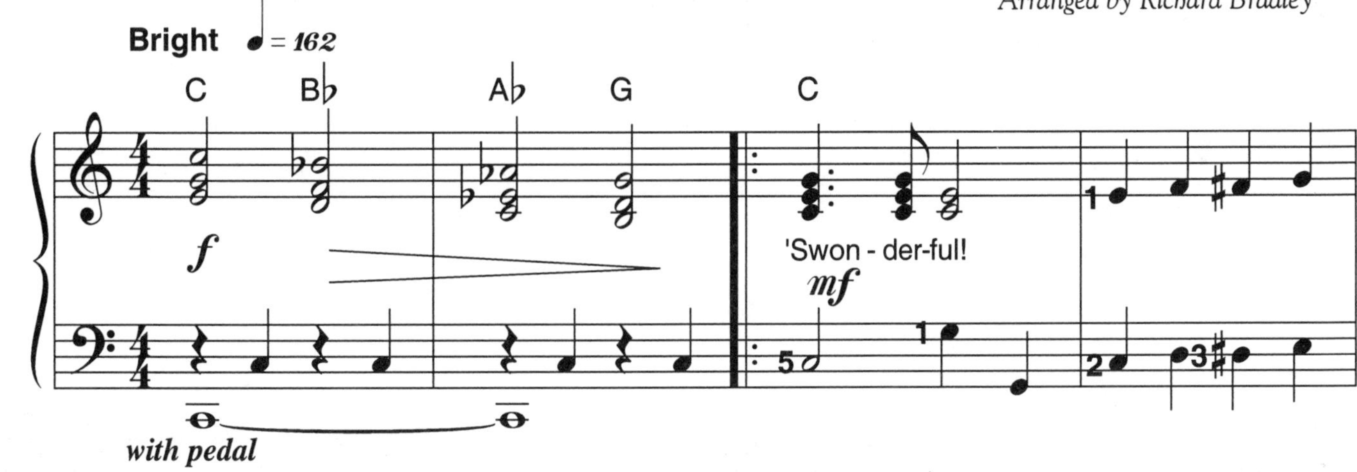

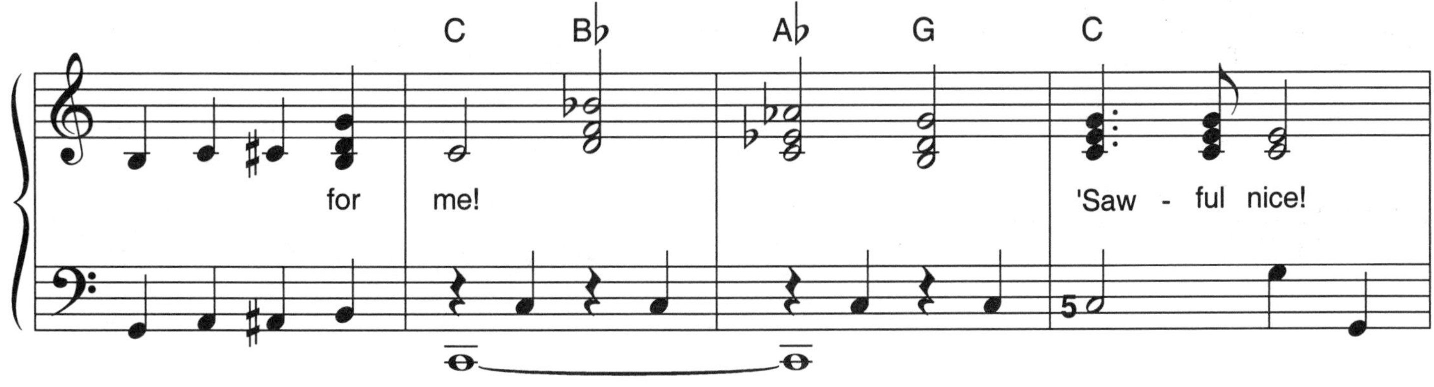

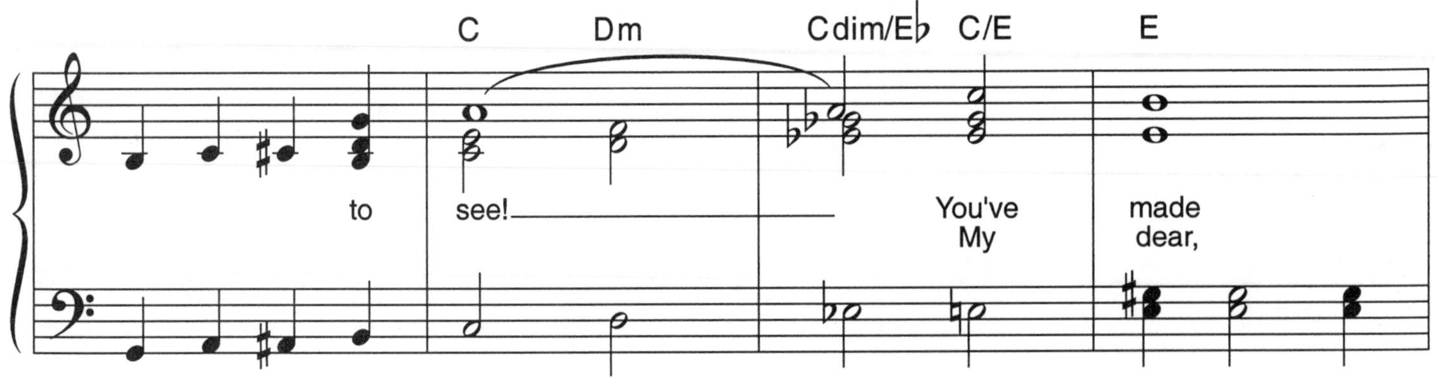
C
Dm
Cdim/E♭
C/E
E
to
see!
You've
My
made
dear,

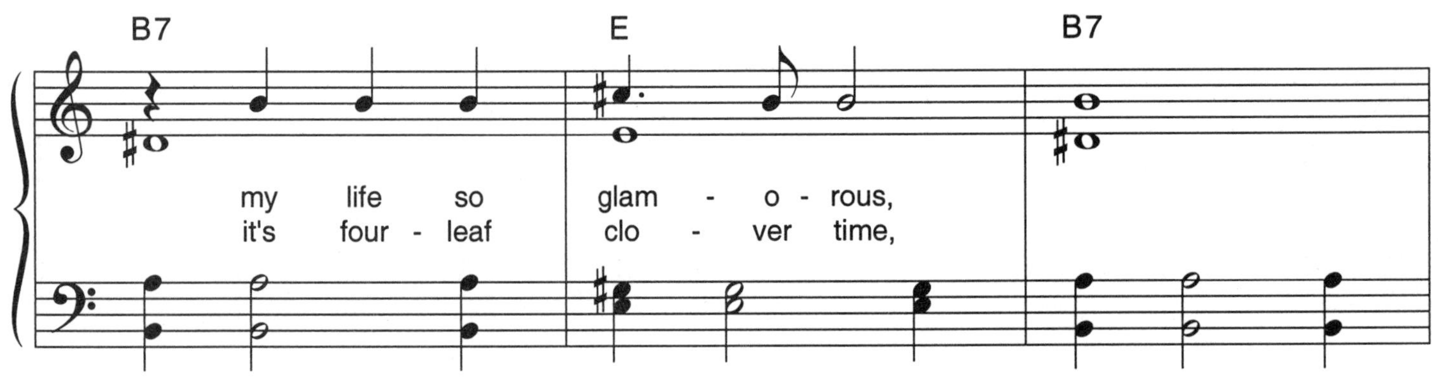
B7
E
B7
my life so
it's four - leaf
glam - o - rous,
clo - ver time,

Em
A7
D7
You can't blame
From now on
me for feel - ing
my heart's work - ing
a - mor - ous.
o - ver - time.

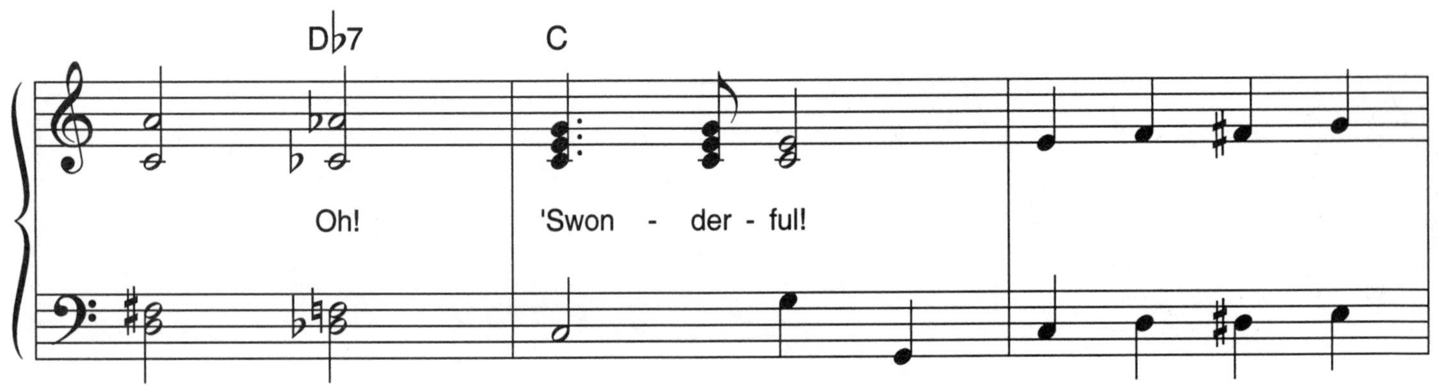
D♭7
C
Oh!
'Swon - der - ful!

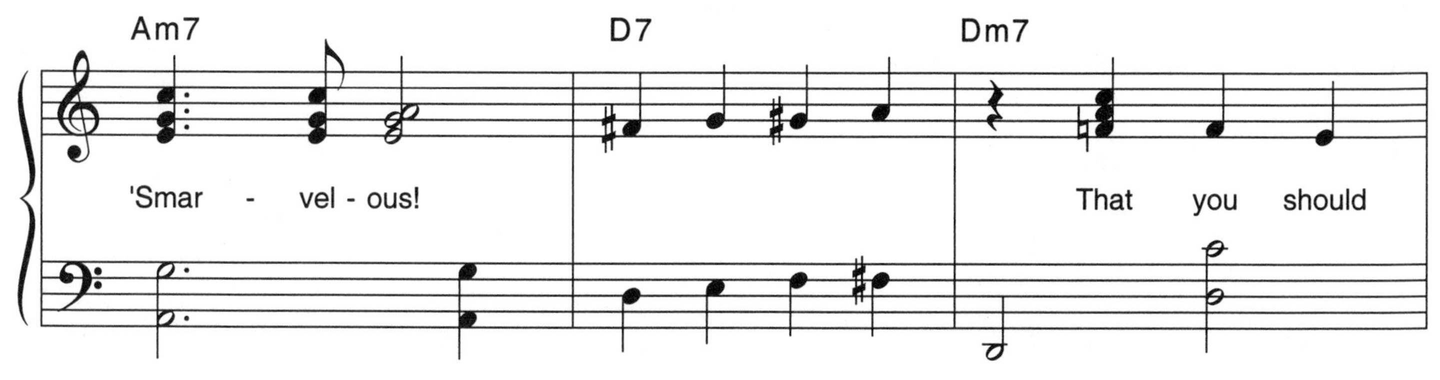
Am7
D7
Dm7
'Smar - vel - ous!
That you should

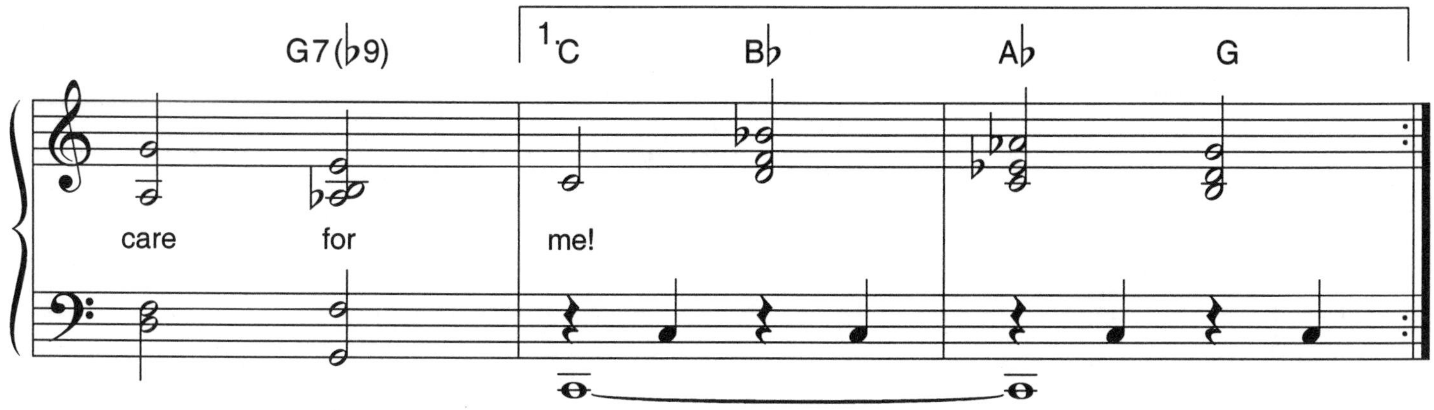
G7(♭9)
1. C
B♭
A♭
G
care for
me!

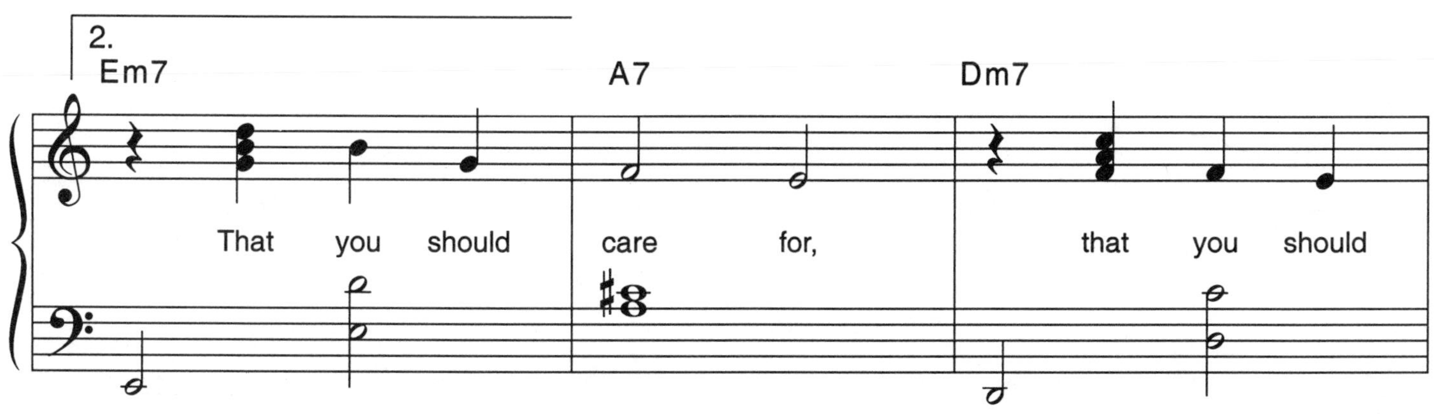
2.
Em7
A7
Dm7
That you should
care for,
that you should

G7(♭9)
C
care for
me!

Once Upon a Time

From the Broadway Musical *All American*

Lyrics by LEE ADAMS
Music by CHARLES STROUSE
Arranged by Richard Bradley

Moderately slow ♩ = 74

B♭ B♭Maj7 C m7 F7sus4 F7

8va
mp

with pedal

B♭ B♭Maj7 B♭6 B♭Maj7 G m G m7

Once up - on a time a girl with moon - light in her eyes

G m G m7 E♭ B♭ B♭Maj7 E♭ D m7

8va

put her hand in mine and said she loved me

E♭ E♭+ C m7 F7 G m G m7

so. But that was once up - on a time,

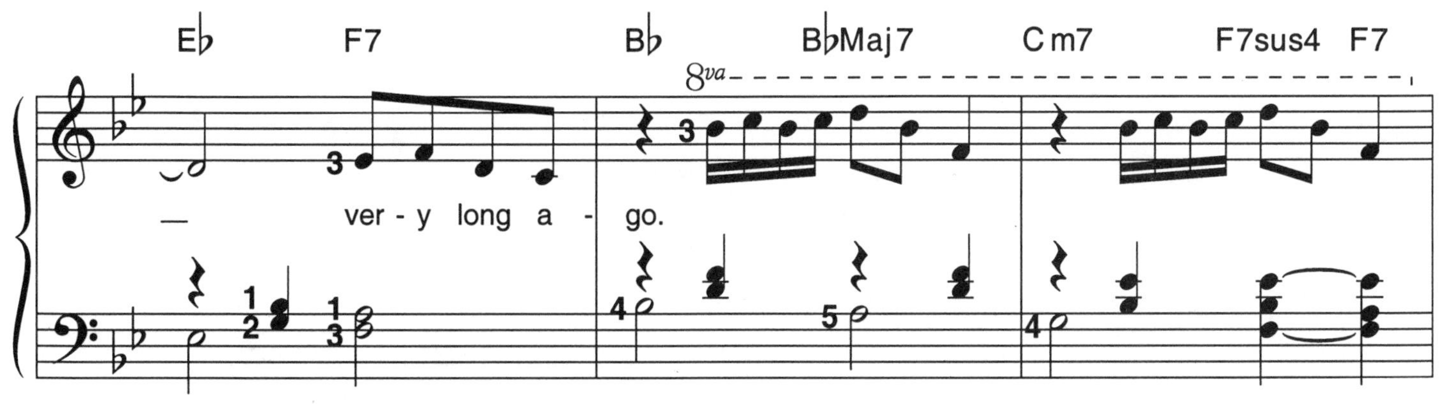
E♭ F7 B♭ B♭Maj7 Cm7 F7sus4 F7
8va
— ver - y long a - go.

B♭ B♭Maj7 B♭6 B♭Maj7 Gm Gm7
Once up - on a hill we sat be - neath a wil - low tree,

Gm Gm7 E♭ B♭ B♭Maj7 E♭ Dm7
8va
count - ing all the stars and wait - ing for the

E♭ E♭+ Cm7 F7 Gm Gm7
dawn. But that was once up - on a time,

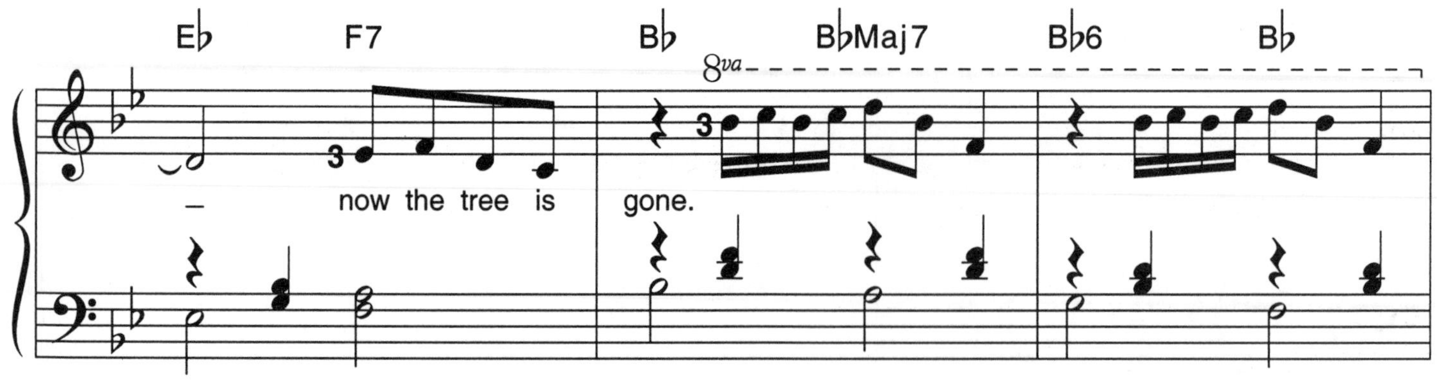
E♭
F7
B♭
B♭Maj7
B♭6
B♭
8va
– now the tree is gone.

Cm7
F7
B♭Maj7
B♭6
Cm7
F7
B♭Maj7
B♭6
How the breeze ruf - fled through her hair,

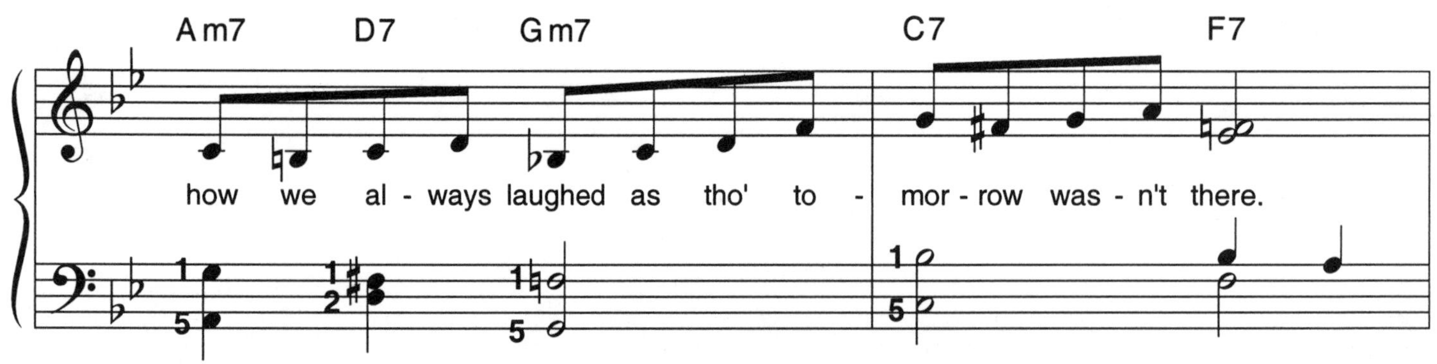
Am7
D7
Gm7
C7
F7
how we al - ways laughed as tho' to - mor - row was - n't there.

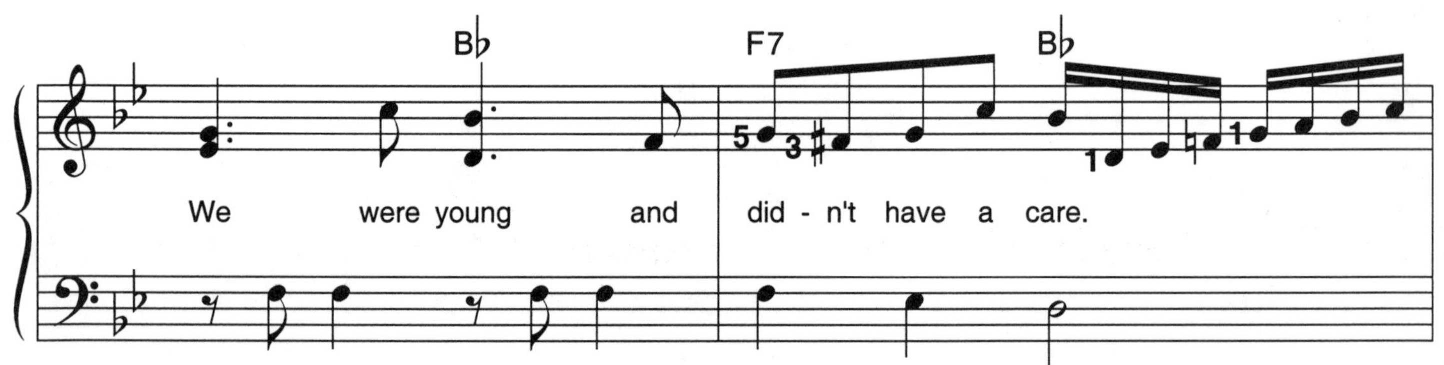
B♭
F7
B♭
We were young and did - n't have a care.

Gm7 C7 F7 B♭ B♭Maj7
Where did it go? Once up - on a time
B♭6 B♭Maj7 Gm Gm7 Gm Gm7
the world was sweet - er than we knew,
8va
E♭ B♭ B♭Maj7 E♭ E♭ E♭+
ev - 'ry - thing was ours, how hap - py we were then.
Cm7 F7 Gm E♭Maj7 Cm9 F7
But some - how once up - on a time nev - er comes a -
B♭ B♭Maj7 B♭6 B♭
gain.
8va

What a Wonderful World

Words and Music by
GEORGE DAVID WEISS and BOB THIELE
Arranged by Richard Bradley

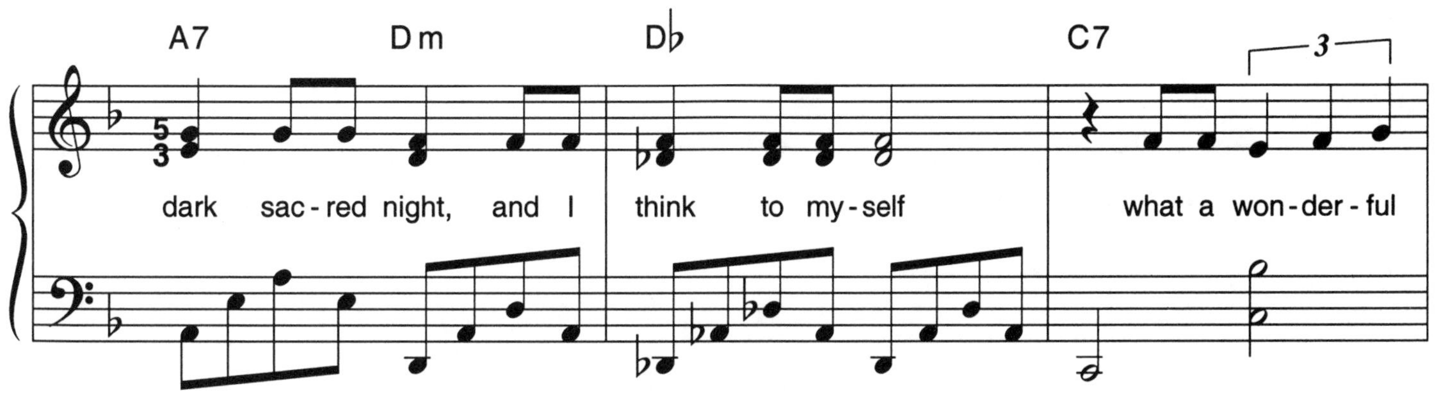
A7
Dm
D♭
C7
3
dark sac-red night, and I think to my-self what a won-der-ful

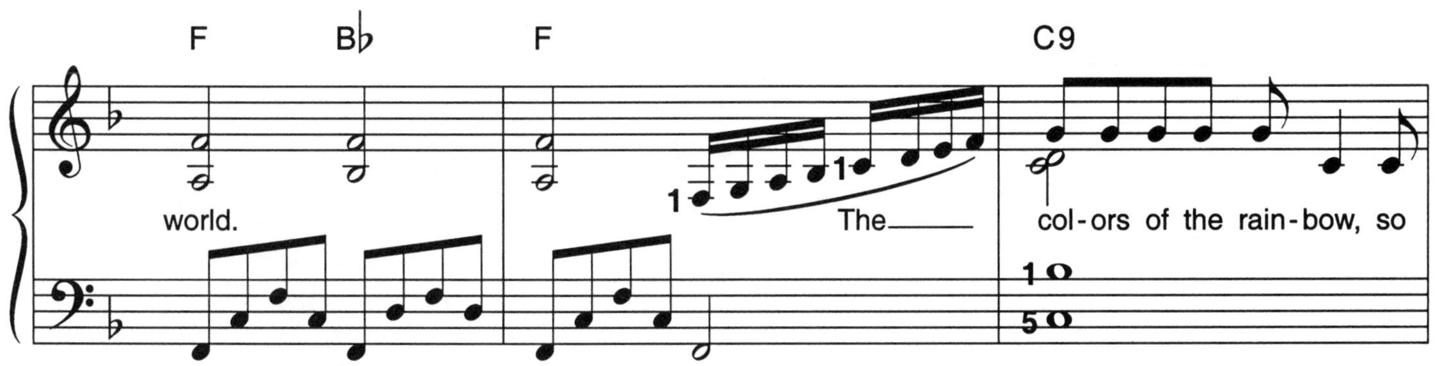
F
B♭
F
C9
world. The colors of the rain-bow, so

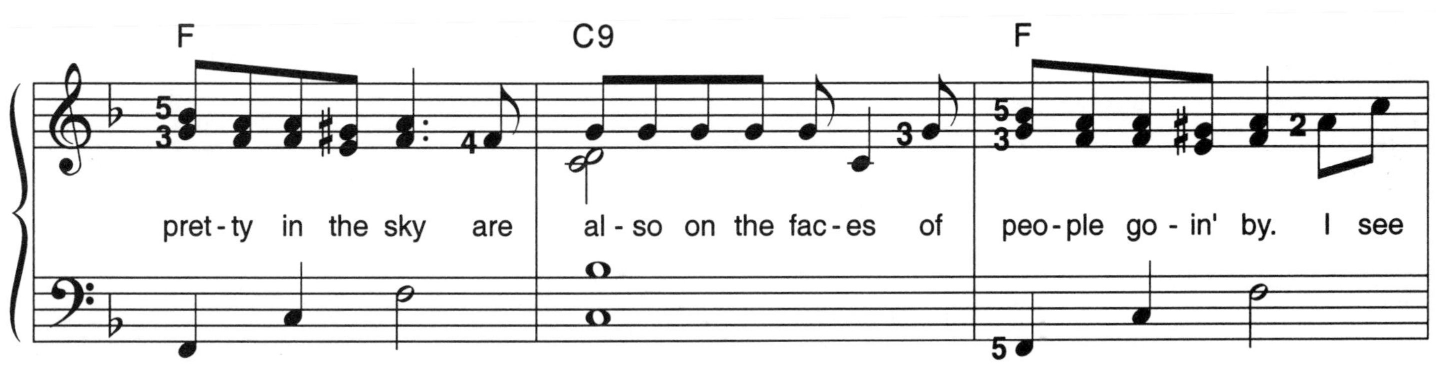
F
C9
F
pret-ty in the sky are al-so on the fac-es of peo-ple go-in' by. I see

Dm
C/E
Dm/F
C/E
Dm
E♭dim
friends shak-in' hands, say-in', "How do you do!" they're real-ly say-in'

Gm Ebdim C7/E C7
F
Am
Bb
Am
"I love you." I hear ba - bies cry, I watch them grow,
Gm7
F
A7
Dm
Db
they'll learn much more than I'll ev - er know and I think to my - self
C7
F
Am7(b5)
D7
what a won - der - ful world. Yes, I
Gm9
G7 Gm7
C7
F
Bb/F
F
think to my - self what a won - der - ful world.

Ebb Tide

Lyric by
CARL SIGMAN

Music by
ROBERT MAXWELL
Arranged by Richard Bradley

L.H.
Dm
E
R.H.
wide? At last we're face to face, and as we
mf
cresc.

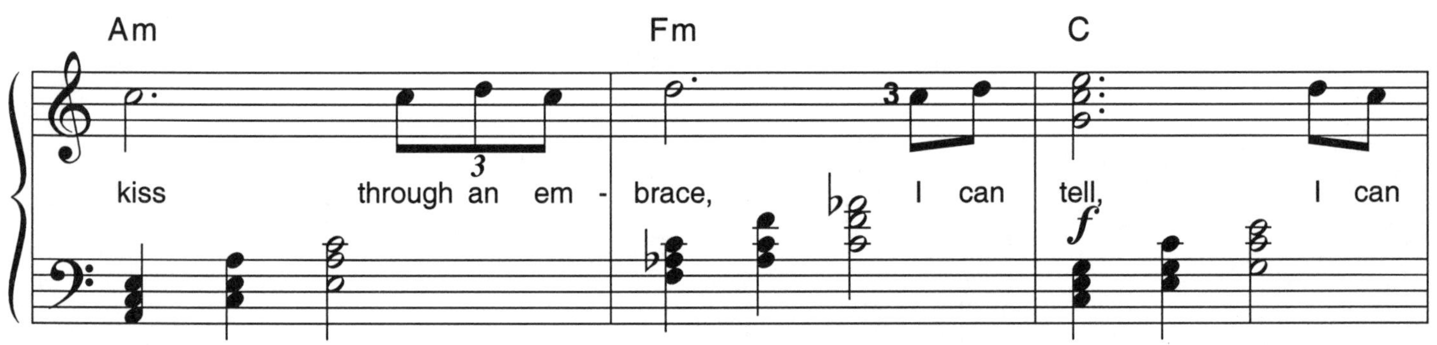
Am
Fm
C
kiss through an em - brace, I can tell, I can
f

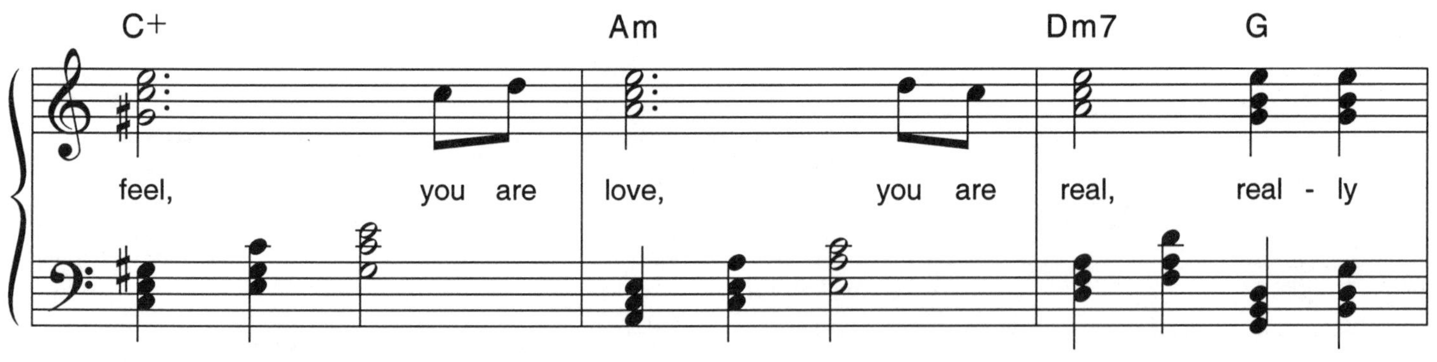
C+
Am
Dm7
G
feel, you are love, you are real, real - ly

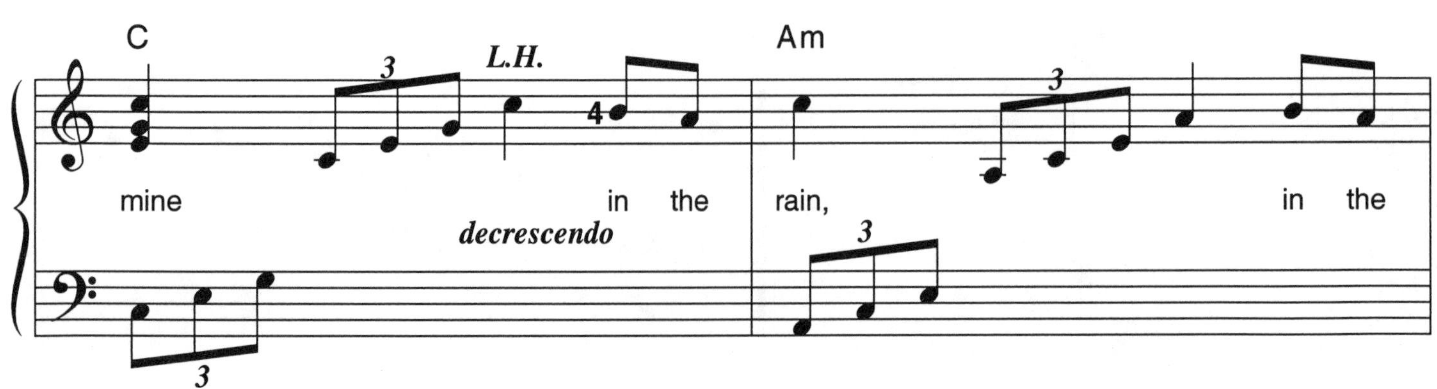
C
L.H.
Am
mine in the rain, in the
decrescendo

Fm
3
dark,
in the
3
Dm
3
G7
5
sun.
Like the
3
C
3
tide
at it's
3
Am
3
ebb,
I'm at
3
Dm
3
4
peace
in the
3
Fm
web
of your
C
3
R.H.
3
arms.
L.H.
3
3
R.H.
3
L.H.
3
L.H.
3
R.H.
3
R.H.
3
L.H.
3
R.H.
3
R.H.
3
L.H.
3
L.H.
3
L.H.

I'm Thru With Love

Words by
GUS KAHN

Music by
MATT MALNECK and FUD LIVINGSTON
Arranged by Richard Bradley

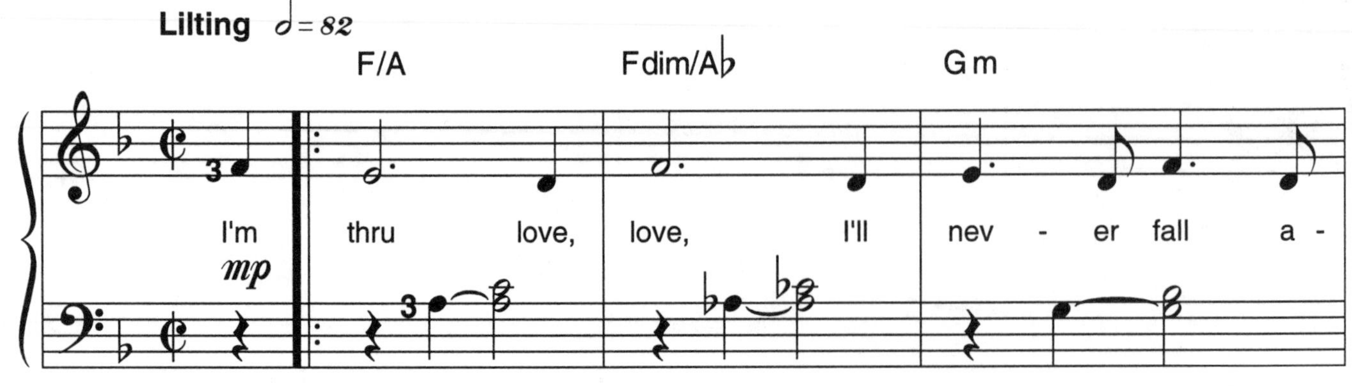

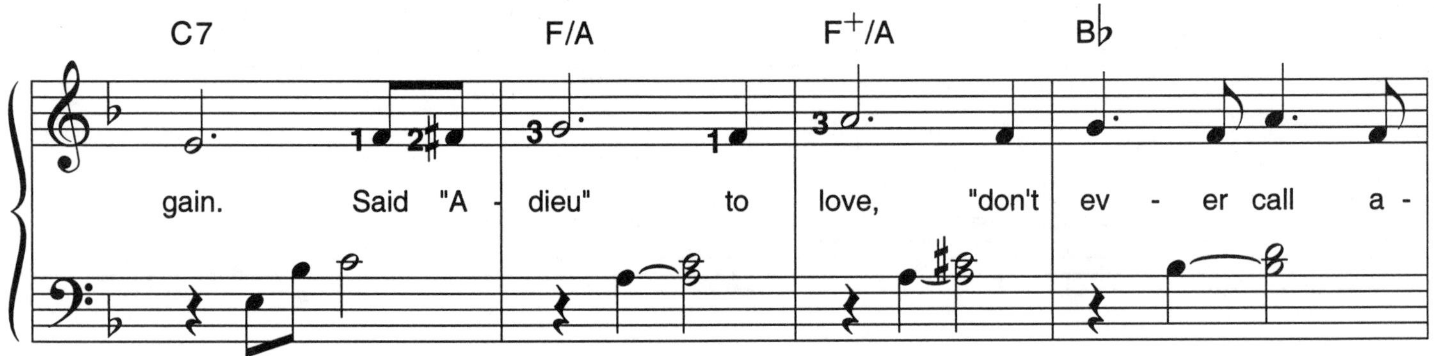

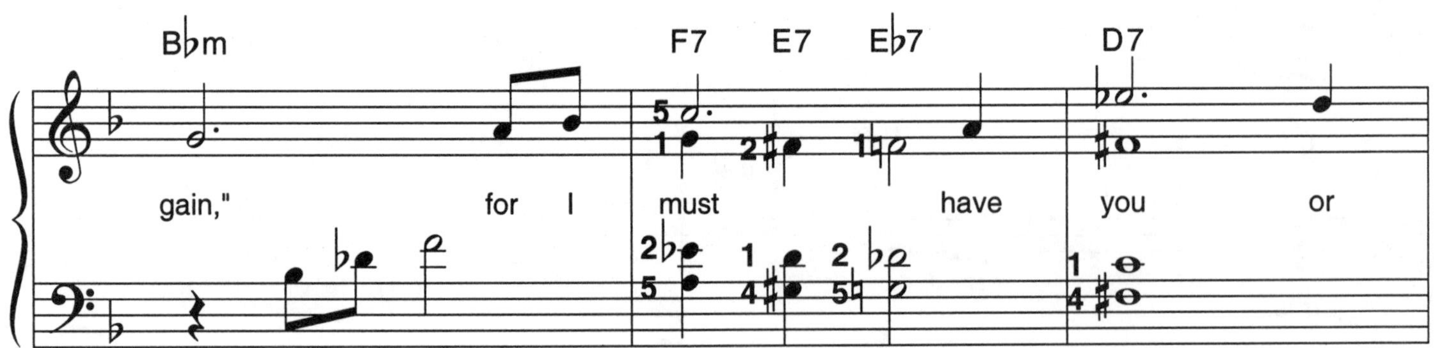

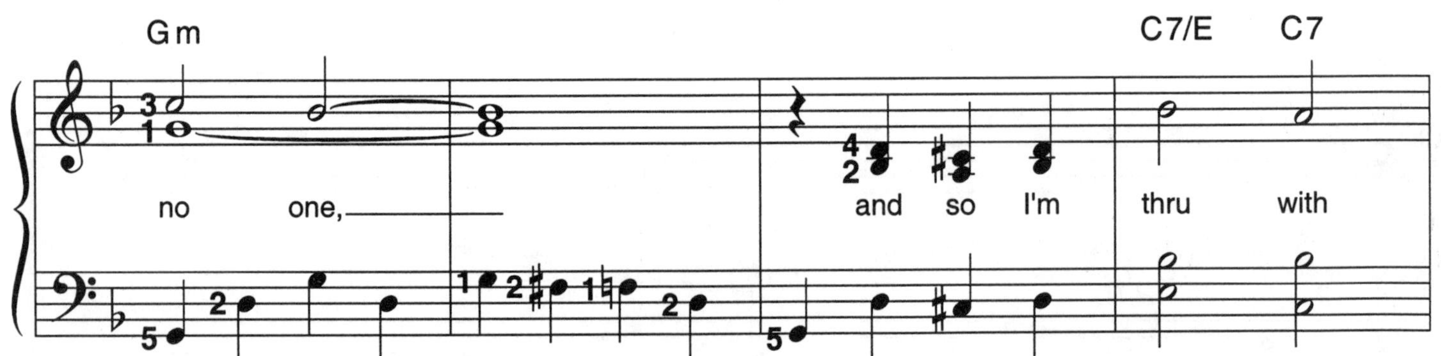

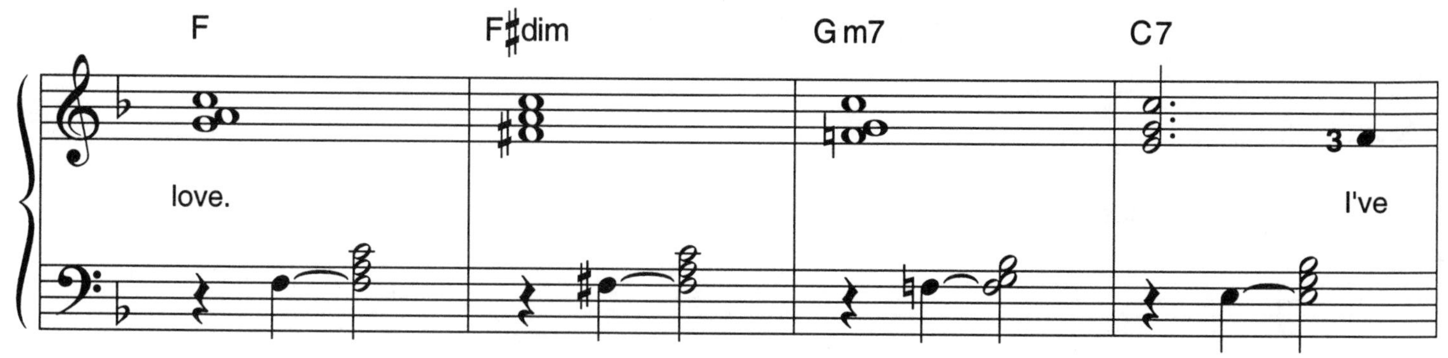
F
F♯dim
Gm7
C7
3
love.
I've

F/A
Fdim/A♭
Gm
C7
1 2
locked my heart, I'll keep my feel - ings there, I have

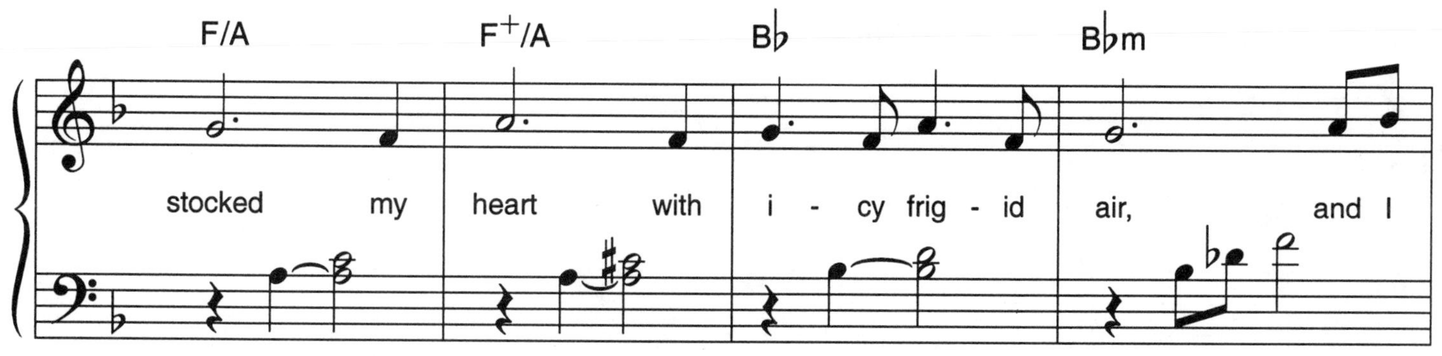
F/A
F+/A
B♭
B♭m
stocked my heart with i - cy frig - id air, and I

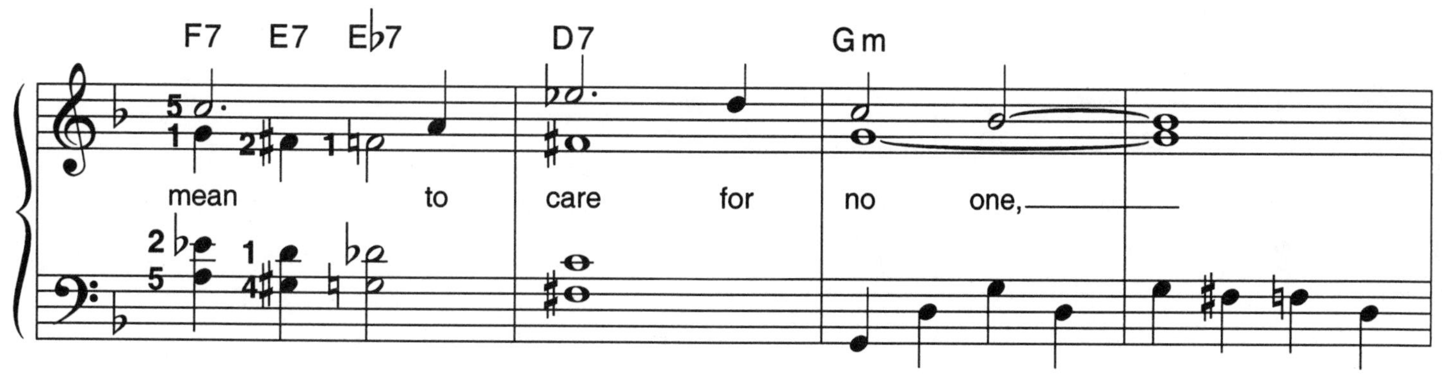
F7 E7 E♭7
D7
Gm
5
1 2 1
mean to care for no one,
2 1
5 4

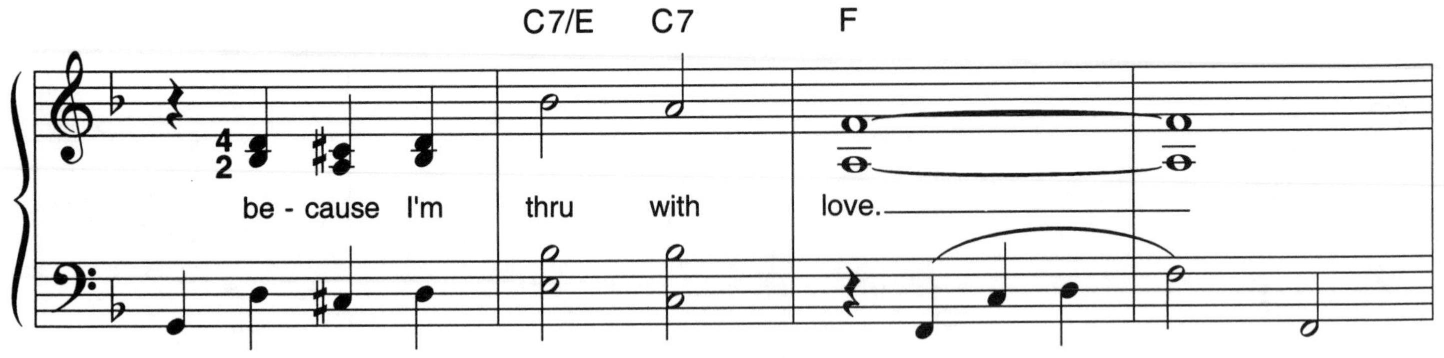
C7/E
C7
F
be - cause I'm
thru
with
love.

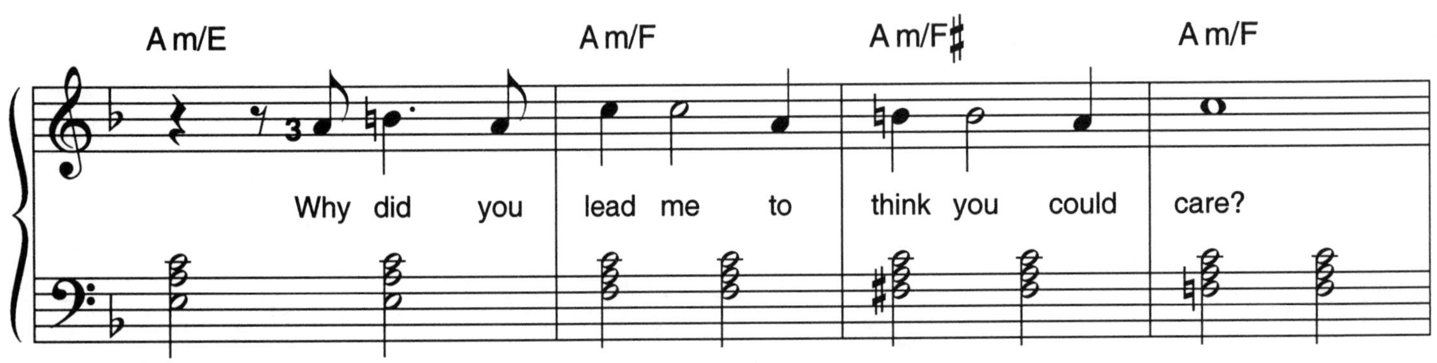
Am/E
Am/F
Am/F♯
Am/F
Why did you
lead me to
think you could
care?

Am/E
Am/F
D7/F♯
mf
You did - n't
need me for
you had your
share

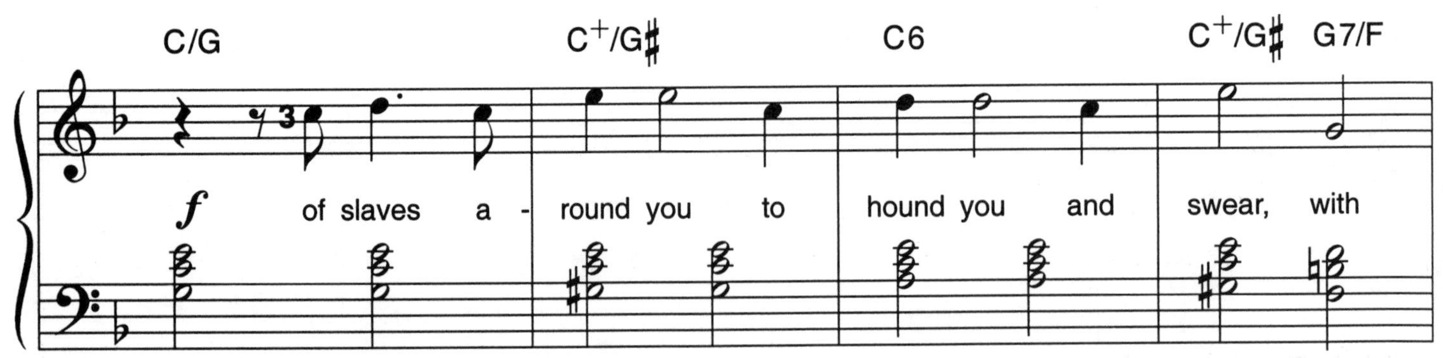
C/G
C+/G♯
C6
C+/G♯
G7/F
f
of slaves a -
round you to
hound you and
swear, with

C/E
Gm/D
Gm7/D
C7/E
C7
deep e - mo - tion, de - vo - tion to you. Good -
mf
G/B
Gdim/B♭
Am
D7
bye to spring, and all it meant to me, it can
G/B
G+/B
C
Cm
nev - er bring the thing that used to be, for I
G7
F♯7
F7
E7
Am
must have you or no one,
D7/F♯
D7
G
GMaj9
and so I'm thru with love.
pp

Ain't Misbehavin'

Words by
ANDY RAZAF

Music by
THOMAS "FATS" WALLER
and HARRY BROOKS
Arranged by Richard Bradley

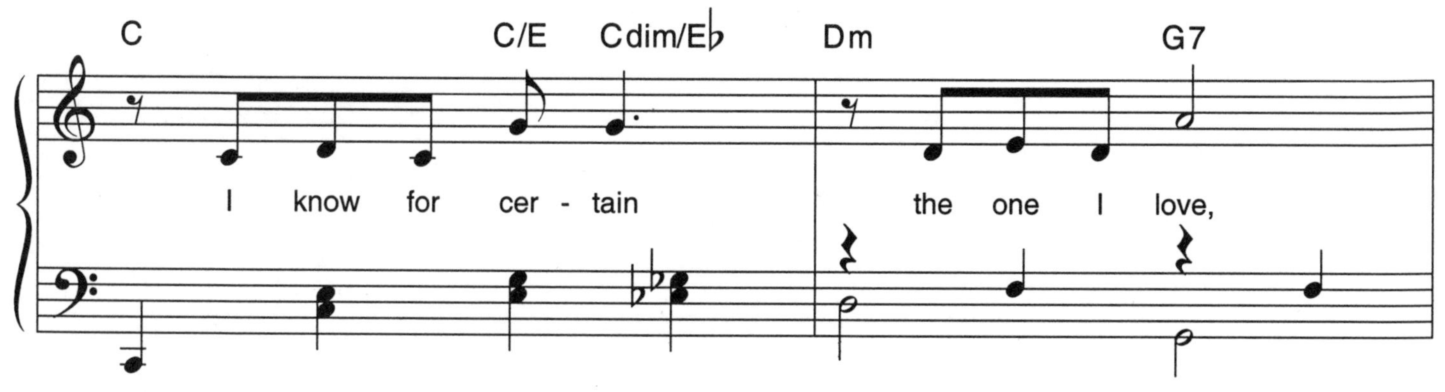
C
C/E
Cdim/E♭
Dm
G7
I know for cer - tain
the one I love,

C
C7/E
F
Fm
3
I'm thru with flirt - in', it's
just you I'm think - ing of,

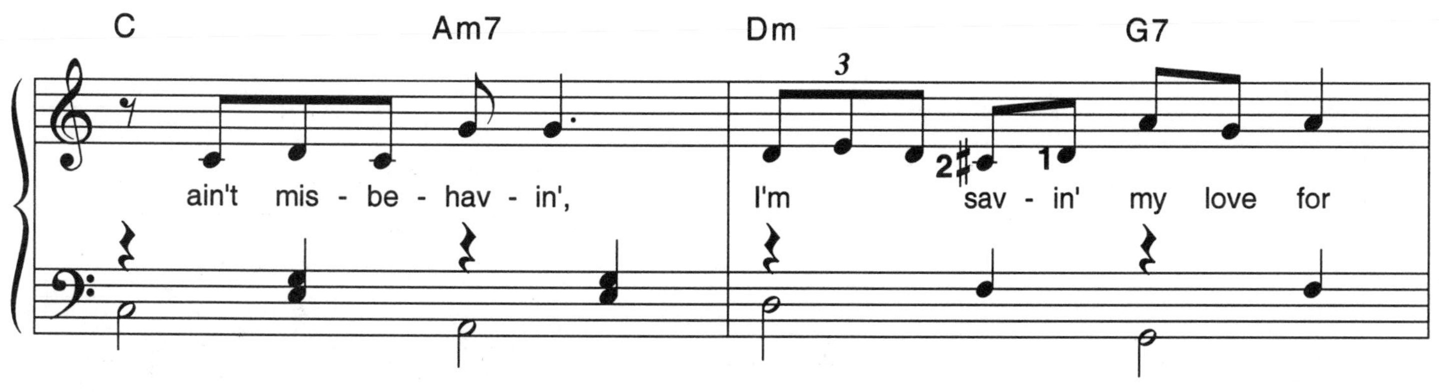
C
Am7
Dm
G7
3
ain't mis - be - hav - in',
I'm sav - in' my love for

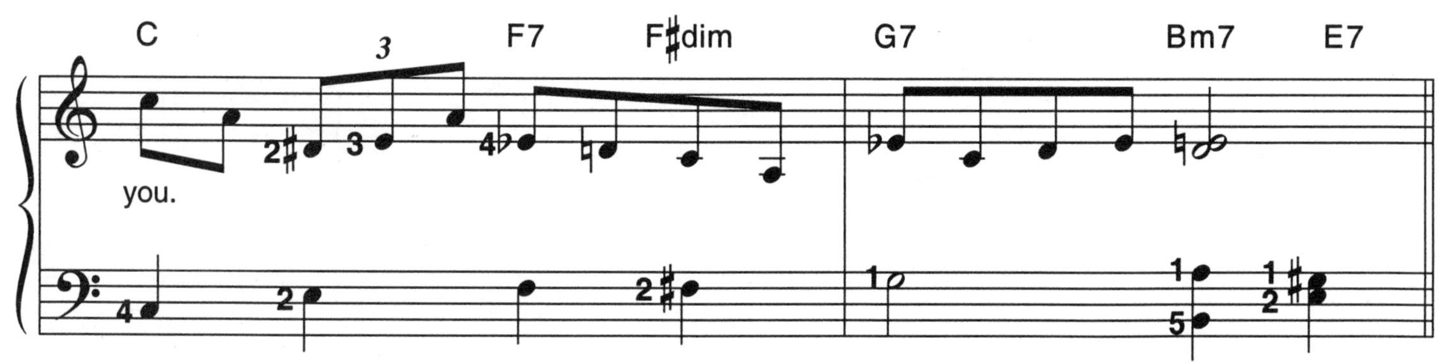
C
F7
F♯dim
G7
Bm7
E7
3
you.

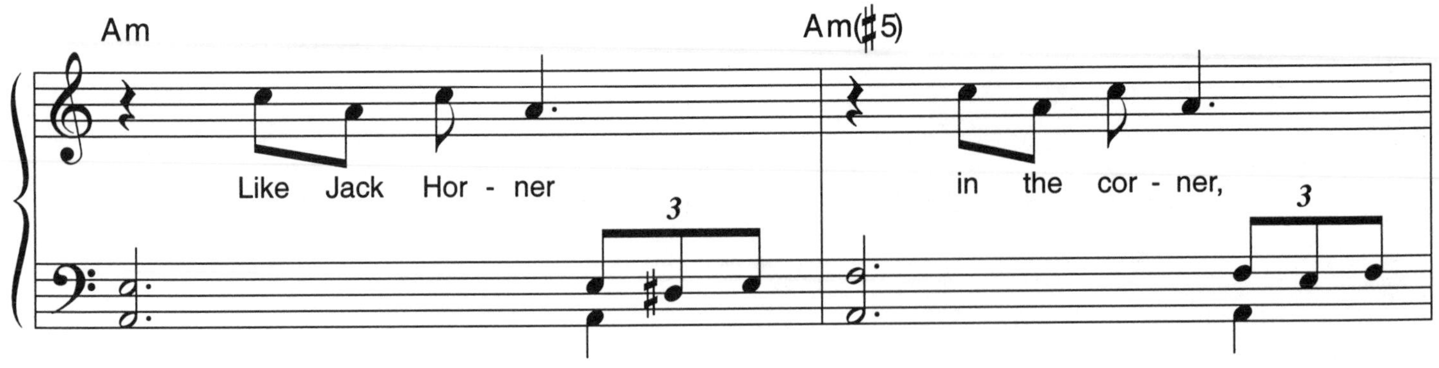
Am
Am(♯5)
Like Jack Hor - ner
in the cor - ner,
3
3

Am6
A7
don't go no - where,
what do I care,
3

G
Em
Am7
D7
your kiss - es
are worth wait - ing
3
3
3

G7
A7
D9
G9
for, be - lieve me.

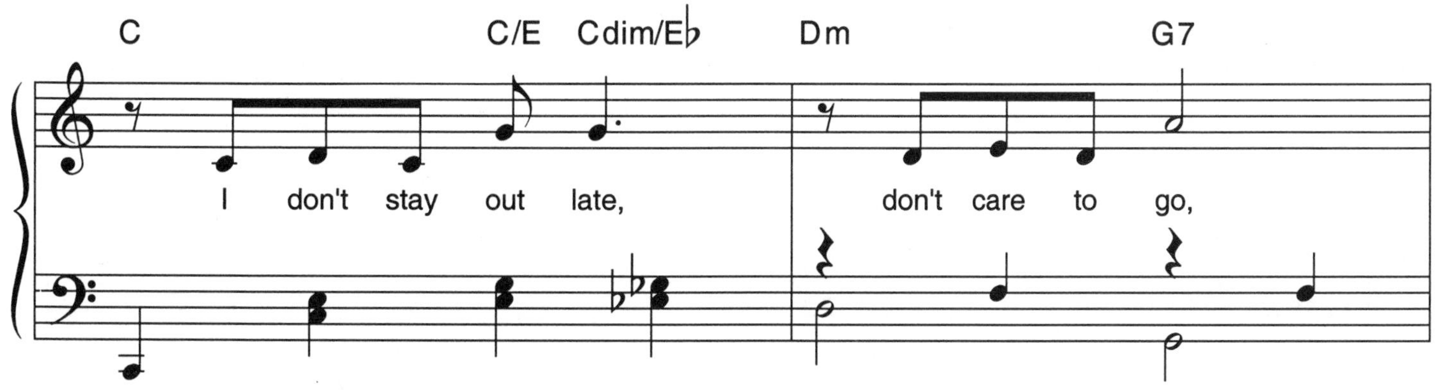
C
C/E
Cdim/E♭
Dm
G7
I don't stay out late,
don't care to go,

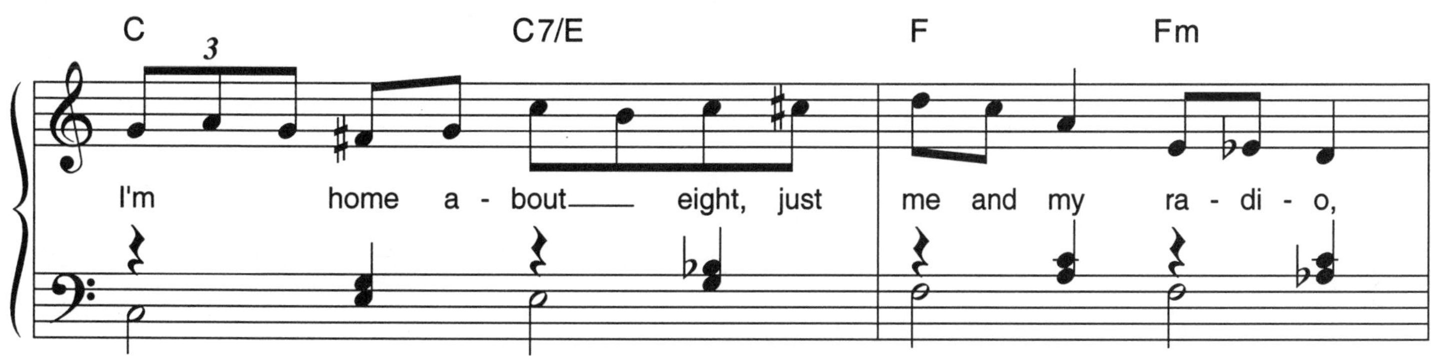
C
C7/E
F
Fm
3
I'm home a - bout eight, just
me and my ra - di - o,

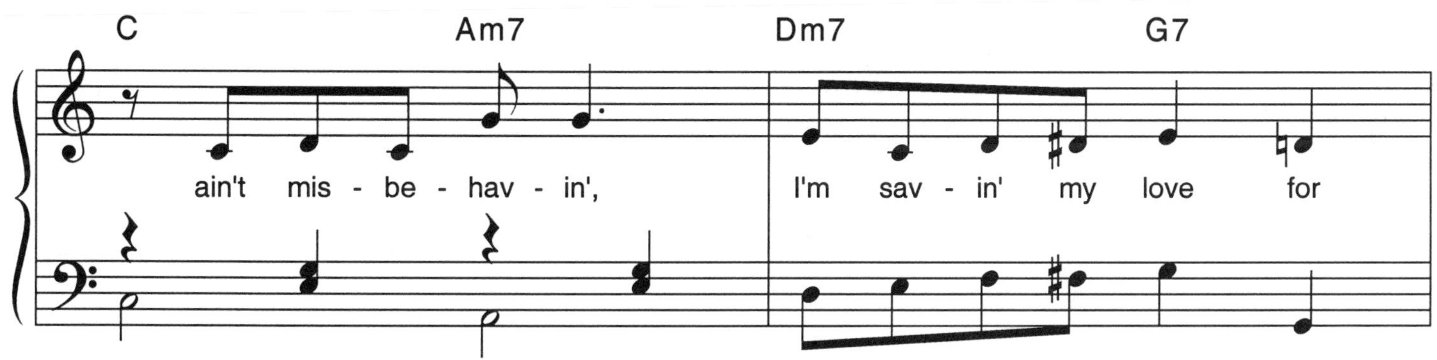
C
Am7
Dm7
G7
ain't mis - be - hav - in',
I'm sav - in' my love for

C
F7
F♯dim
C
D♭9
C13
3
2
3
4
you.

He Loves and She Loves

From the Broadway Musical *Manhattan*

Music and Lyrics by
GEORGE GERSHWIN
and IRA GERSHWIN
Arranged by Richard Bradley

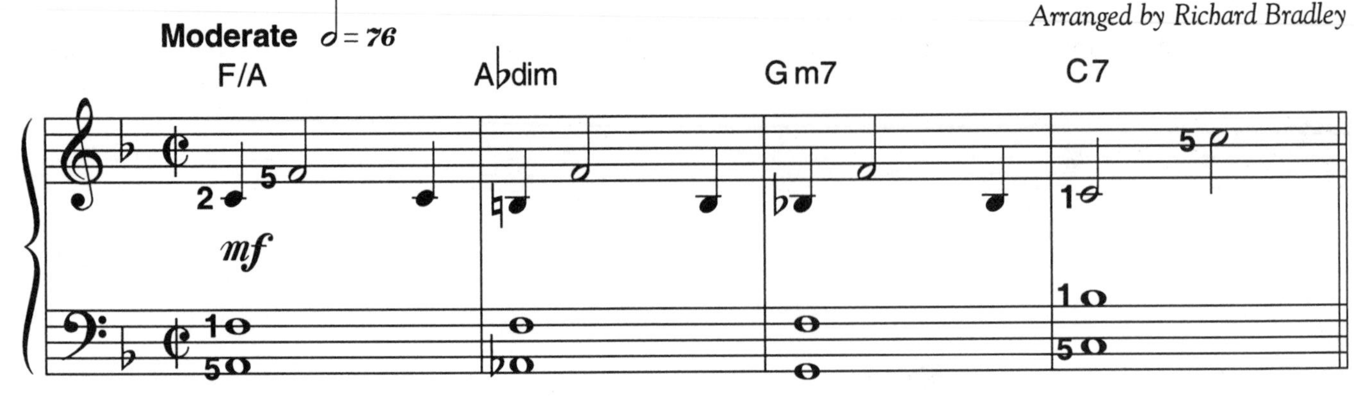

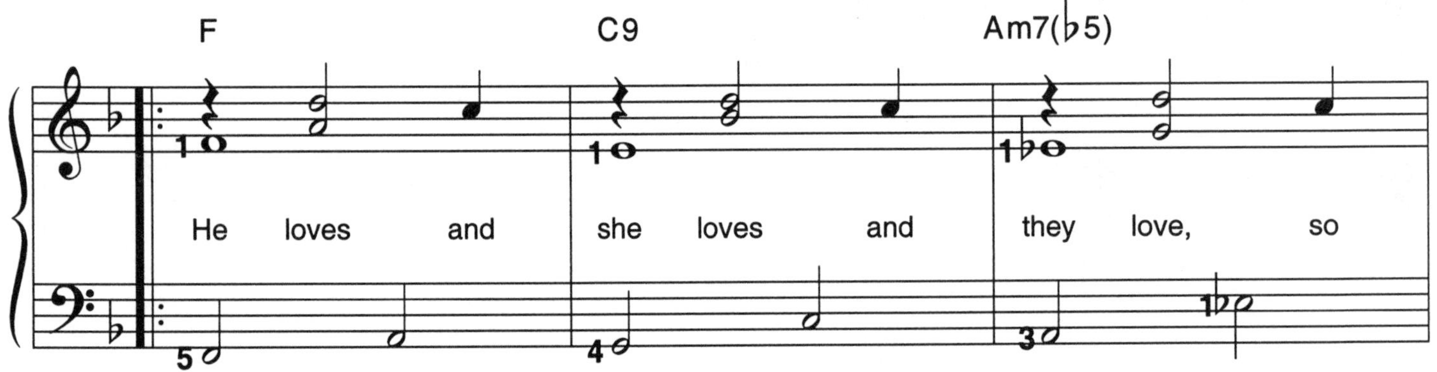

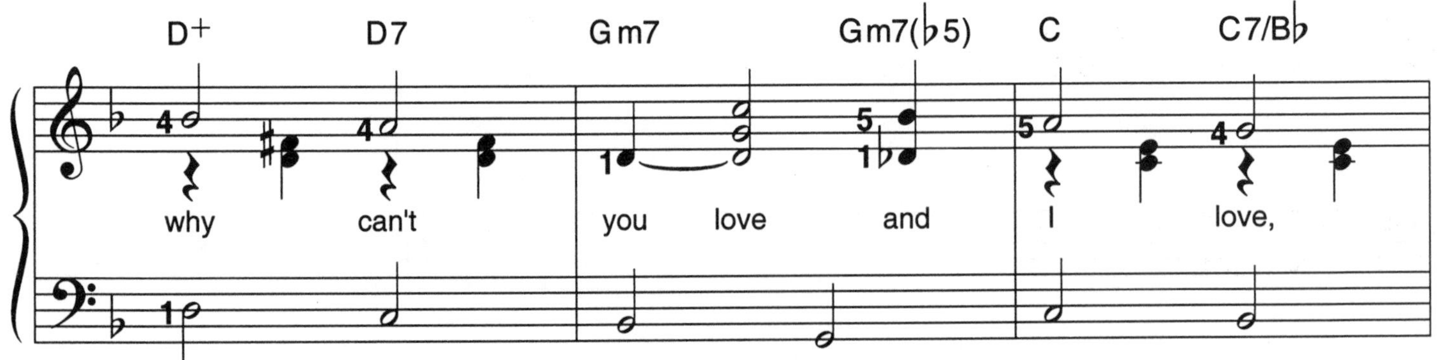

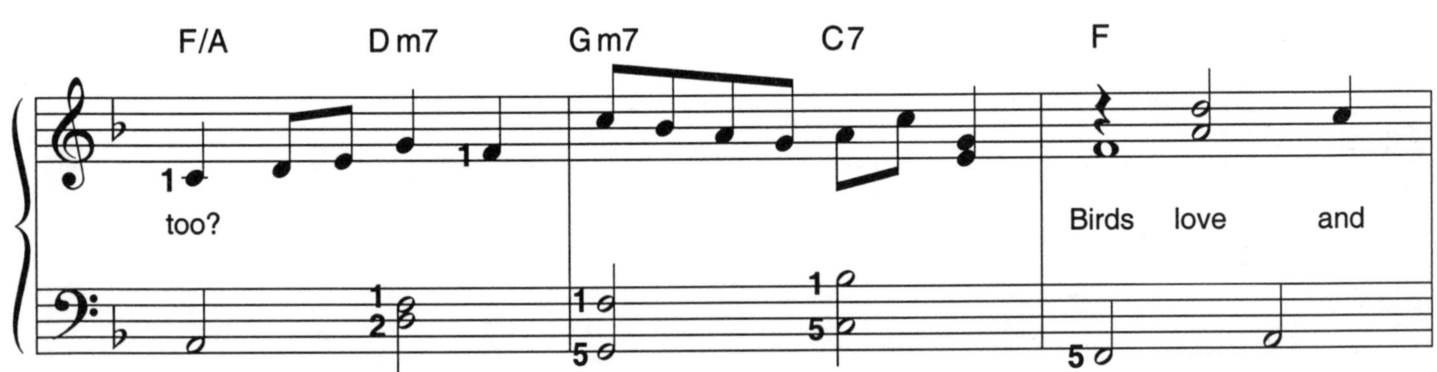

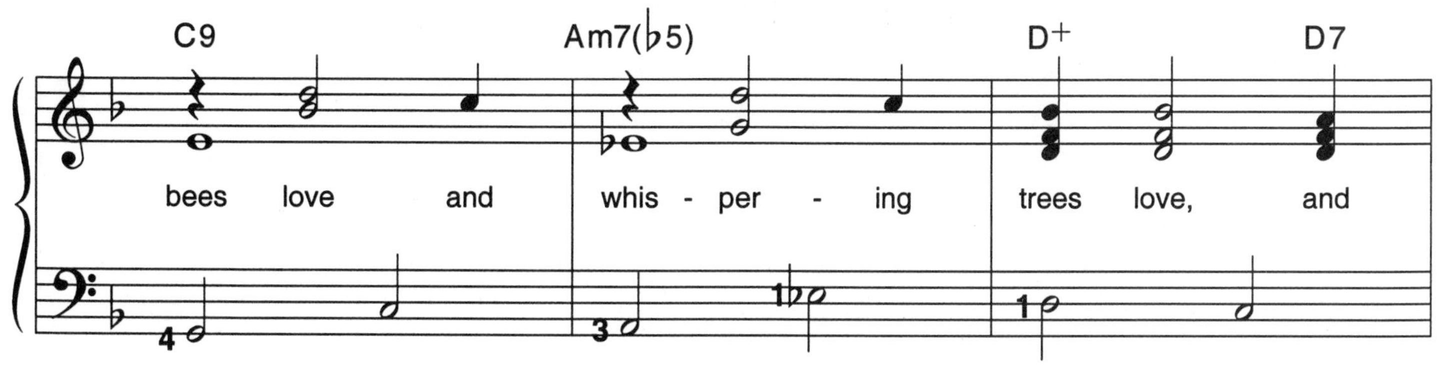
C9
Am7(♭5)
D+
D7
bees love and whis - per - ing trees love, and

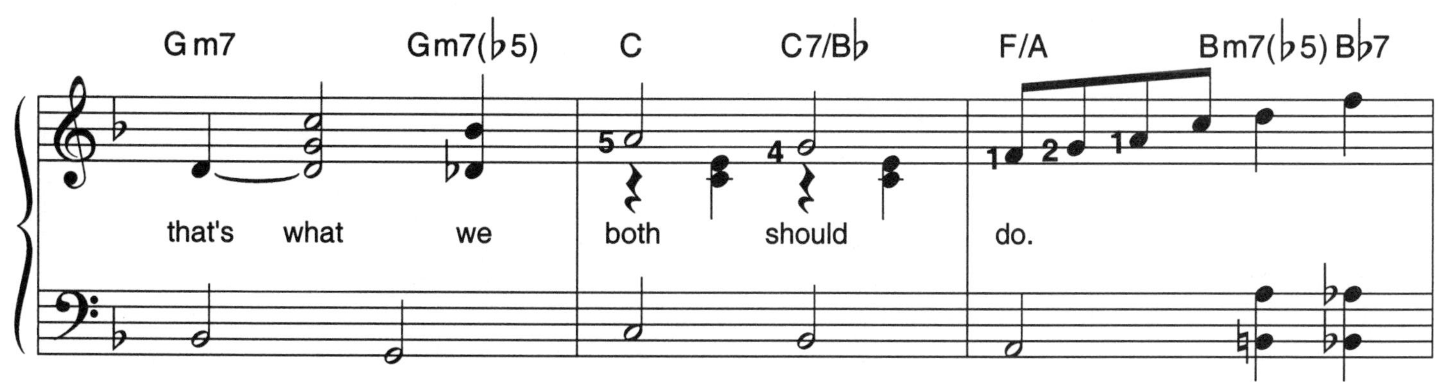
Gm7
Gm7(♭5)
C
C7/B♭
F/A
Bm7(♭5) B♭7
that's what we both should do.

Am7 A♭7 Gm7 C7(♯5)
F
Cm7
F6
Oh, I al - ways knew, some - day

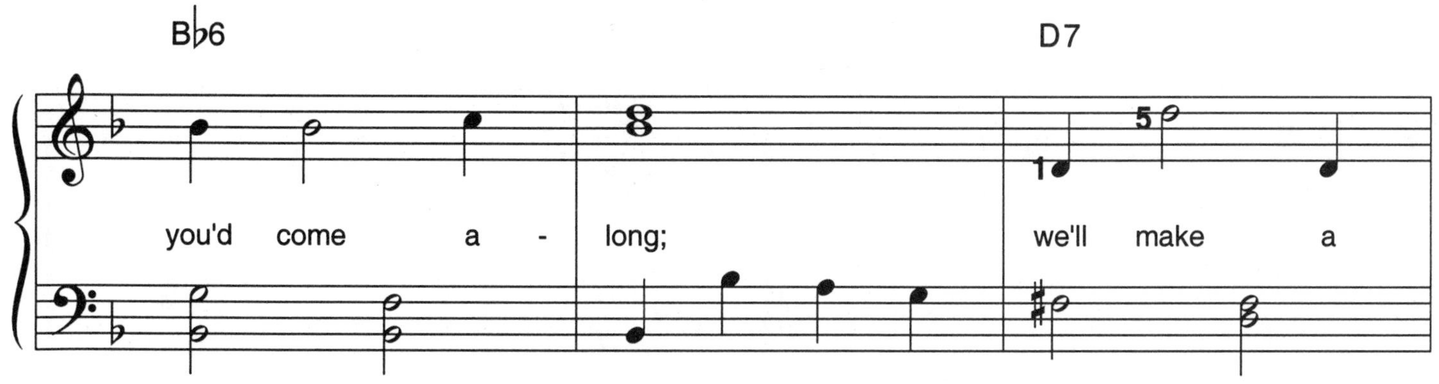
B♭6
D7
you'd come a - long; we'll make a

Am7
D7
Gm
Gm7/F
C9/E
Gm7
C7
two - some that just can't go wrong, hear me:

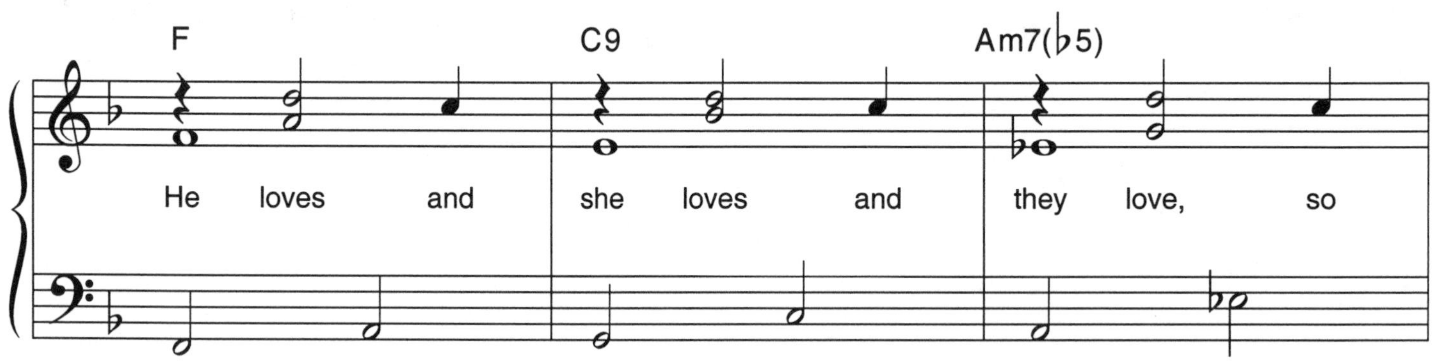
F
C9
Am7(♭5)
He loves and she loves and they love, so

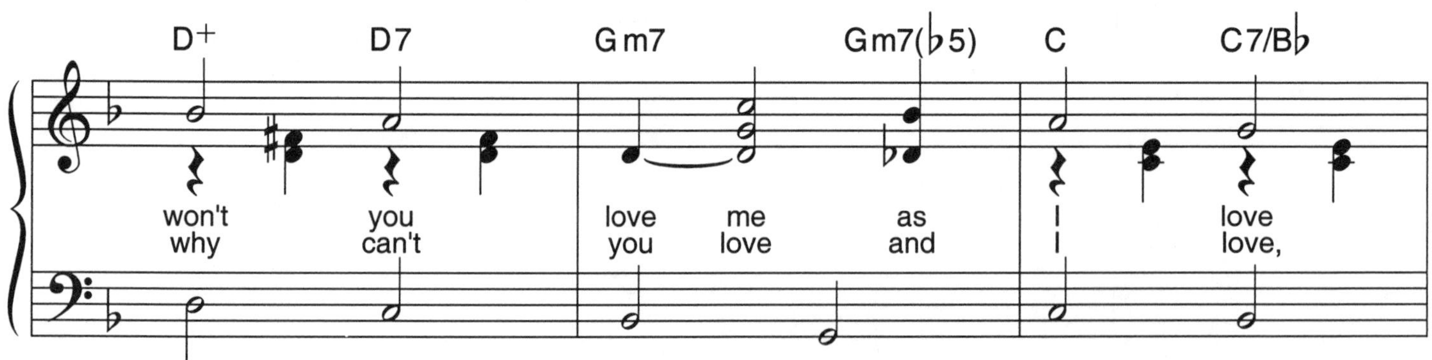
D+
D7
Gm7
Gm7(♭5)
C
C7/B♭
won't you love me as I love
why can't you love and I love,

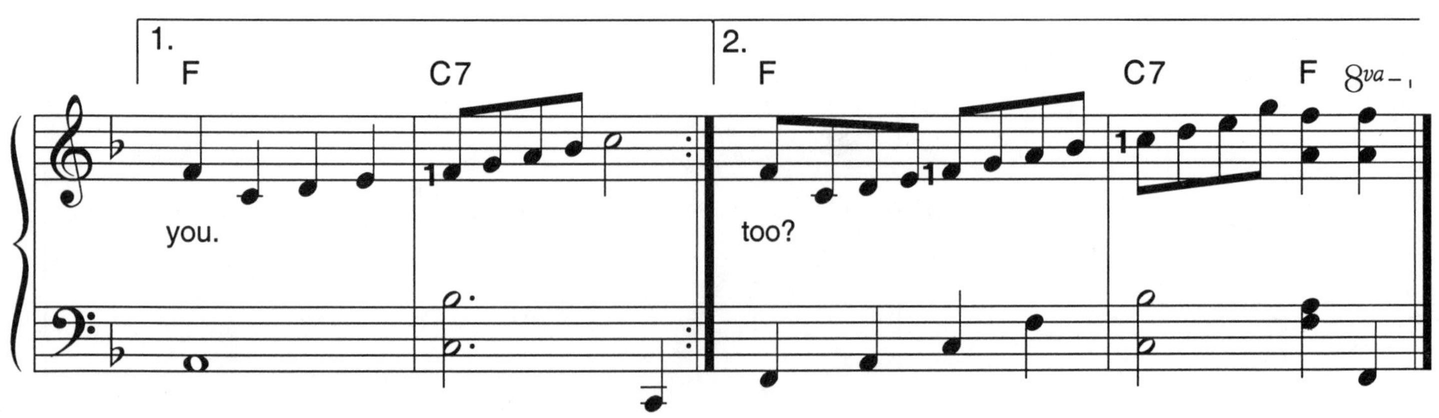
1.
2.
F
C7
F
C7
F
8va
you.
too?

Love and Marriage

Words by
SAMMY CAHN

Music by
JAMES VAN HEUSEN
Arranged by Richard Bradley

B♭m7 E♭7 A♭ A♭Maj7
it's an il - lu - sion. Try, try,

A♭6 C
try and you will on - ly come

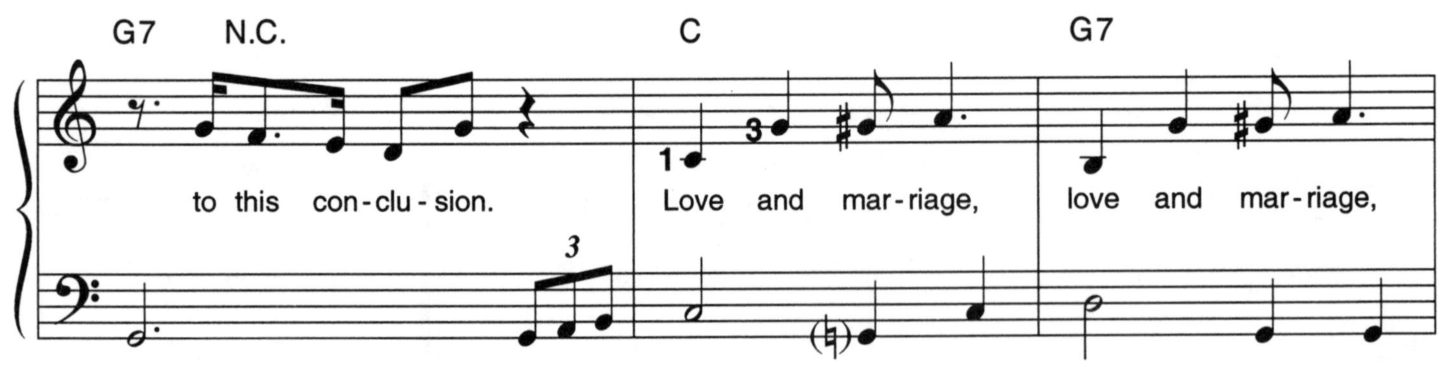
G7 N.C. C G7
to this con-clu - sion. Love and mar-riage, love and mar-riage,

C C7/B♭ F/A Fm C/E
go to-geth - er like a horse and car-riage. Dad was told by

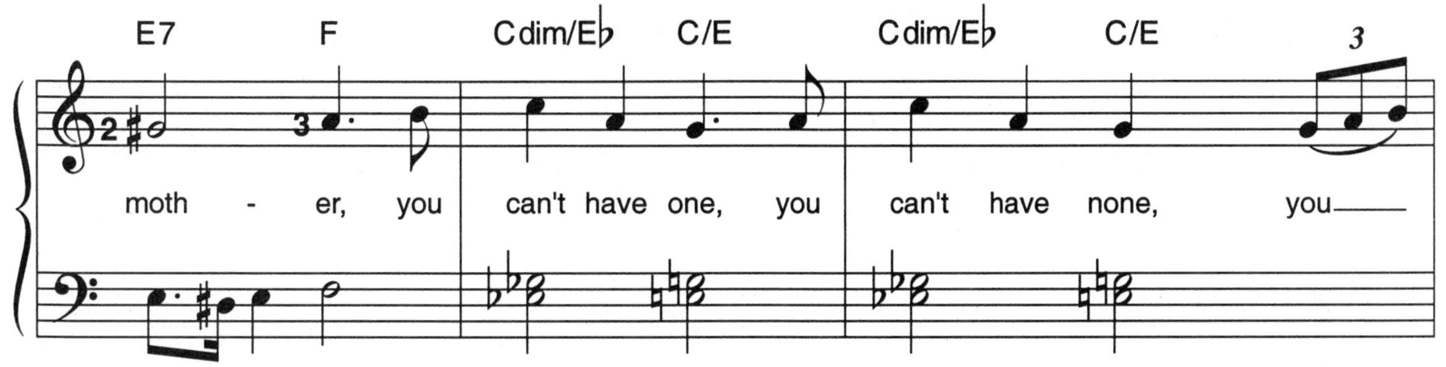

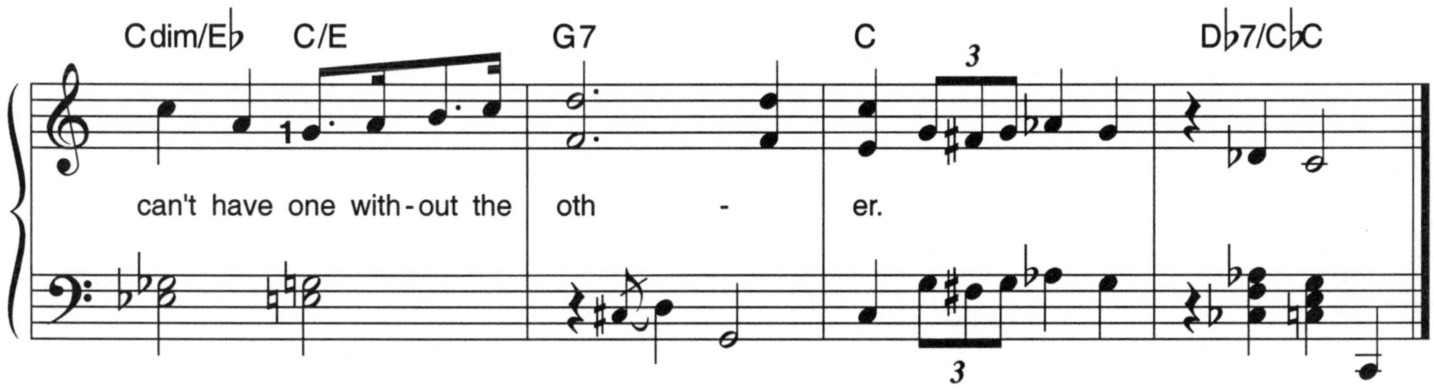

Verse 2:
Love and marriage,
Love and marriage,
It's an institute you can't disparage,
Ask the local gentry
And they will say it's elementary.

Sunrise, Sunset

From the Broadway Musical *Fiddler on the Roof*

Lyrics by SHELDON HARNICK
Music by JERRY BOCK
Arranged by Richard Bradley

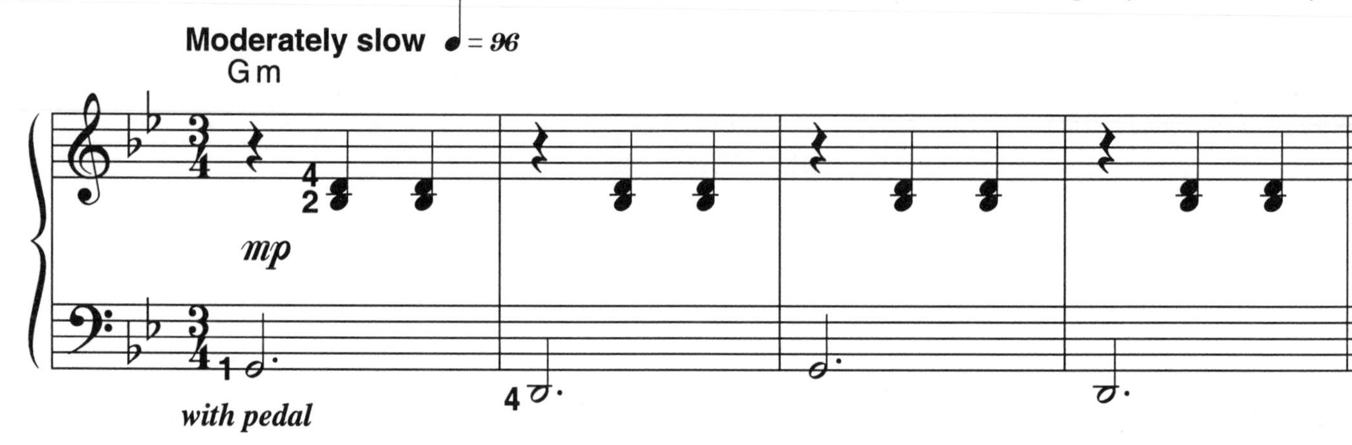

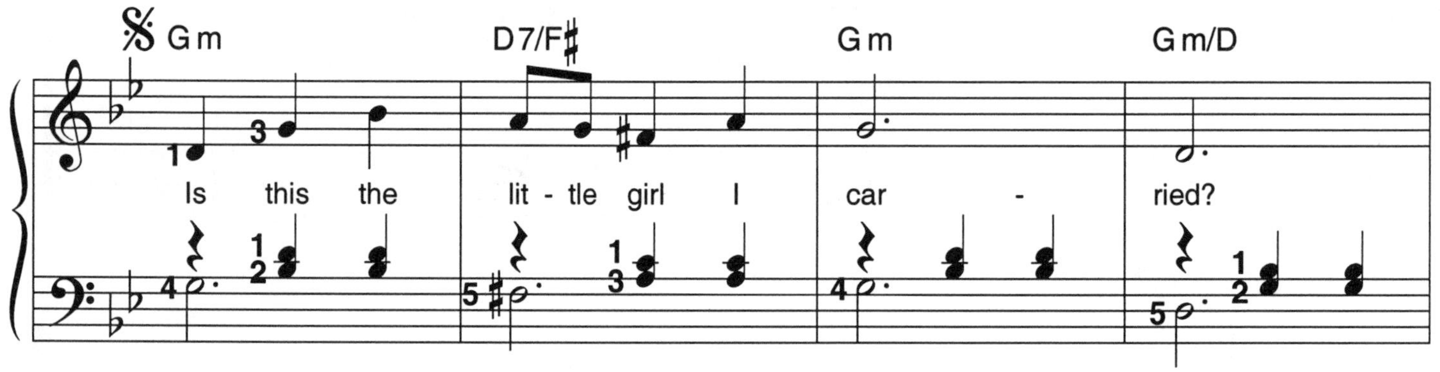

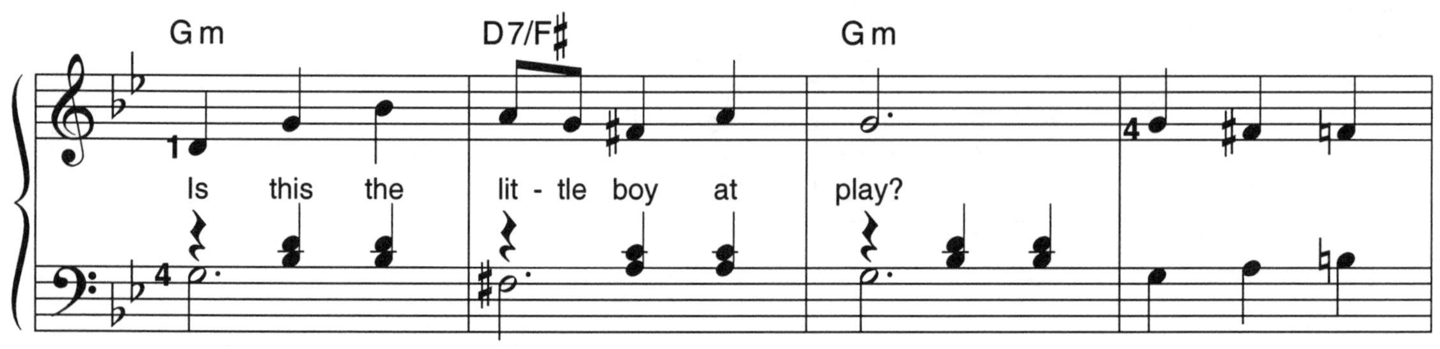

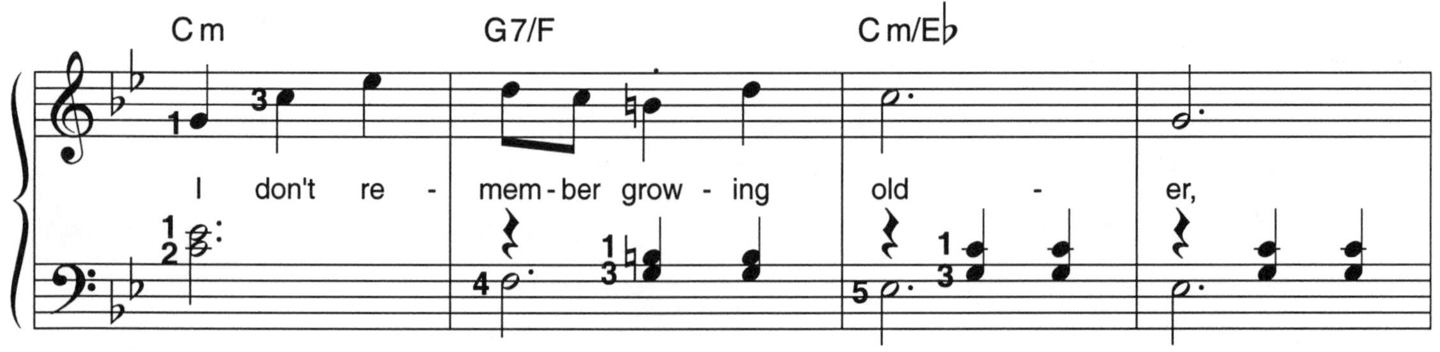

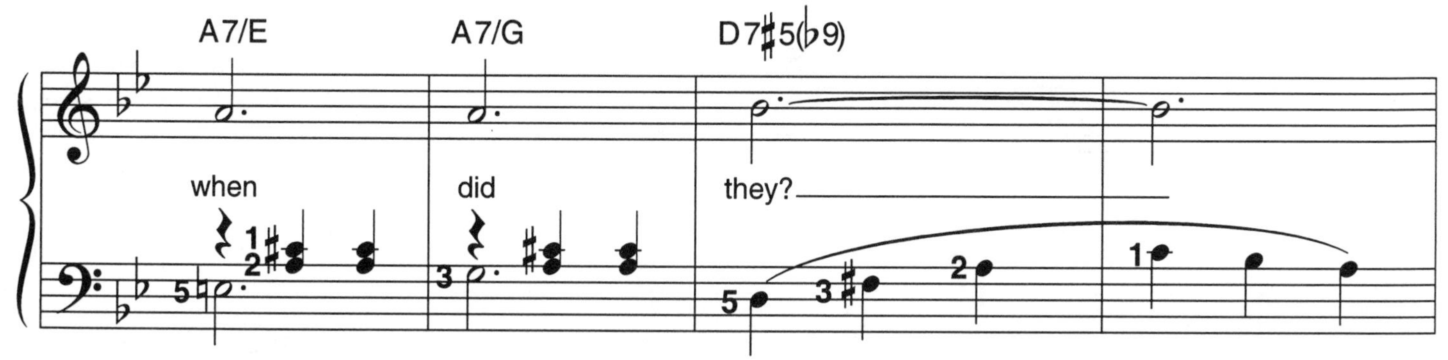
A7/E
A7/G
D7♯5(♭9)
when
did
they?

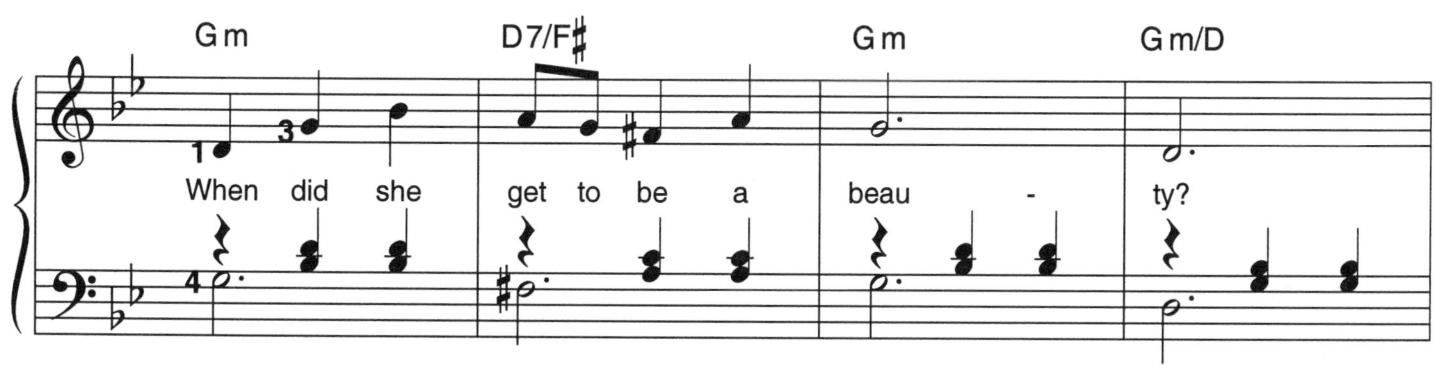
Gm
D7/F♯
Gm
Gm/D
When did she get to be a beau - ty?

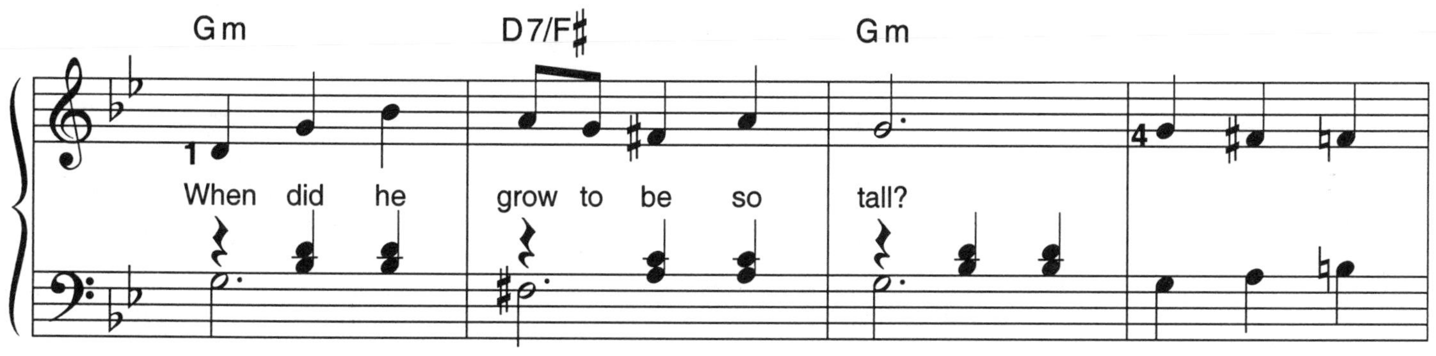
Gm
D7/F♯
Gm
When did he grow to be so tall?

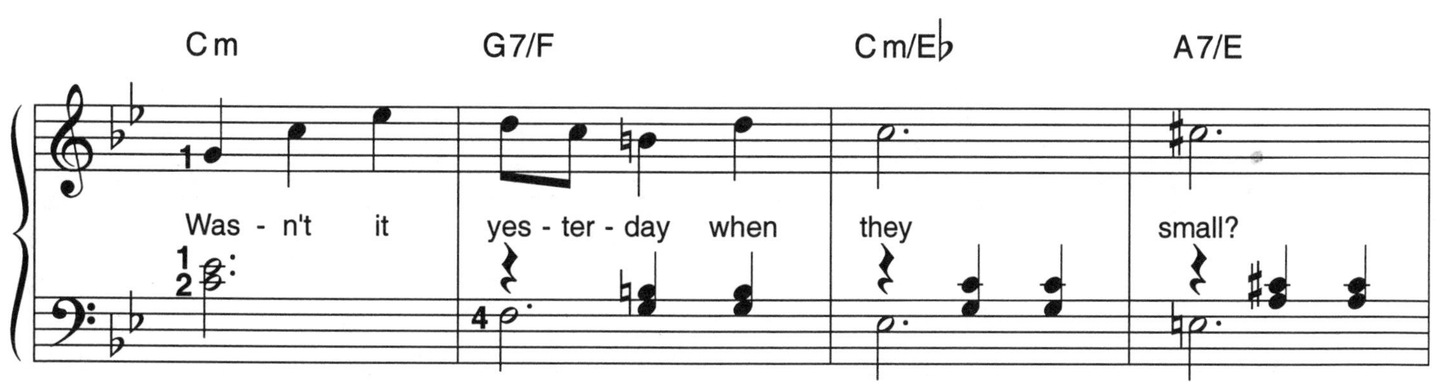
Cm
G7/F
Cm/E♭
A7/E
Was - n't it yes - ter - day when they small?

D
D7
D6
D
small?
Gm
D
Gm
D
Sun - rise, sun - set, sun - rise, sun - set,
Sun - rise, sun - set, sun - rise, sun - set,
Gm
G7
swift - ly flow the days.
swift - ly fly the years.
1.
Cm7
F7
B♭Maj7/A
B♭6/G
Seed - lings turn o - ver - night to sun - flow'ers,
Am7
D7
Gm
blos - som - ing e - ven as we gaze.

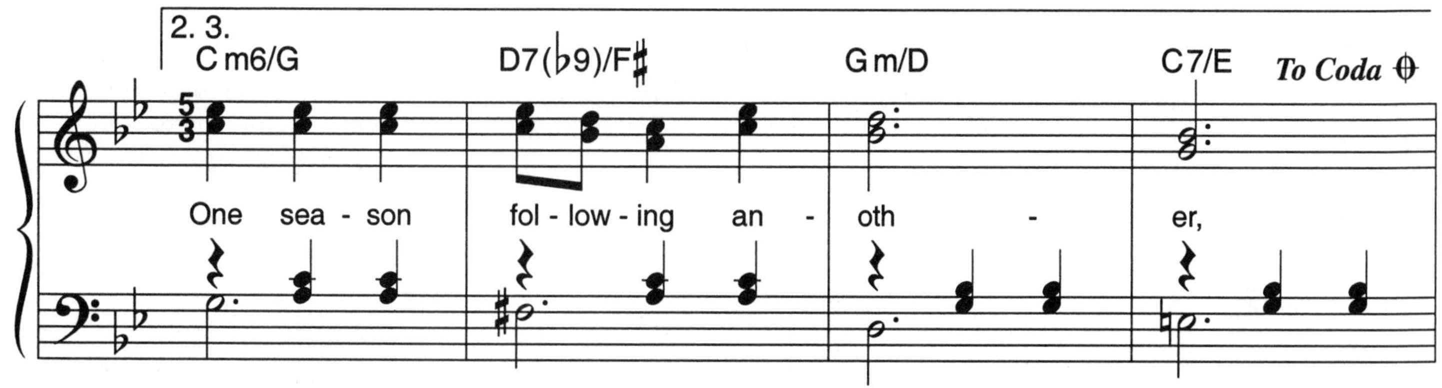

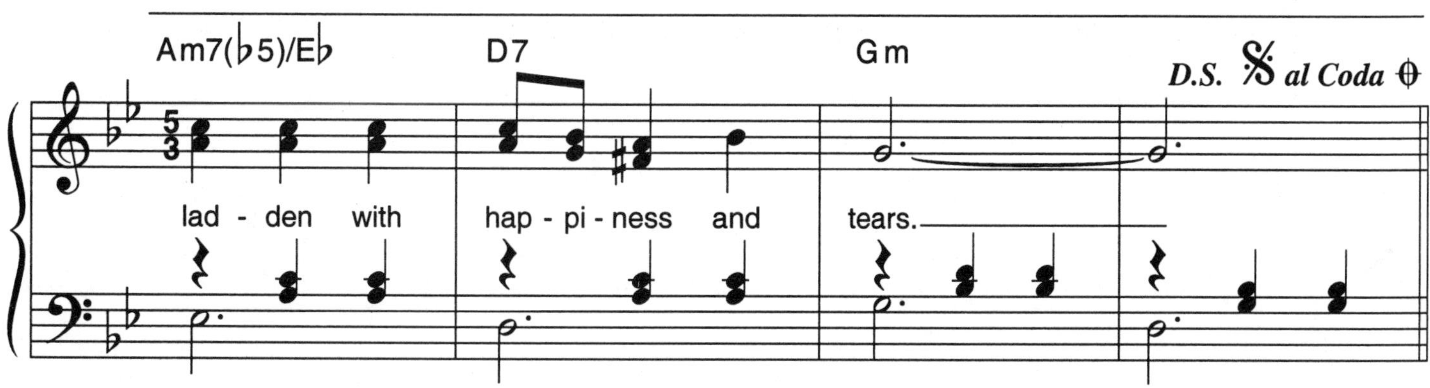

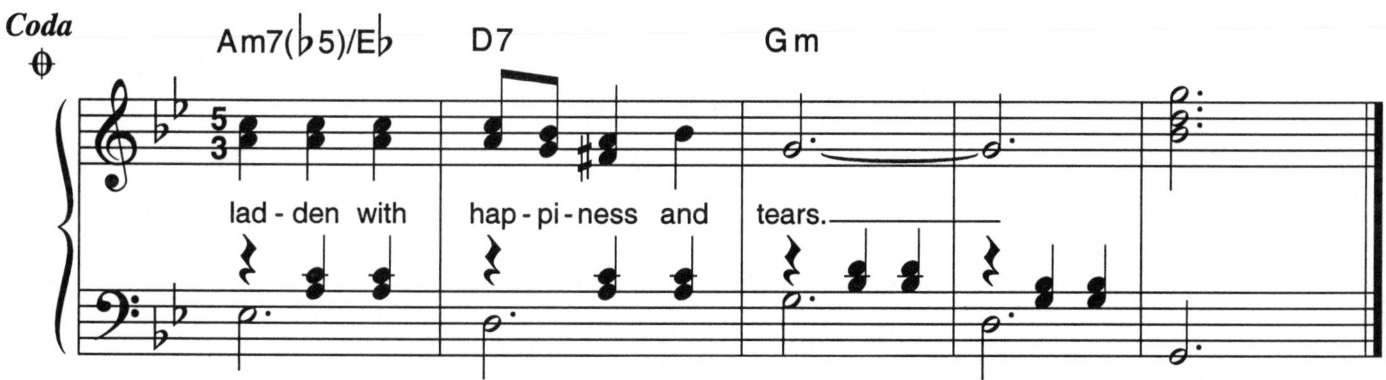

Verse 2:
Now is the little boy a bridegroom?
Now is the little girl a bride?
Under the canopy I see them, side by side.
Place the gold ring around her finger,
Share the sweet wine and break the glass;
Soon the full circle will have come to pass.

On a Clear Day
(You Can See Forever)

From the Broadway Musical
On a Clear Day You Can See Forever

Lyrics by ALAN JAY LERNER
Music by BURTON LANE
Arranged by Richard Bradley

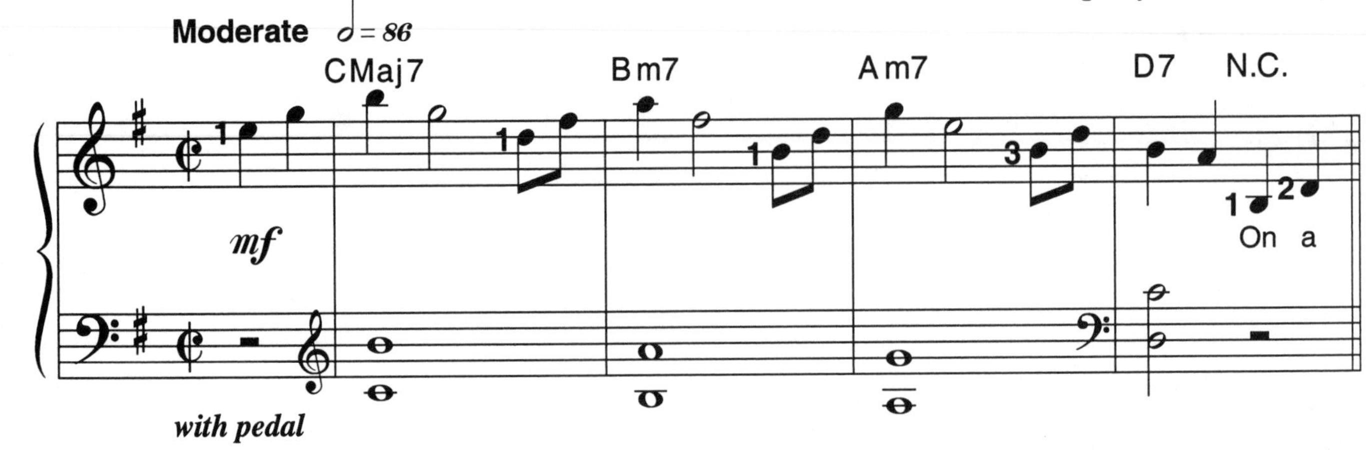

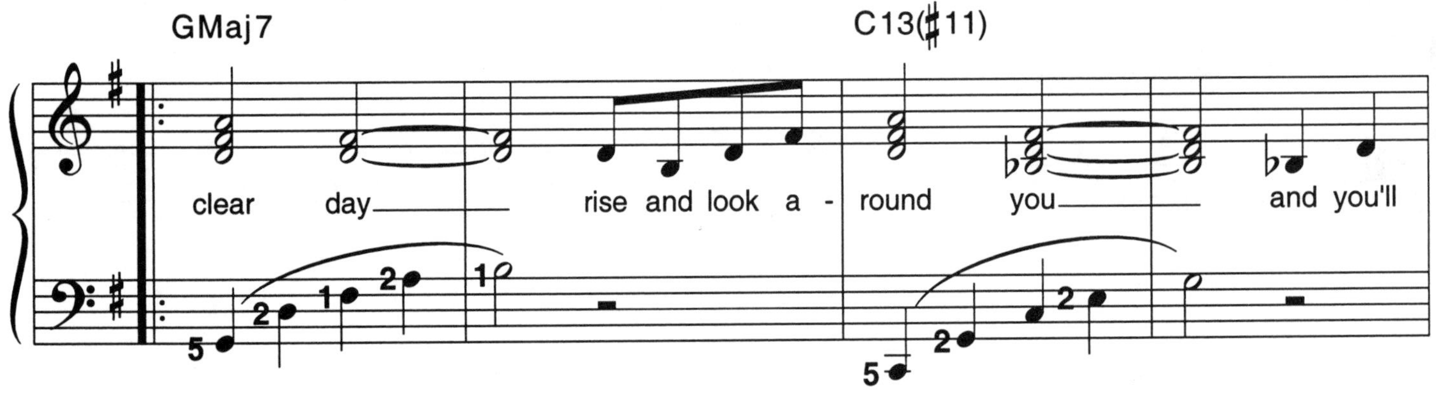

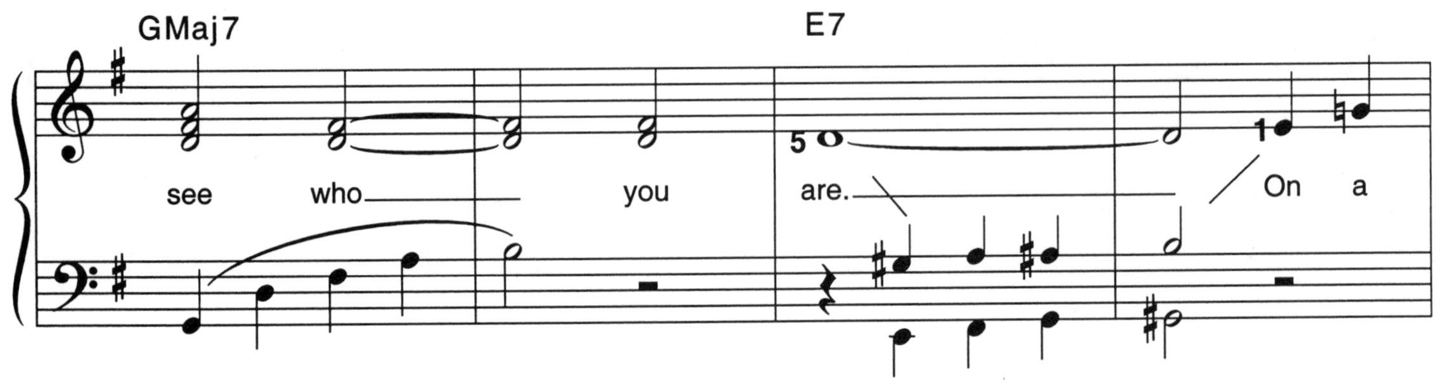

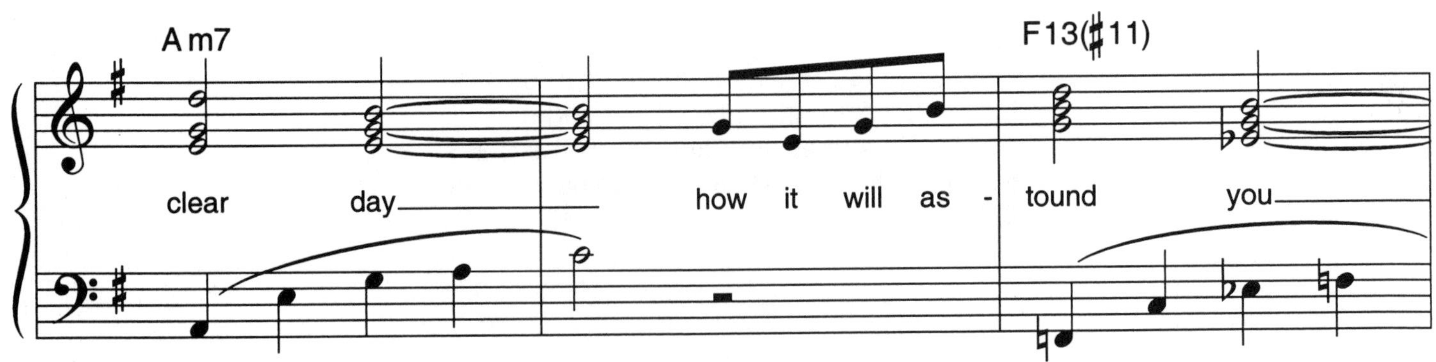

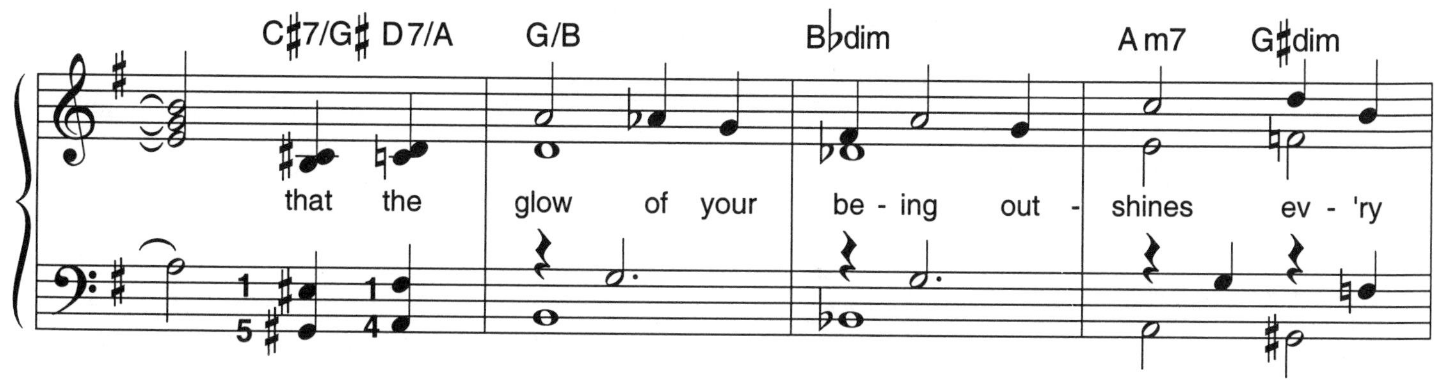
C♯7/G♯ D7/A
G/B
B♭dim
Am7
G♯dim
that the glow of your be - ing out - shines ev - 'ry

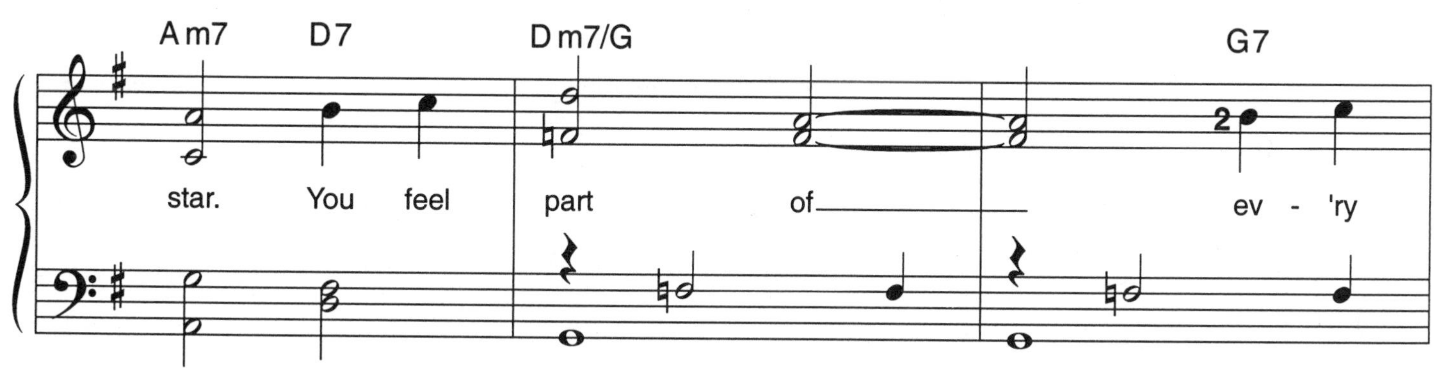
Am7
D7
Dm7/G
G7
star. You feel part of ev - 'ry

Dm7/G
G7
CMaj7
Bm7
moun - tain, sea and shore. You can hear, from far and

A7/C♯
D7
near, a world you've nev - er heard be - fore. And on a

Gdim GMaj7
G
Bm7sus4 E9
Bm
E9
clear day,
on that
clear day
you can

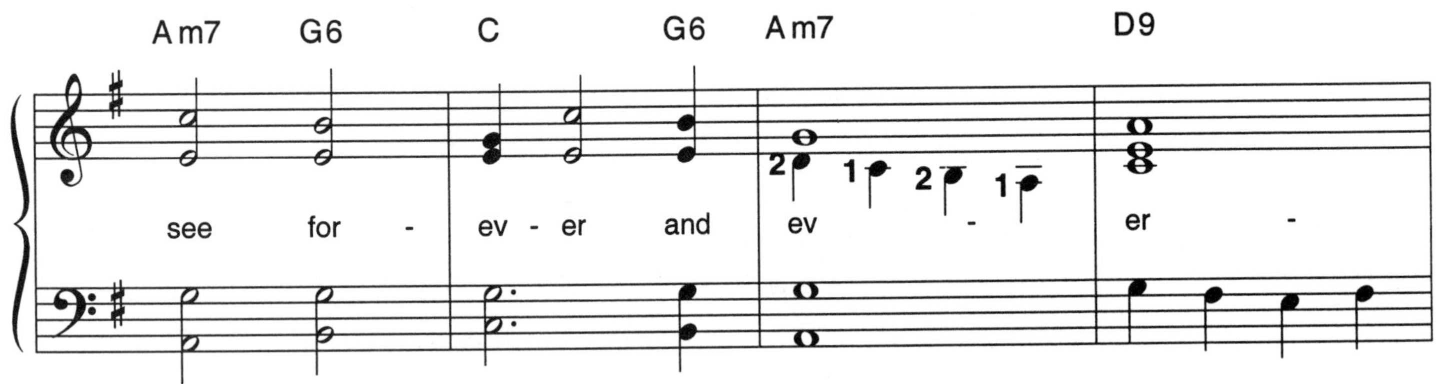
Am7 G6
C
G6 Am7
D9
see for -
ev - er and
ev -
er -

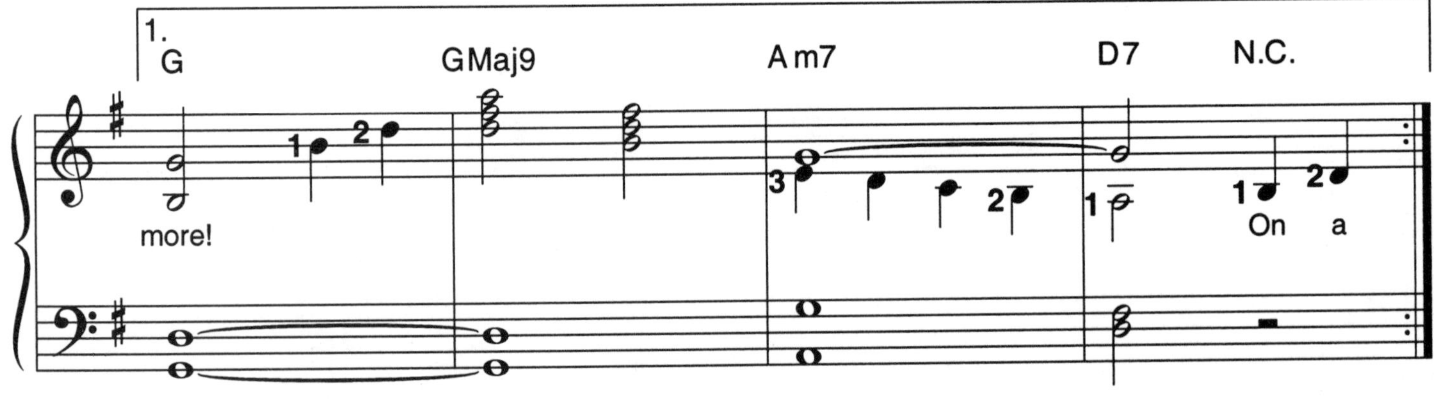
1.
G
GMaj9
Am7
D7 N.C.
more!
On a

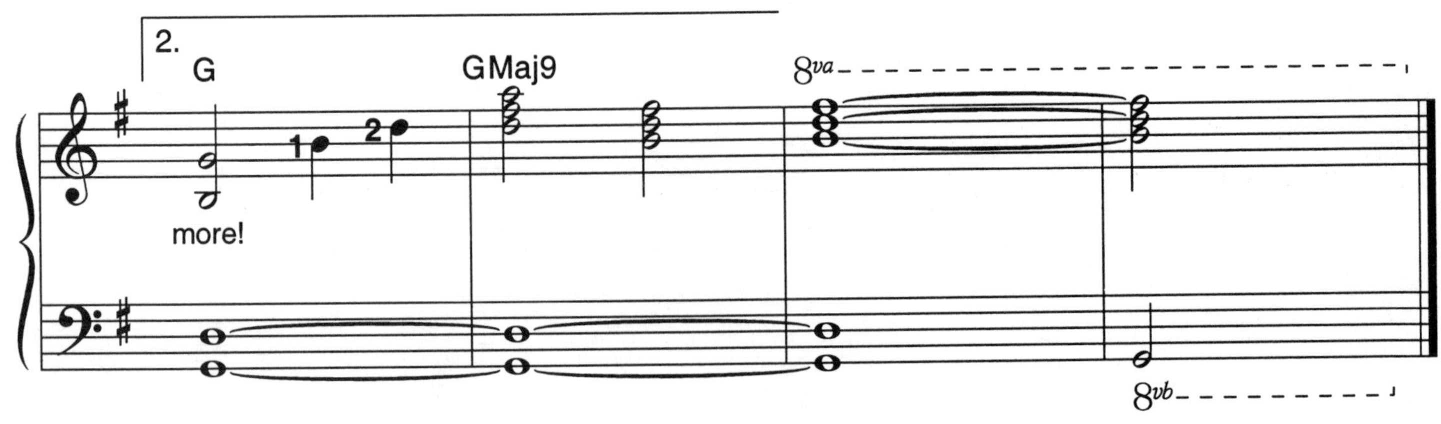
2.
G
GMaj9
8va
more!
8vb

The Summer Knows

From the Motion Picture *Summer of '42*

Words by MARILYN and ALAN BERGMAN
Music by MICHEL LEGRAND
Arranged by Richard Bradley

C7
3
F2
F
which you lie. The sum - mer knows, the
R.H.
mf

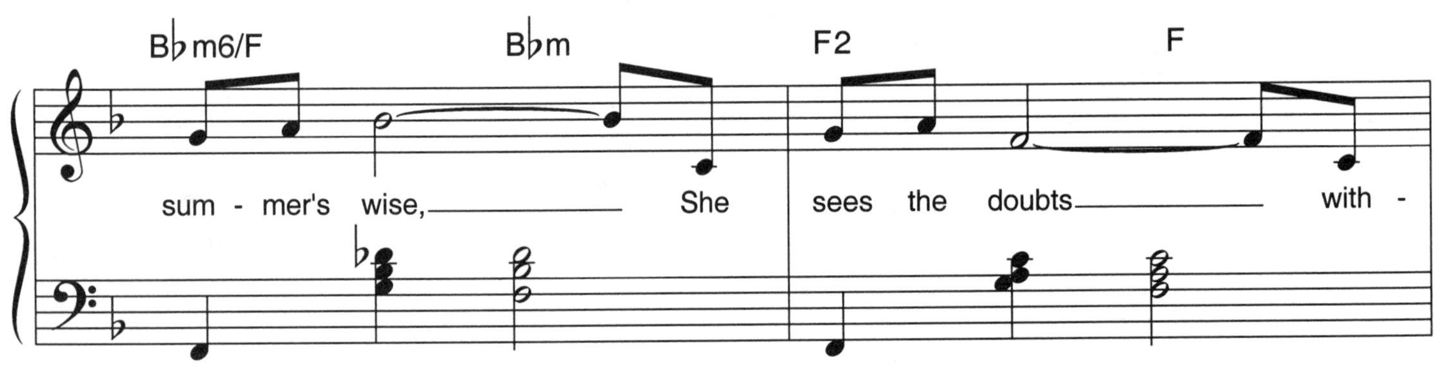
B♭m6/F
B♭m
F2
F
sum - mer's wise, She sees the doubts with -

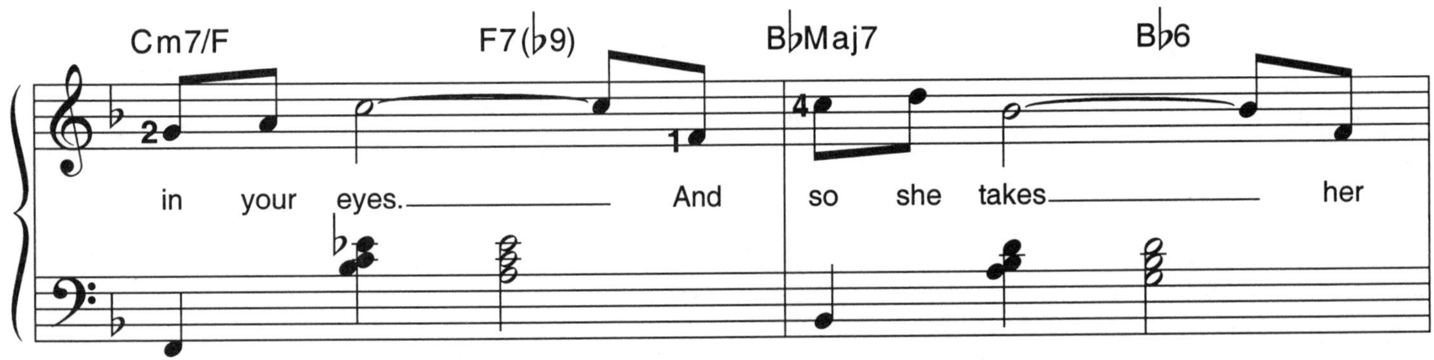
Cm7/F
F7(♭9)
B♭Maj7
B♭6
in your eyes. And so she takes her

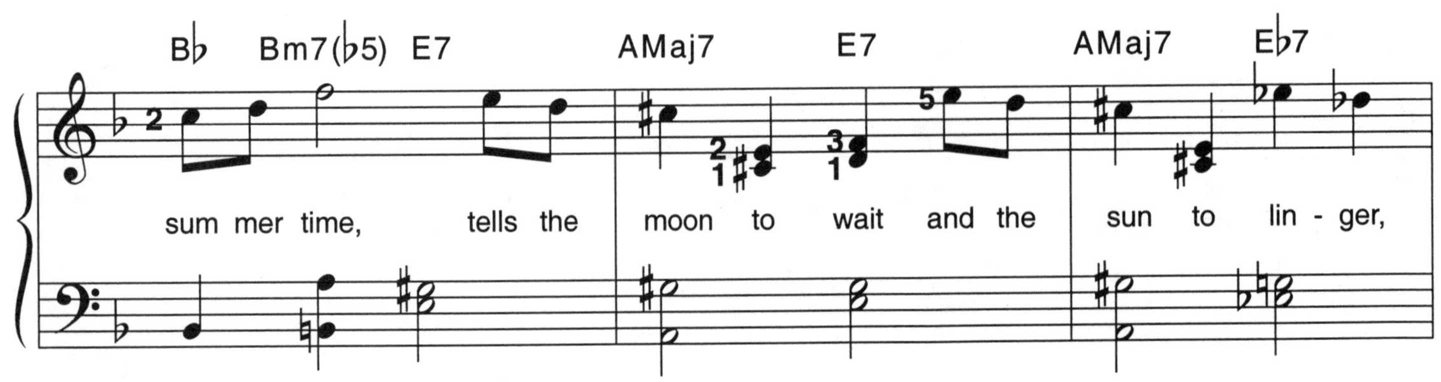
B♭ Bm7(♭5) E7
AMaj7
E7
AMaj7
E♭7
sum mer time, tells the moon to wait and the sun to lin - ger,

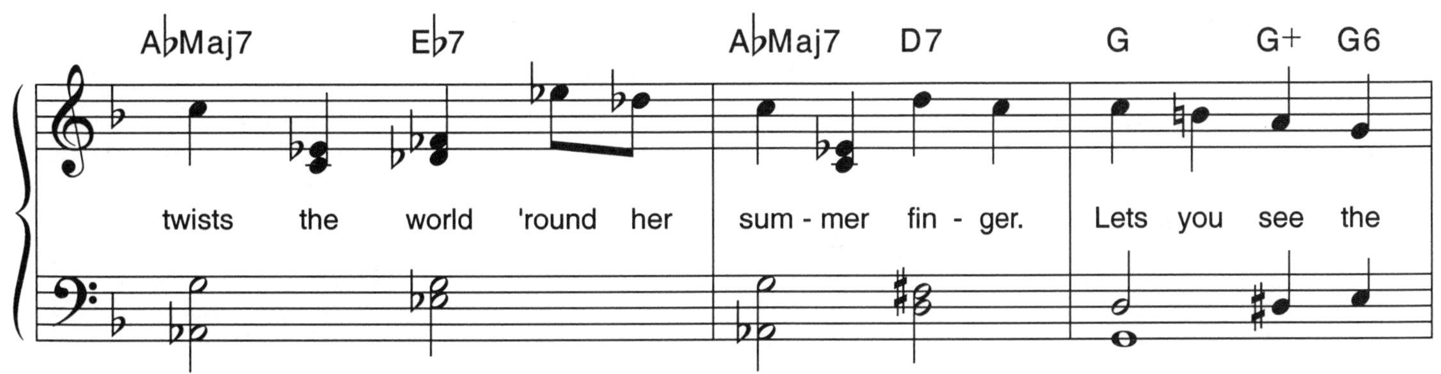
A♭Maj7
E♭7
A♭Maj7
D7
G
G+
G6
twists the world 'round her sum - mer fin - ger. Lets you see the

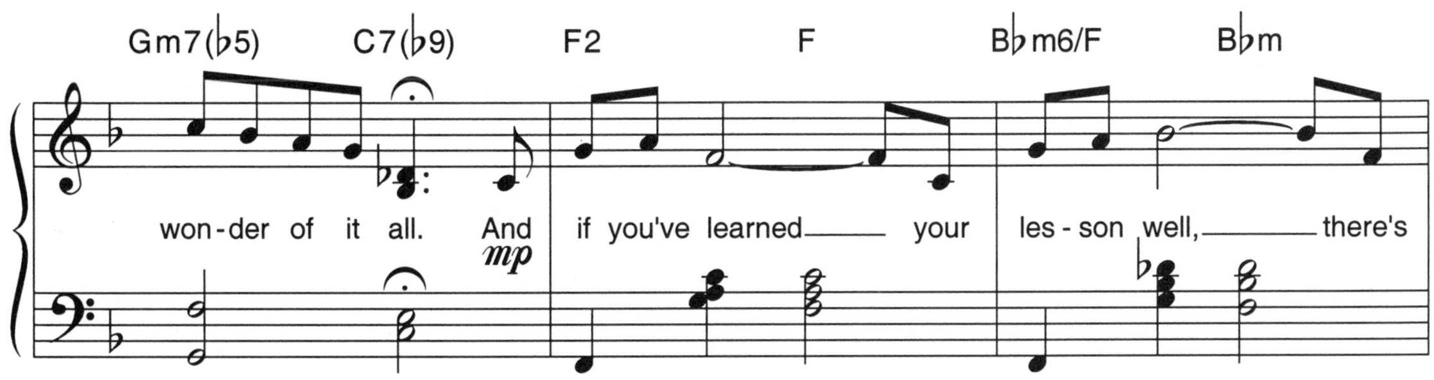
Gm7(♭5)
C7(♭9)
F2
F
B♭m6/F
B♭m
won-der of it all. And if you've learned your les - son well, there's
mp

F2
F
B♭m6/F
B♭m
Fm
lit - tle more for her to tell, one last ca - ress, it's
p

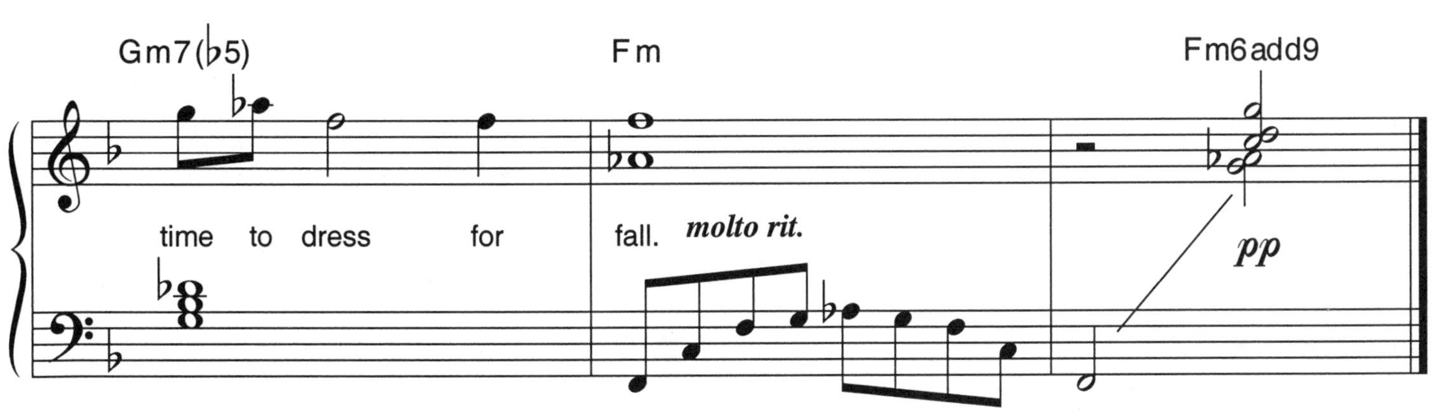
Gm7(♭5)
Fm
Fm6add9
time to dress for fall.
molto rit.
pp

Theme from Ice Castles

(Through the Eyes of Love)

From the Motion Picture *Ice Castles*

Lyrics by CAROL BAYER SAGER
Music by MARVIN HAMLISCH
Arranged by Richard Bradley

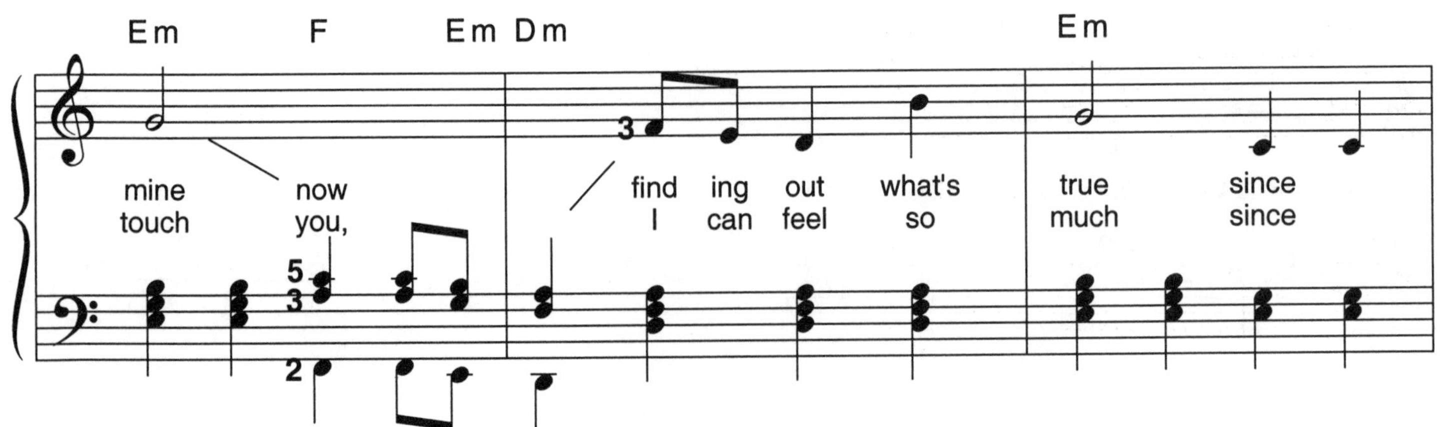

F
E
Am
D7
I
found
you
look - ing
I
found
you
look - ing

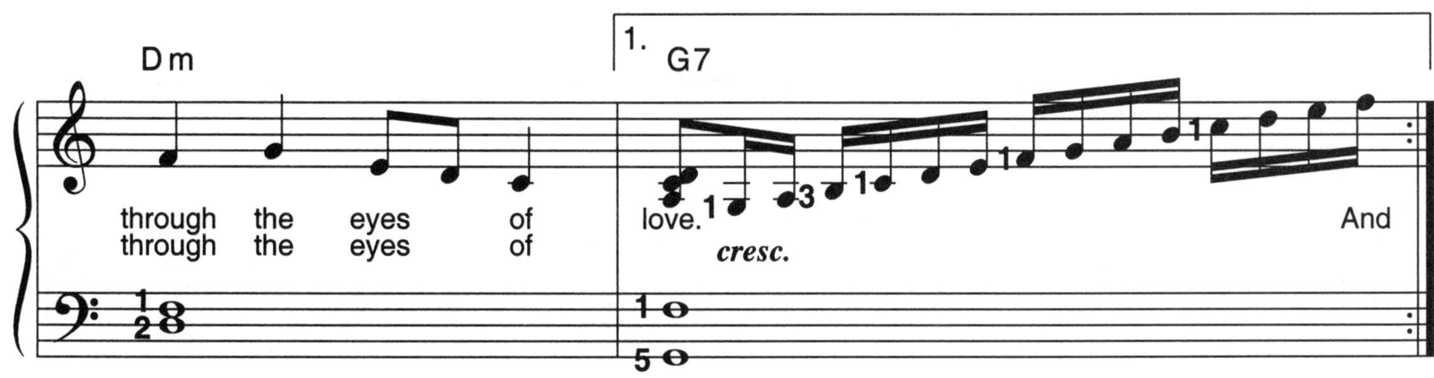
Dm
1.
G7
through the eyes of
love.
And
through the eyes of
cresc.

2.
F
C
Am
Em
F
love.
And
now
I
do be - lieve that
mp

Em
Dm
C
ev - en in the storm we'll find some light.

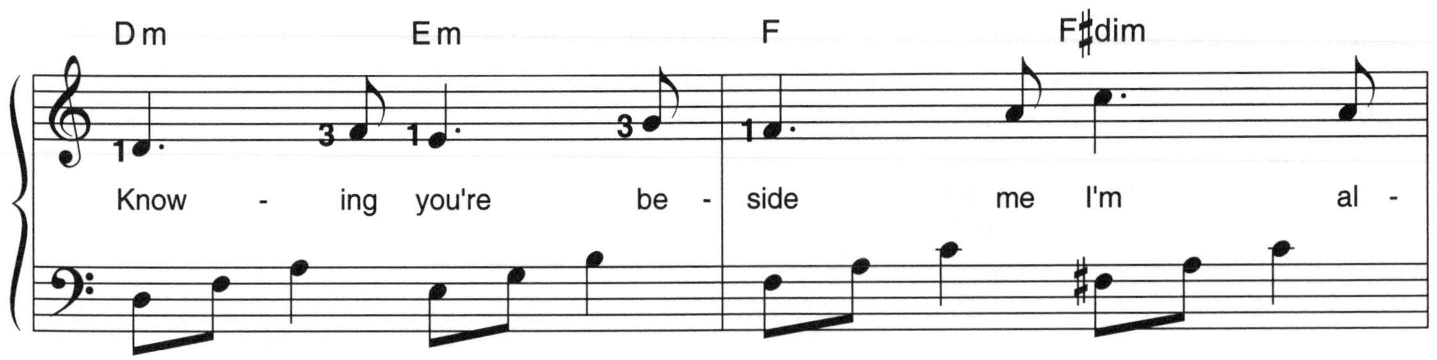
Dm
Em
F
F♯dim
Know - ing you're be - side me I'm al -

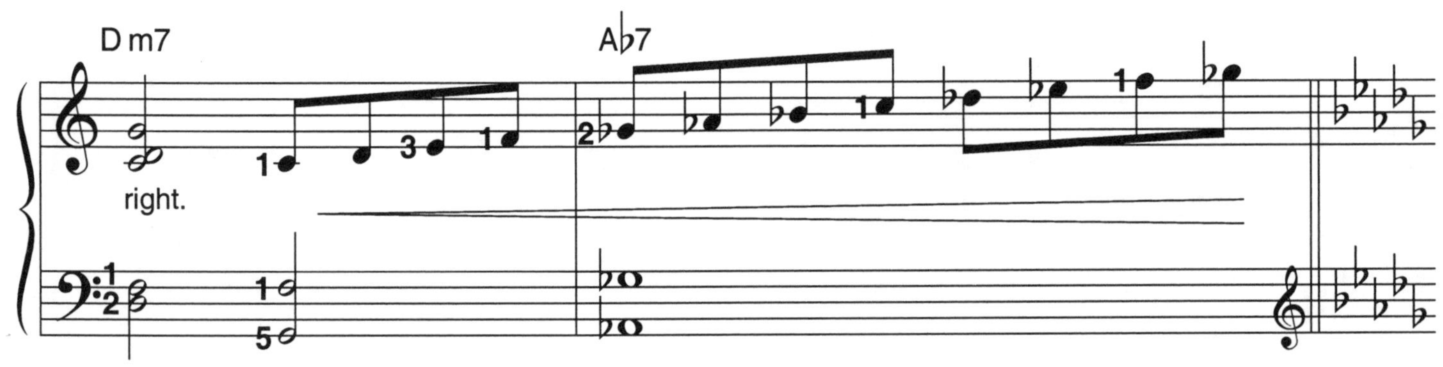
Dm7
A♭7
right.

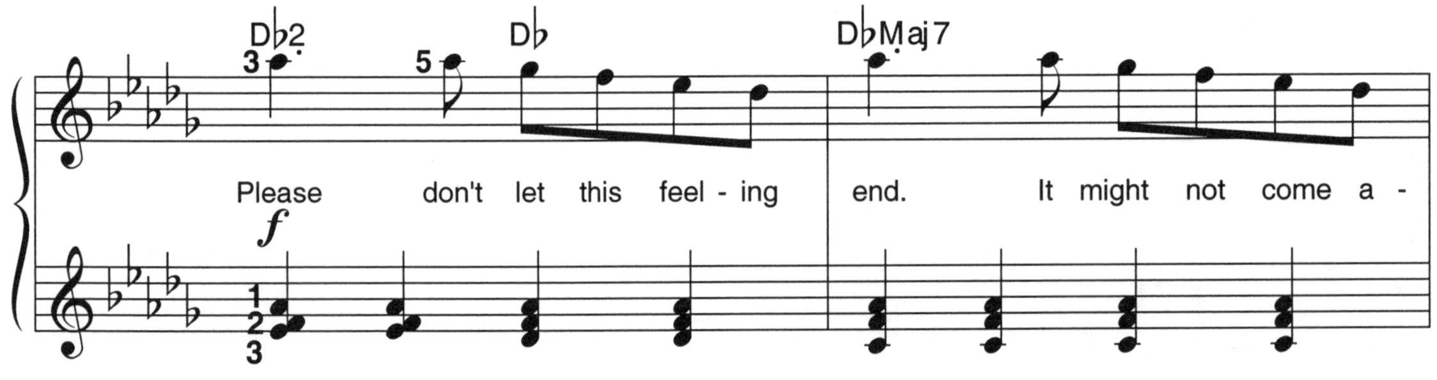
D♭2
D♭
D♭Maj7
Please don't let this feel - ing end. It might not come a -

D♭7
G♭
Fm
gain, and I want to re - mem - ber

E♭m
Fm
G♭
Fm
E♭m
how it feels to
touch you,
how I feel so
Fm
G♭
F
much since
I
found
B♭m
E♭7
E♭m
D♭
you
look-ing
through the eyes of
love.

Don't Get Around Much Anymore

Lyric by
BOB RUSSELL

Music by
DUKE ELLINGTON
Arranged by Richard Bradley

C
N.C.
A7
club.
got as far as the
door,
N.C.
D7
G7
they'd have asked me a - bout you,
don't get a-round much an-y-
C
F
more.
Dar - ling, I
Fm
C
C9
Caug
guess, my
mind's more at
ease; But

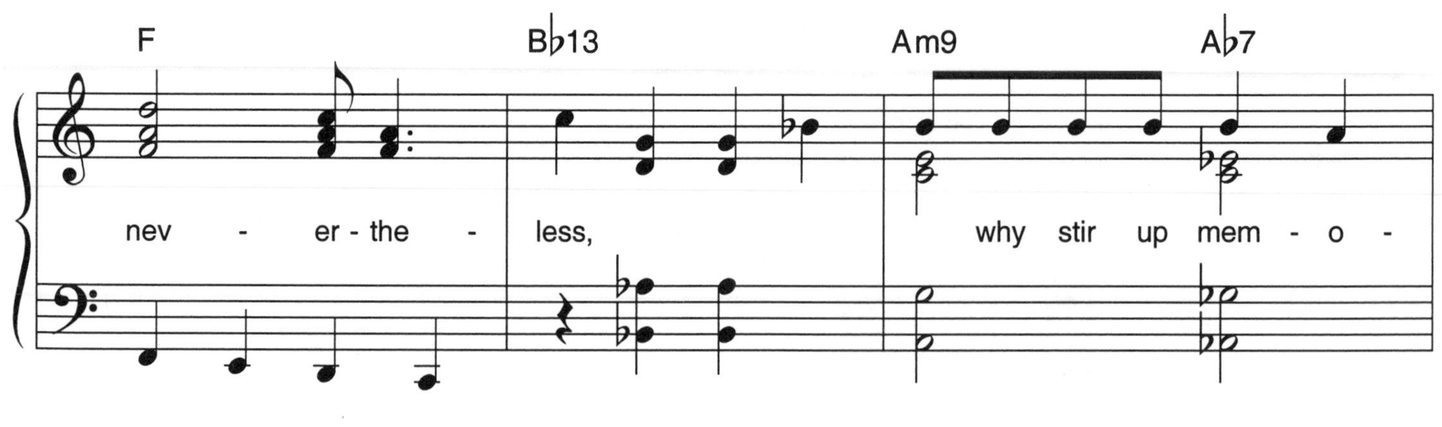
F
B♭13
Am9
A♭7
nev - er - the - less,
why stir up mem - o -

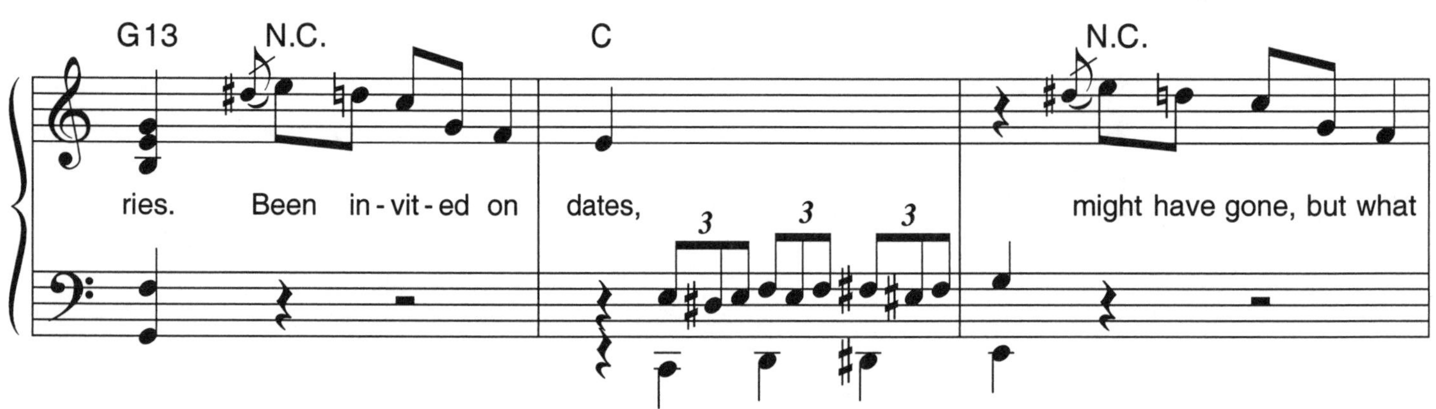
G13
N.C.
C
N.C.
ries. Been in - vit - ed on dates,
might have gone, but what

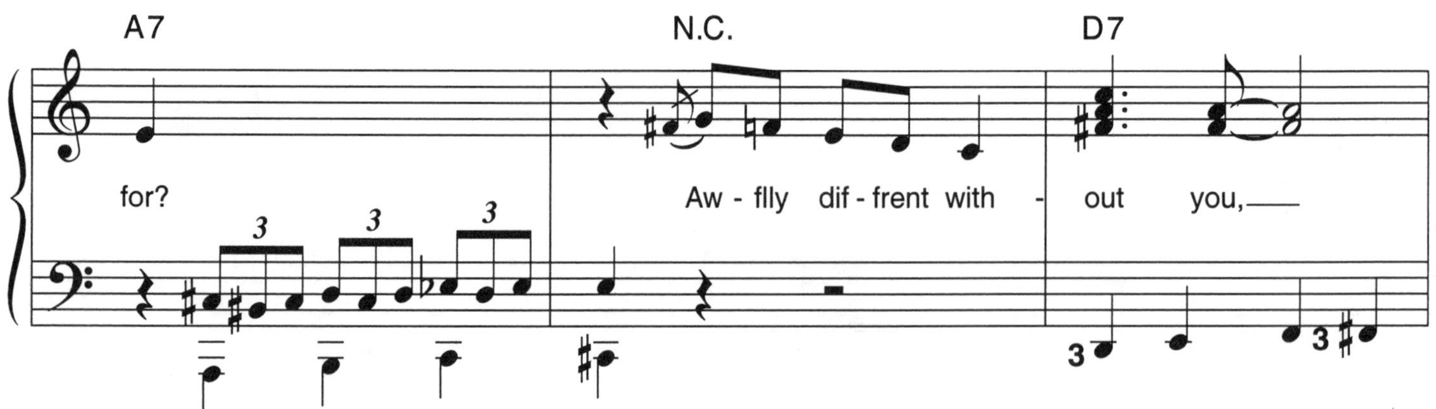
A7
N.C.
D7
for?
Aw - flly dif - frent with - out you,

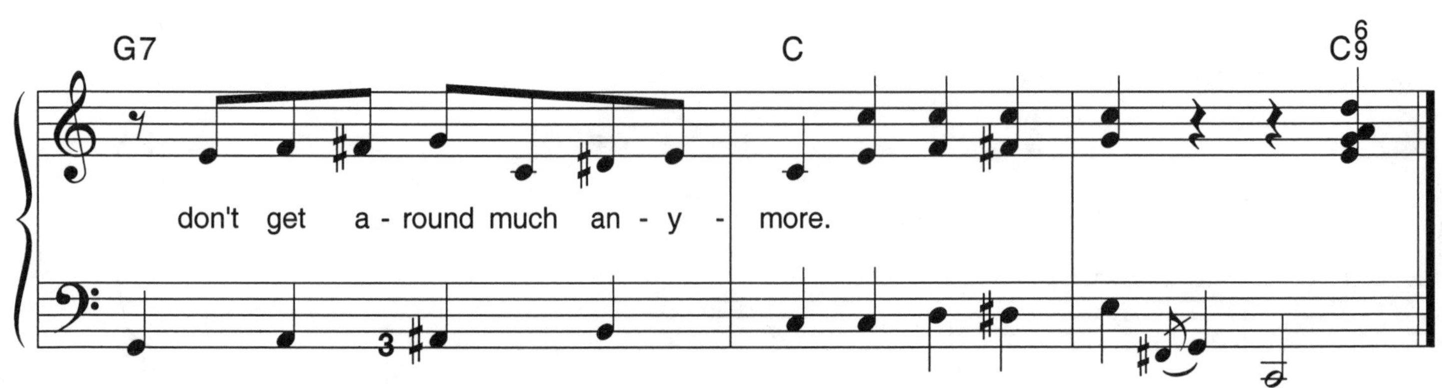
G7
C
C6/9
don't get a - round much an - y - more.

Hey, Look Me Over

From the Broadway Musical *Wildcat*

Music by CY COLEMAN
Lyrics by CAROLYN LEIGH
Arranged by Richard Bradley

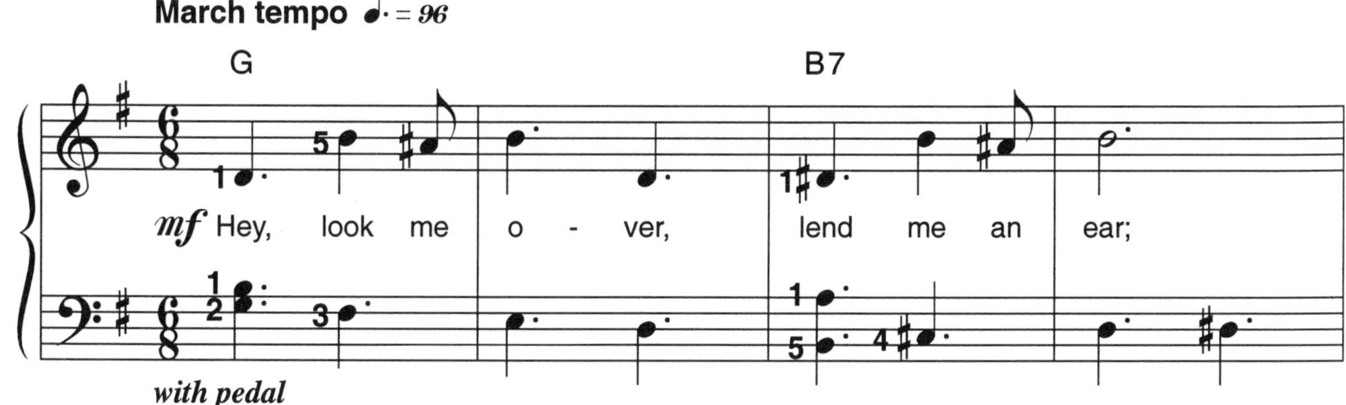

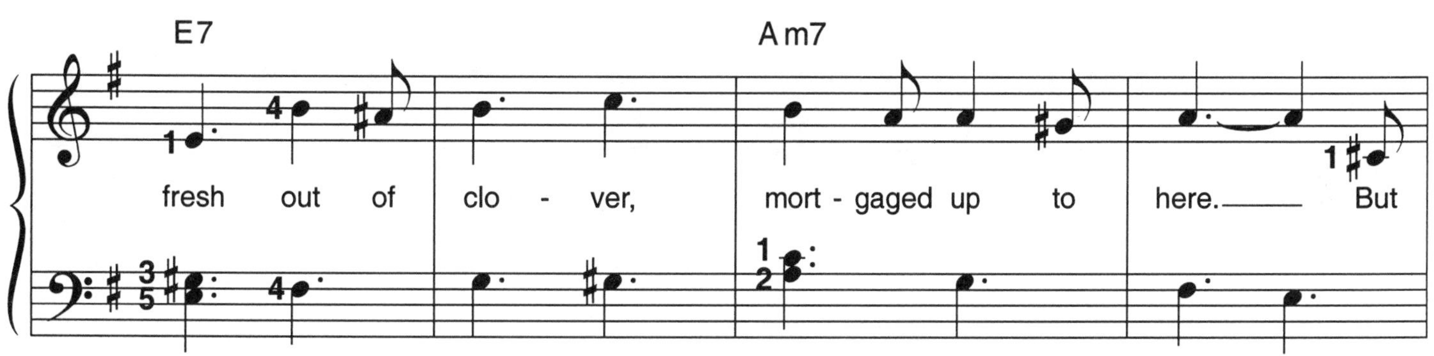

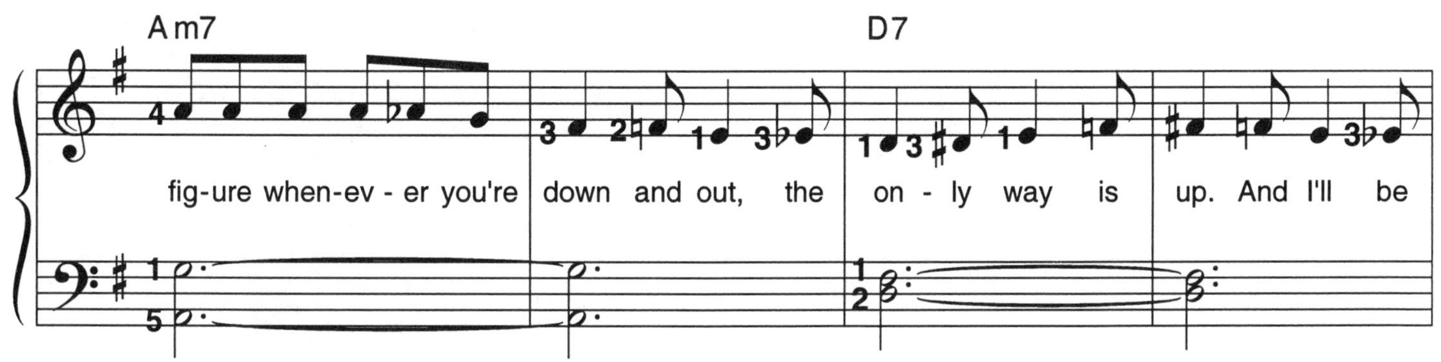

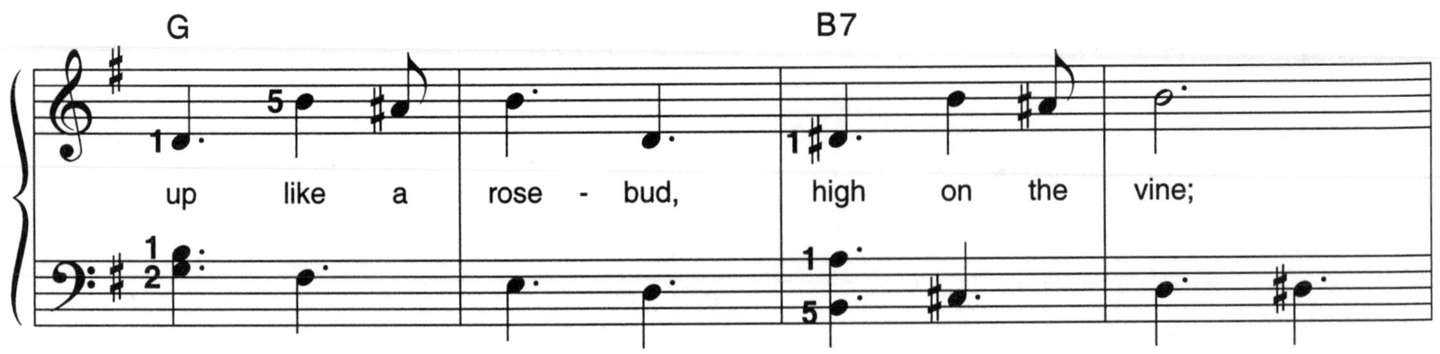
G
B7
up like a rose - bud, high on the vine;

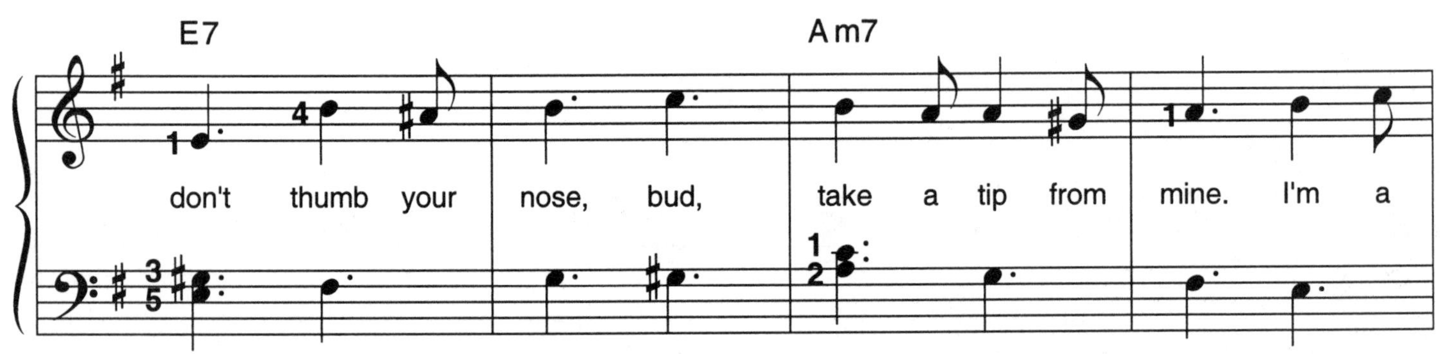
E7
Am7
don't thumb your nose, bud, take a tip from mine. I'm a

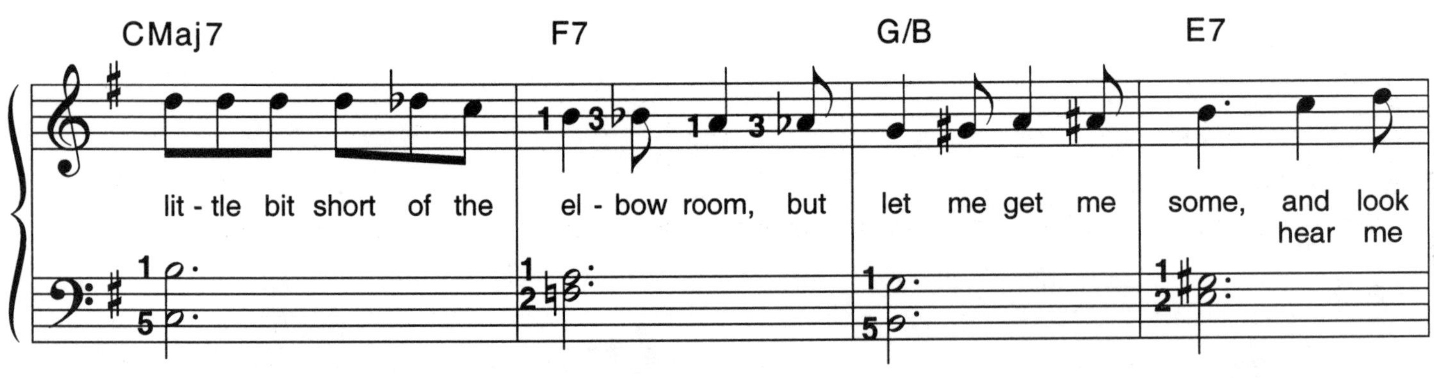
CMaj7
F7
G/B
E7
lit - tle bit short of the el - bow room, but let me get me some, and look
hear me

Am7
D7
G
Fine
out, world, here I come.
shout, world, here I come.

G
No - bod - y in the world was ev - er with - out a pray'r;

F
how can you win the world, if no - bod - y knows you're there.

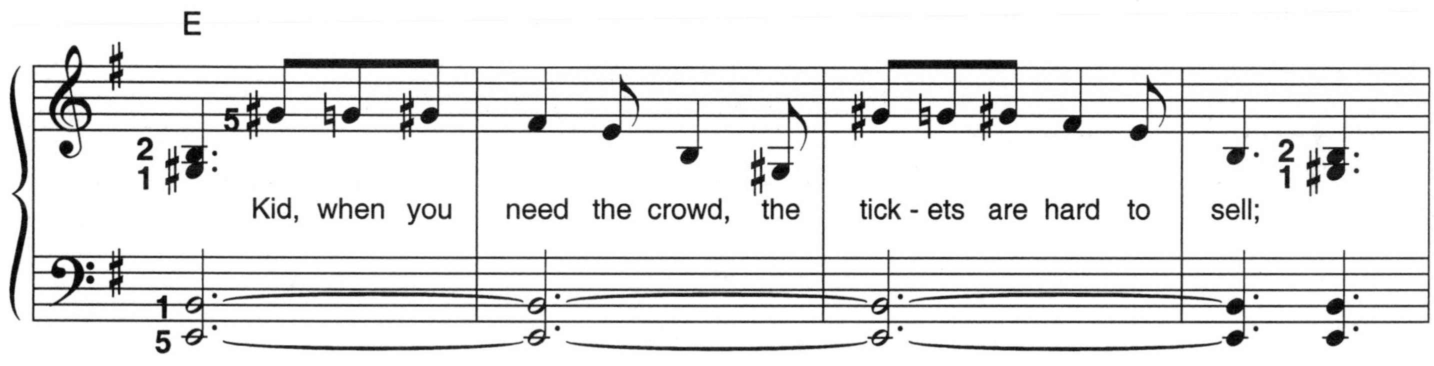
E
Kid, when you need the crowd, the tick - ets are hard to sell;

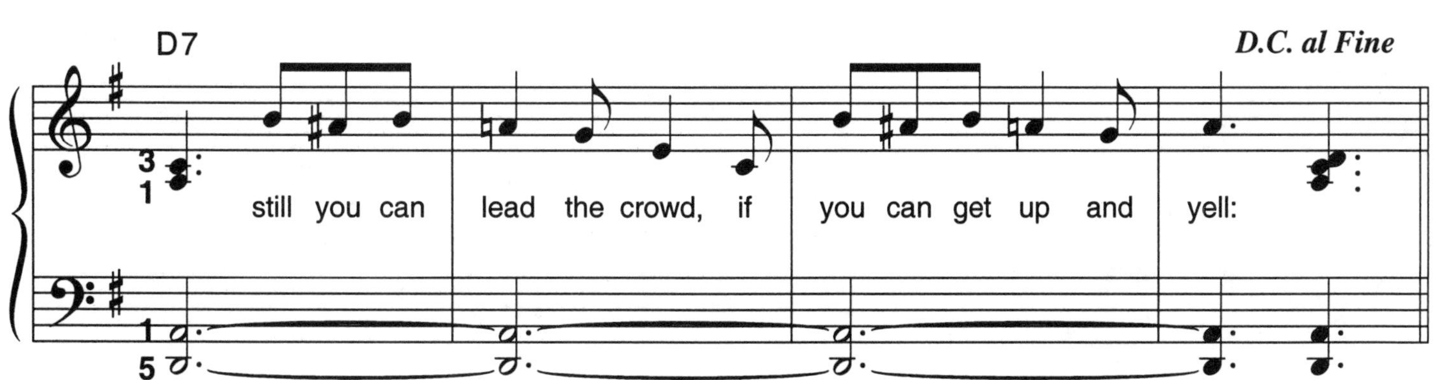
D7
D.C. al Fine
still you can lead the crowd, if you can get up and yell:

Ten Cents a Dance

From the Broadway Musical *Simple Simon*

Words by LORENZ HART
Music by RICHARD RODGERS
Arranged by Richard Bradley

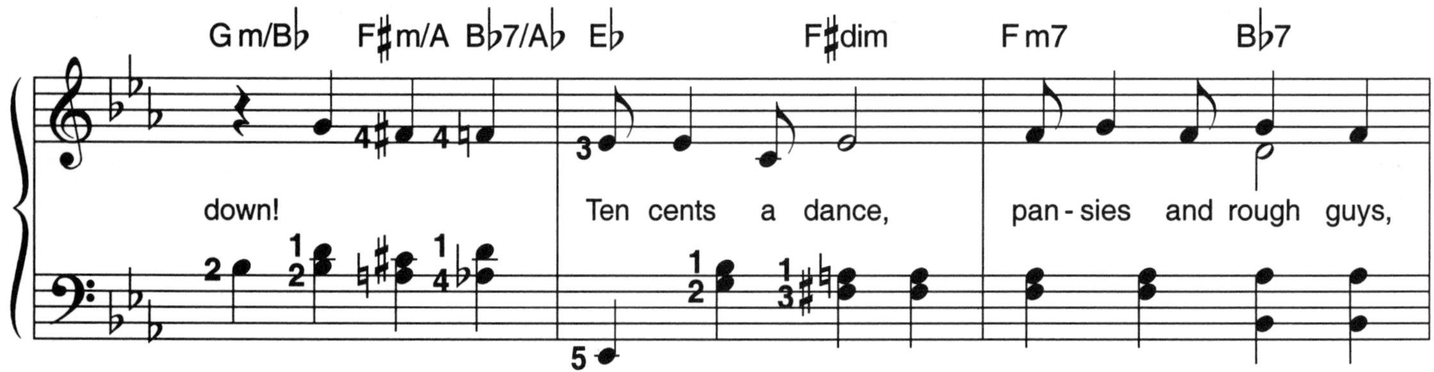

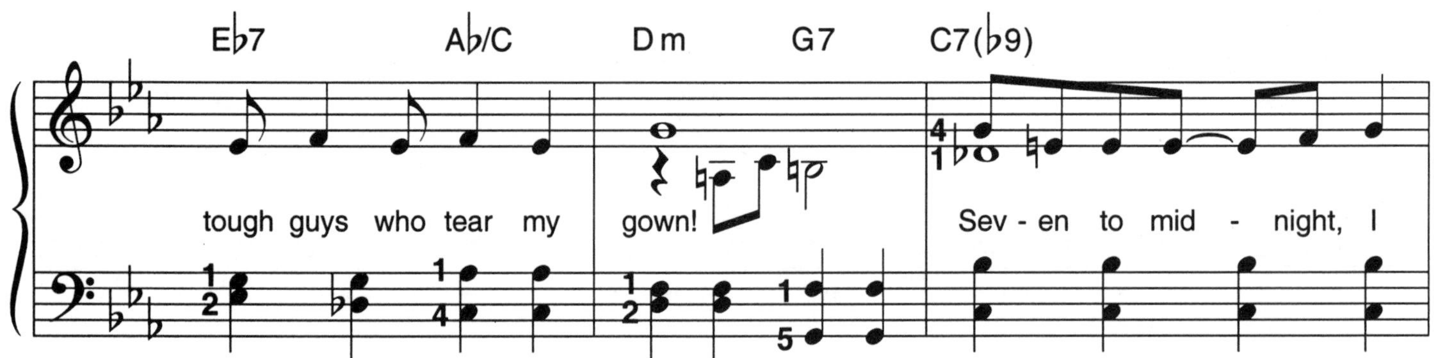

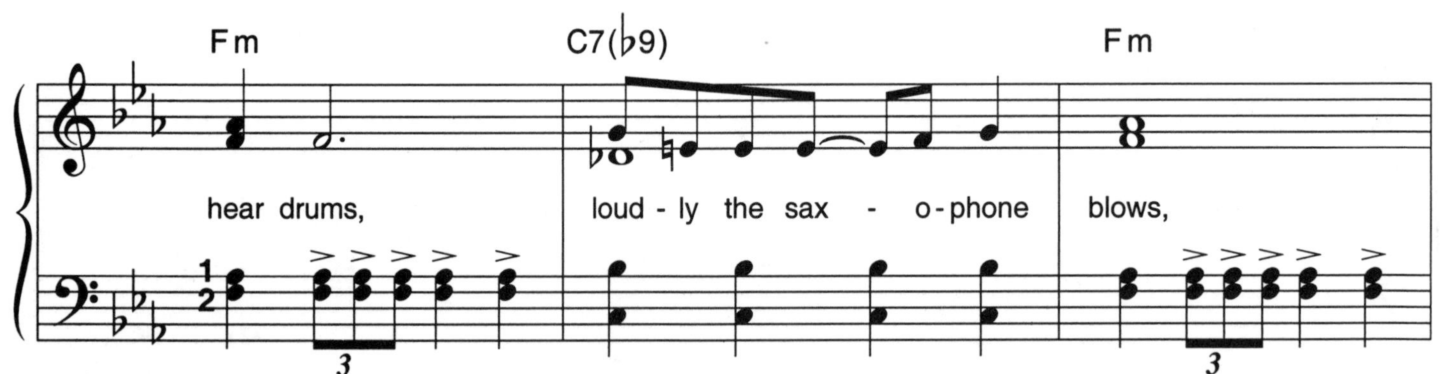

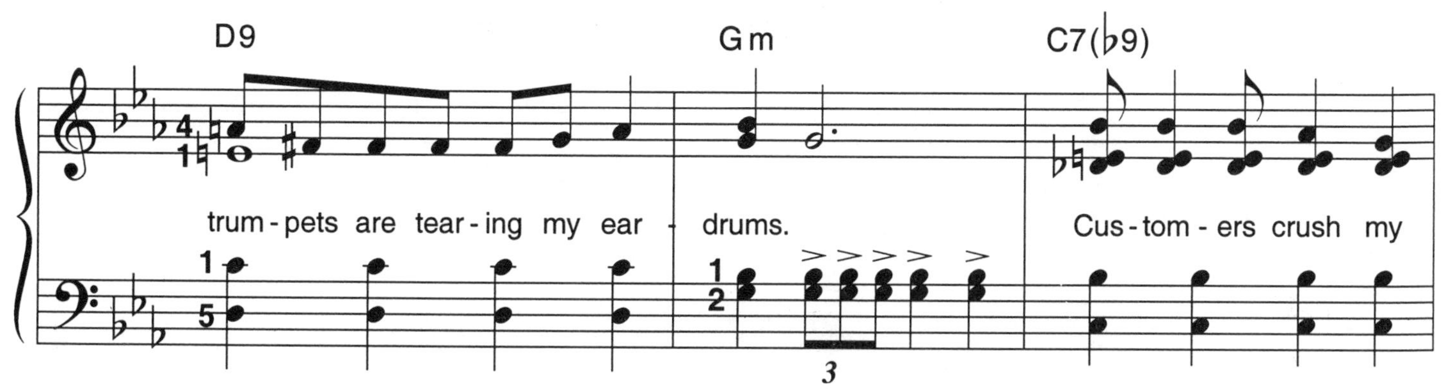
D9
Gm
C7(♭9)
trum-pets are tear-ing my ear - drums.
Cus-tom-ers crush my

F7
B♭7
E♭
F♯dim
Fm7
B♭7
toes.
Some-times I think
I've found my he - ro,

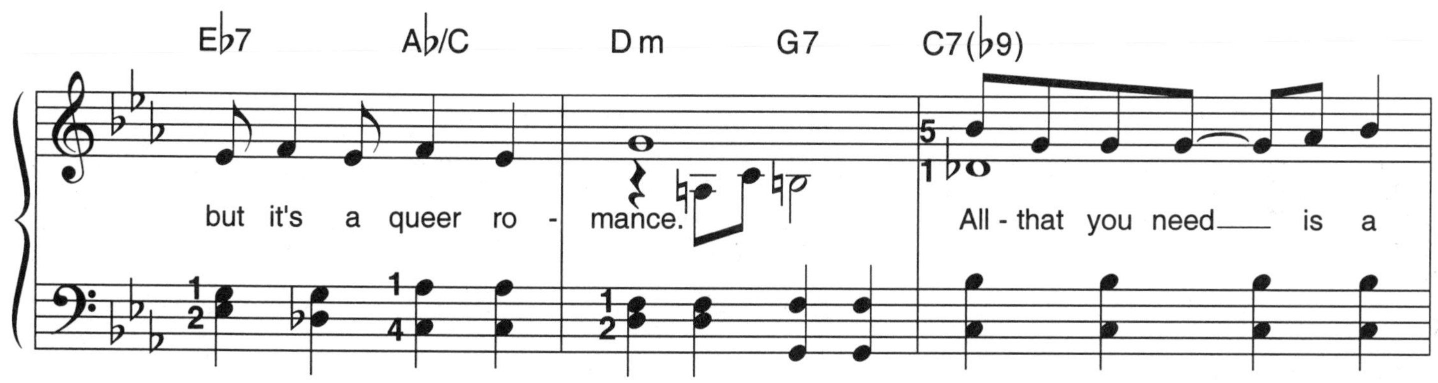
E♭7
A♭/C
Dm
G7
C7(♭9)
but it's a queer ro - mance.
All-that you need is a

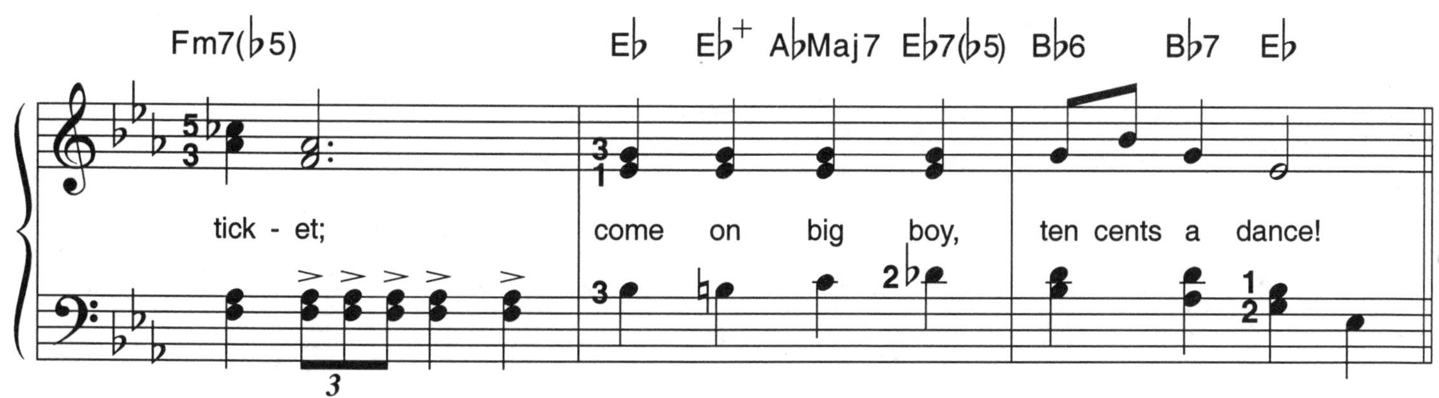
Fm7(♭5)
E♭
E♭+
A♭Maj7
E♭7(♭5)
B♭6
B♭7
E♭
tick - et;
come on big boy,
ten cents a dance!

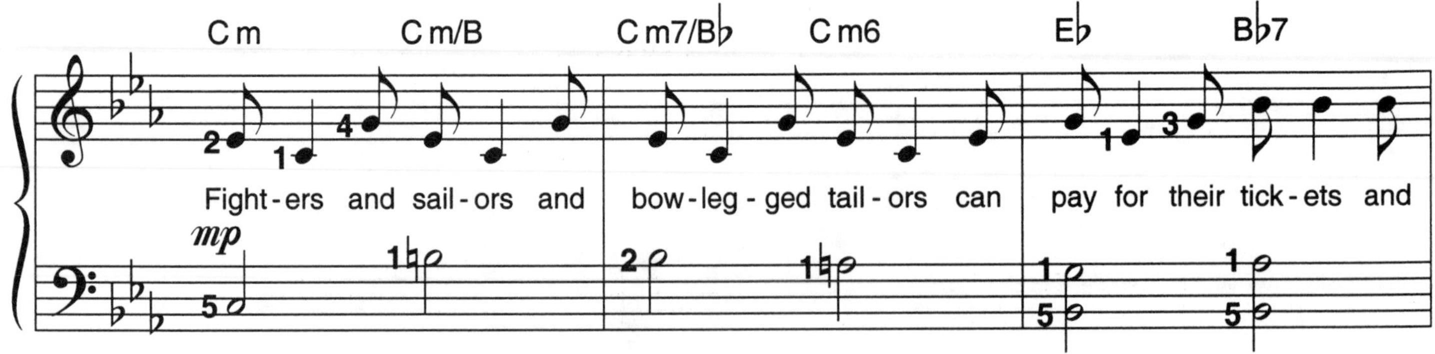
Cm
Cm/B
Cm7/B♭
Cm6
E♭
B♭7
Fight-ers and sail-ors and bow-leg-ged tail-ors can pay for their tick-ets and
mp

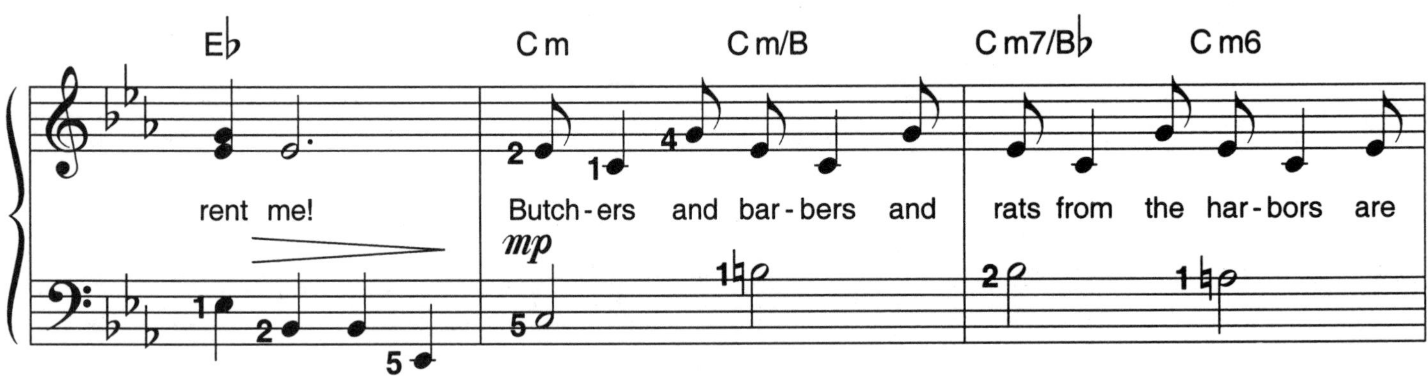
E♭
Cm
Cm/B
Cm7/B♭
Cm6
rent me! Butch-ers and bar-bers and rats from the har-bors are
mp

E♭
B♭9
E♭
Gm
sweet-hearts my good luck has sent me. Though I've a cho-rus of
mp

Am
D
el-der-ly beaux stock-ings are por-rous with holes at the toes.

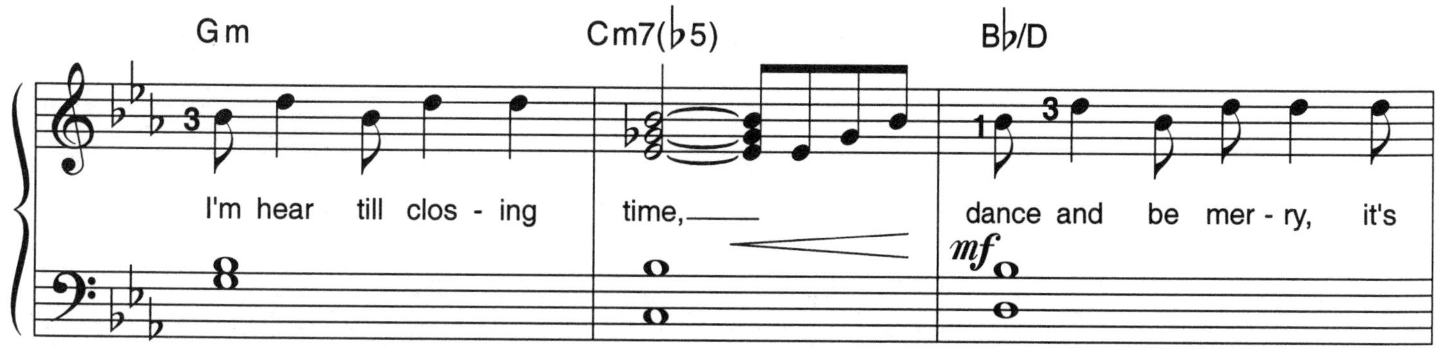
Gm
Cm7(♭5)
B♭/D
I'm hear till clos - ing time,
dance and be mer - ry, it's
mf

F7
B♭7
E♭
F♯dim
Fm7
B♭7
on - ly a dime.
Some-times I think
I've found my he - ro,

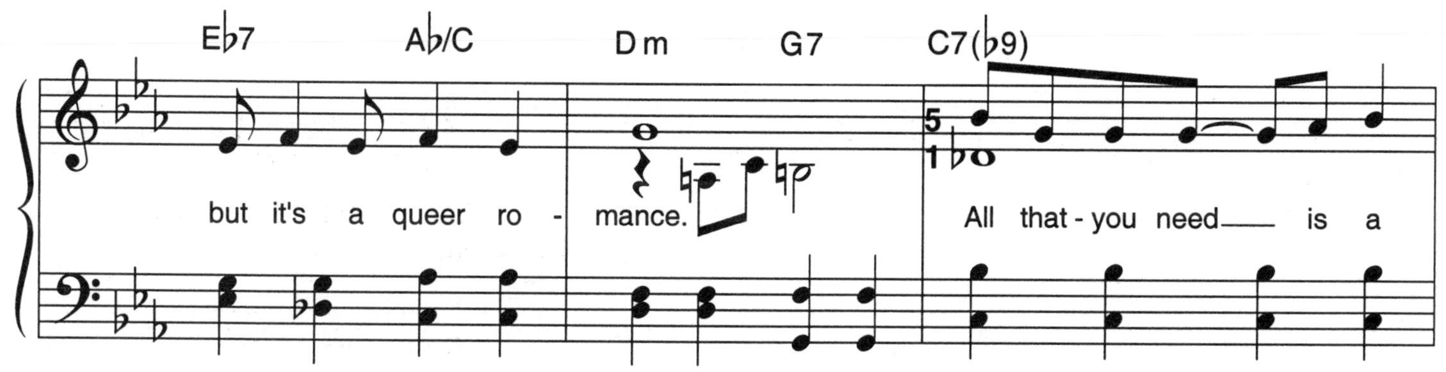
E♭7
A♭/C
Dm
G7
C7(♭9)
but it's a queer ro - mance.
All that - you need is a

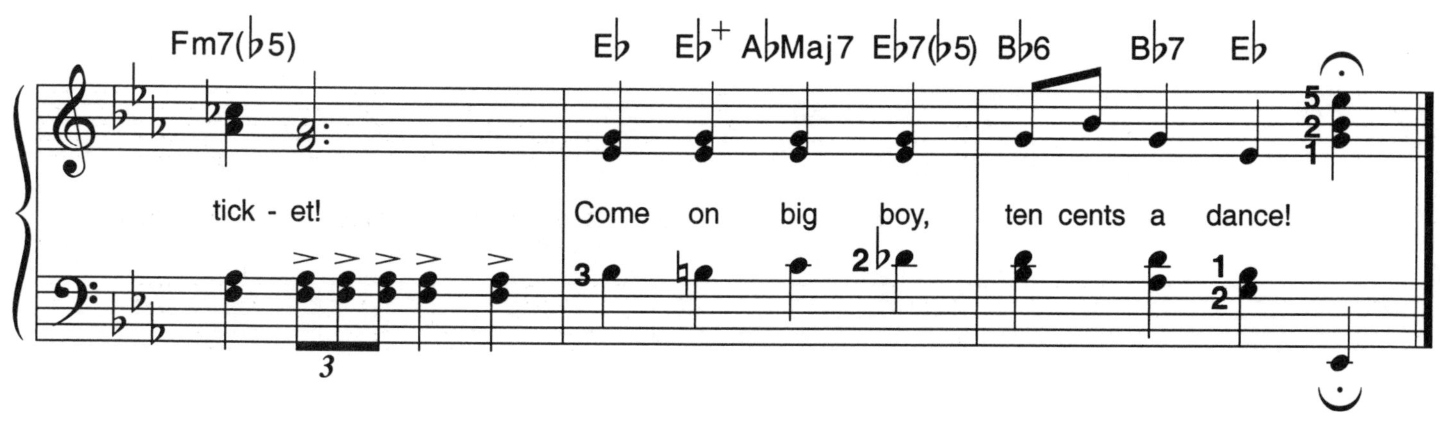
Fm7(♭5)
E♭
E♭+
A♭Maj7
E♭7(♭5)
B♭6
B♭7
E♭
tick - et!
Come on big boy,
ten cents a dance!

Charade

From the Motion Picture *Charade*

Words by JOHNNY MERCER
Music by HENRY MANCINI
Arranged by Richard Bradley

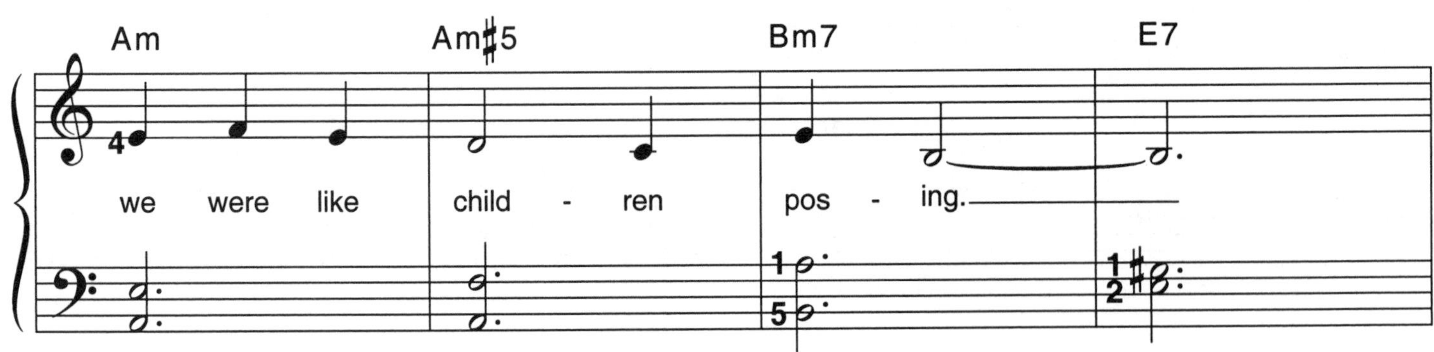

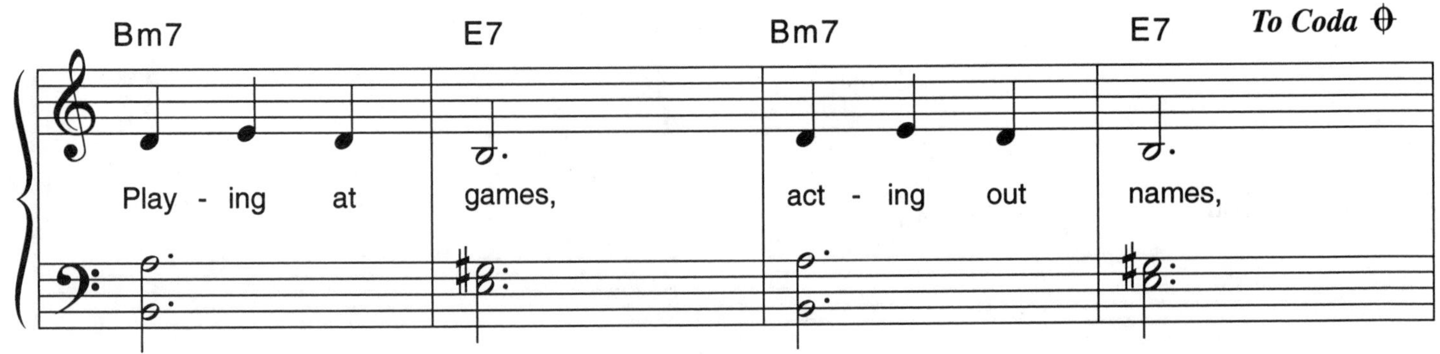

Bm7
E7
Am
Am♯5
guess - ing the parts we played.

1.
2.
Am6
Am♯5
Am♯5
Dm7
mf
Fate

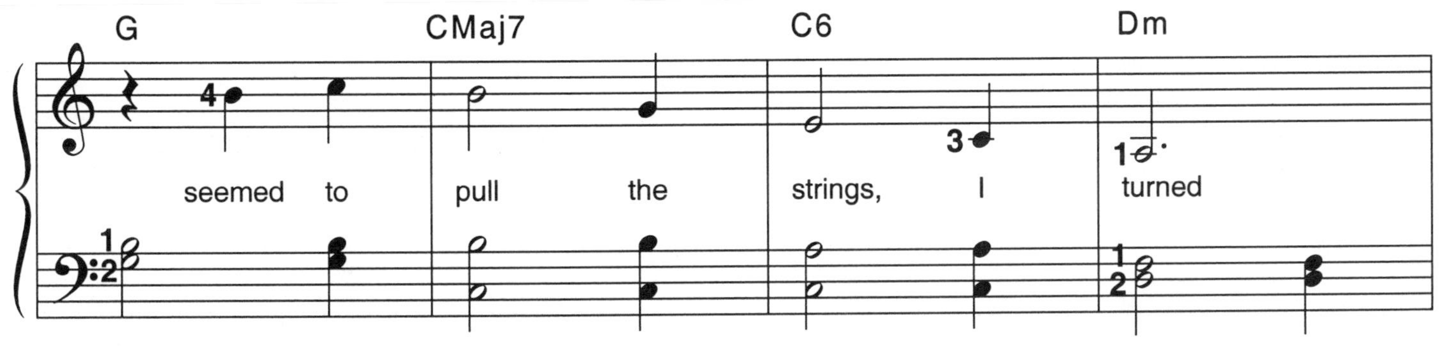
G
CMaj7
C6
Dm
seemed to pull the strings, I turned

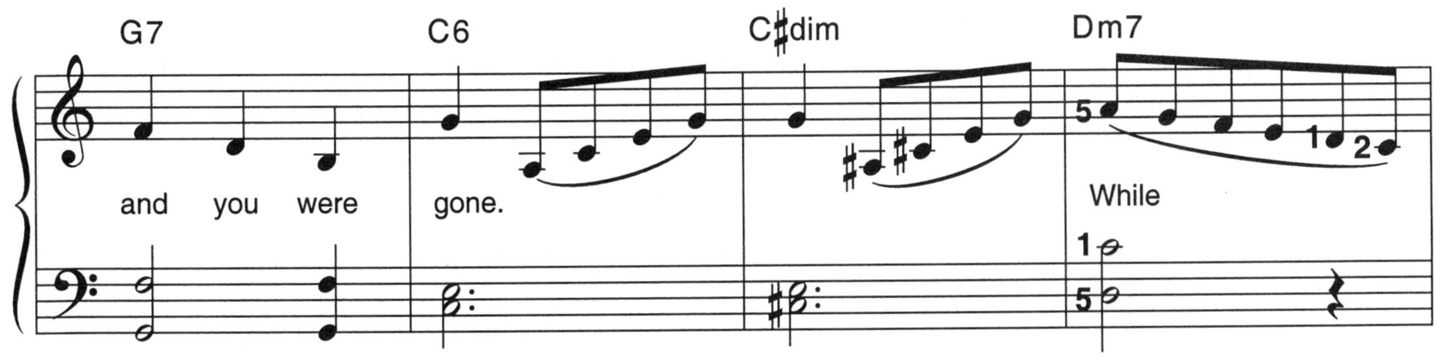
G7
C6
C♯dim
Dm7
and you were gone.
While

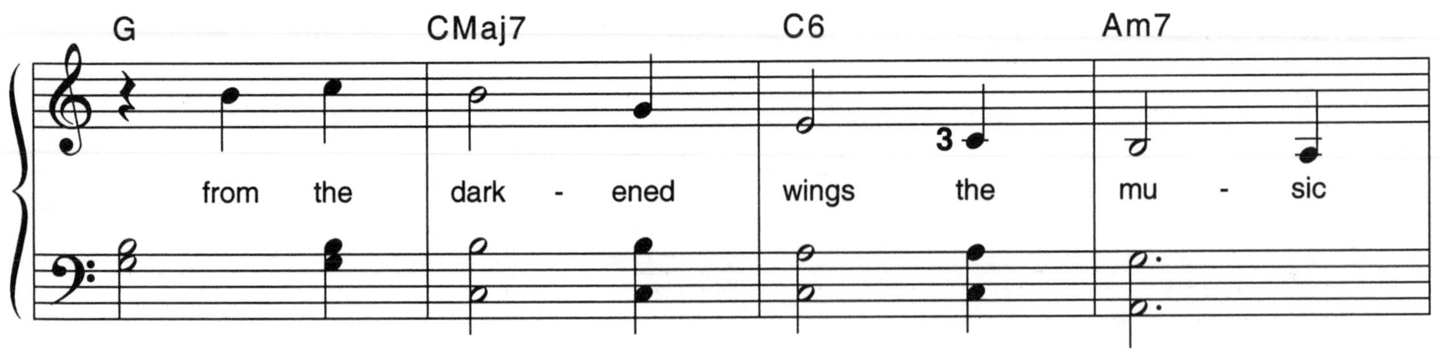
G
CMaj7
C6
Am7
3
from the
dark - ened
wings the
mu - sic

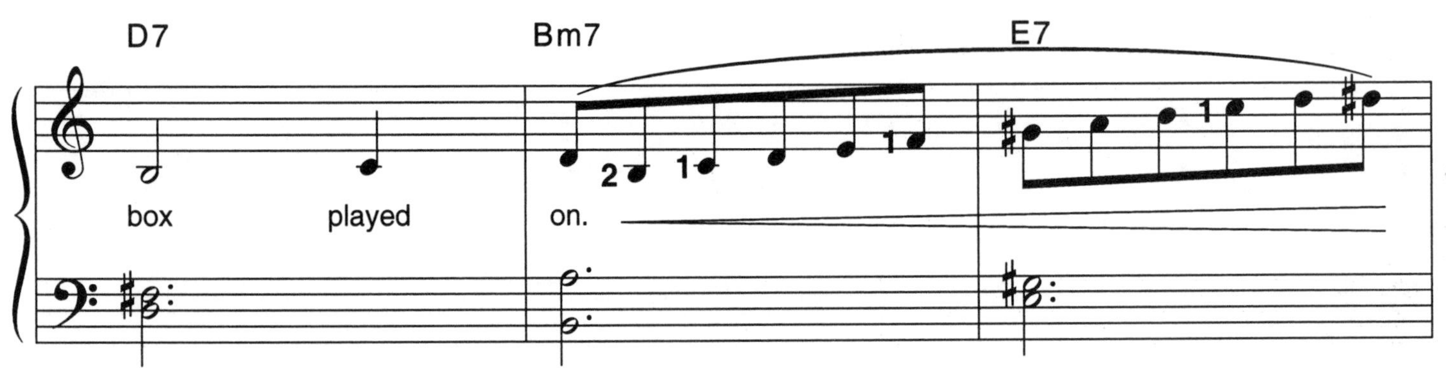
D7
Bm7
E7
2
1
1
1
box played
on.

Am
Am♯5
Am6
Am♯5
4
5
f

D.S. 𝄋 al Coda 𝄌
Am
Am♯5
Am6
Am♯5
4
mp

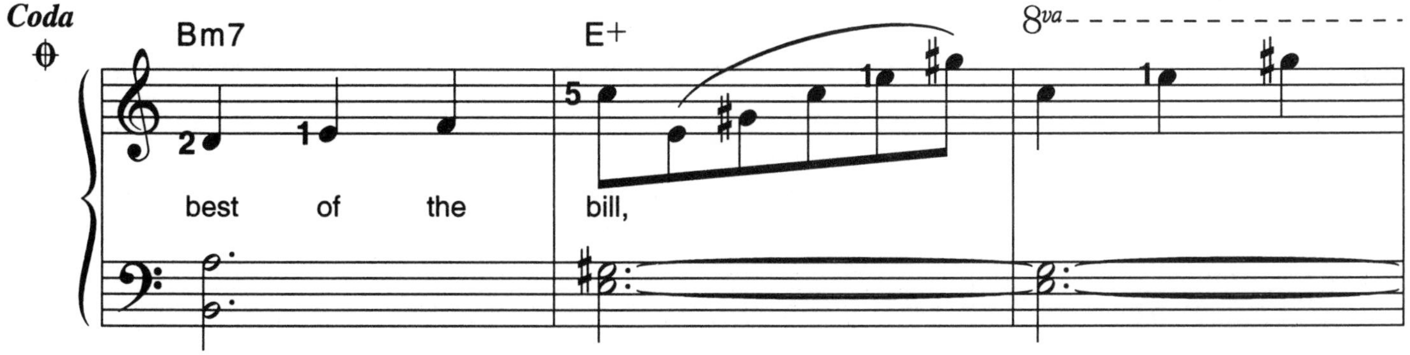

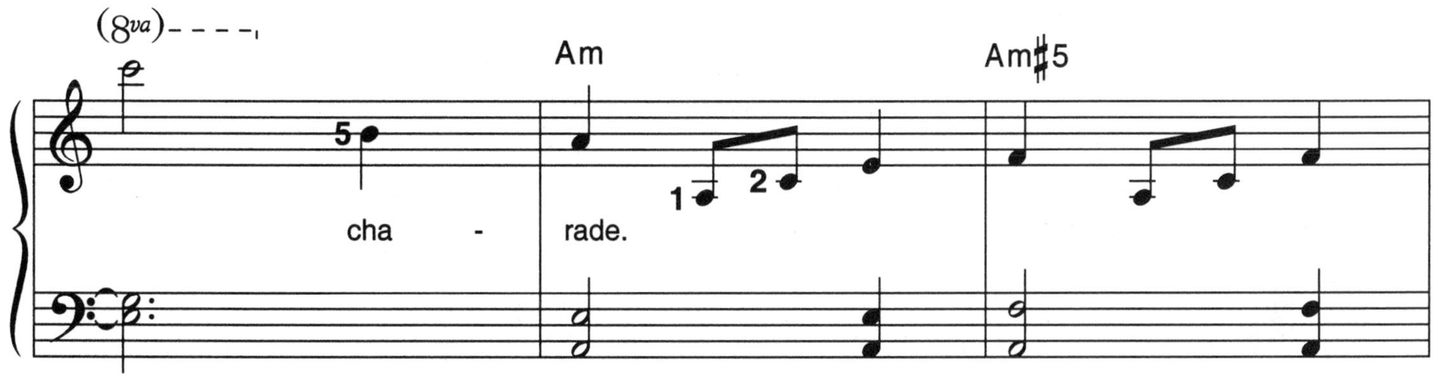

Verse 2:
Oh, what a hit we made.
We came on next to closing.
Best on the bill, lovers until
Love left the masquerade.

Verse 3:
Sad little serenade,
Song of my heart's composing.
I hear it still, I always will,
Best of the bill,
Charade.

Love Makes the World Go 'Round

From the Broadway Musical *Carnival*

Words and Music by
BOB MERRILL
Arranged by Richard Bradley

Fm7
B♭7
E♭
B♭7
if no one loves you now.
E♭
A♭
E♭
High in some si - lent sky,
A♭
E♭Maj7
B♭7
love sings a sil - ver song,
Fm7
B♭7
mak - ing the earth whirl soft - ly,
Fm7
B♭9
E♭
A♭
E♭
love makes the world go 'round.

Someone To Watch Over Me

From the Broadway Musical *Oh, Kay!*

Words by IRA GERSHWIN
Music by GEORGE GERSHWIN
Arranged by Richard Bradley

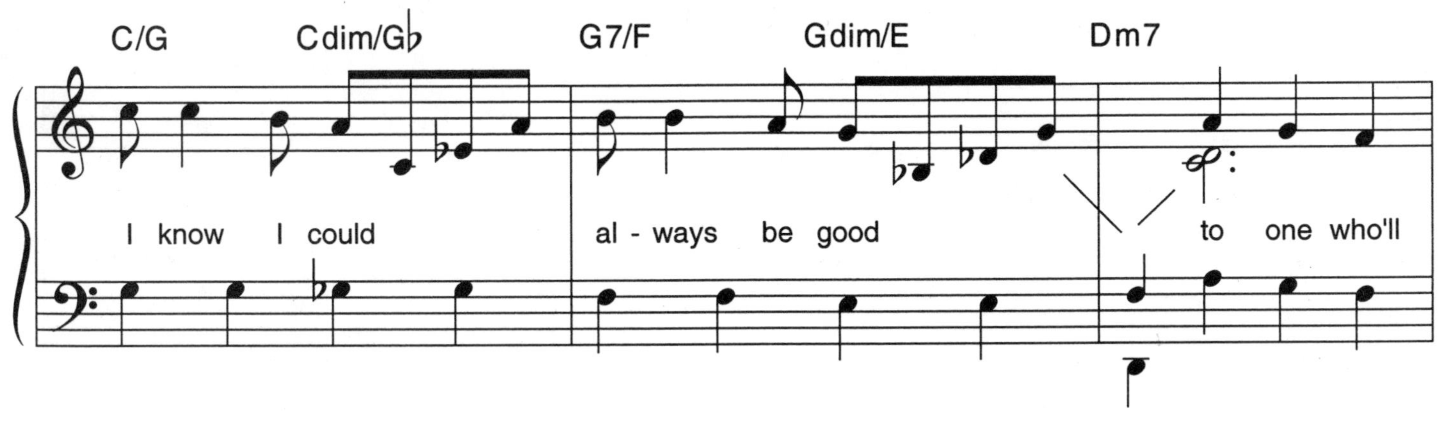
C/G
Cdim/G♭
G7/F
Gdim/E
Dm7
I know I could
al - ways be good
to one who'll

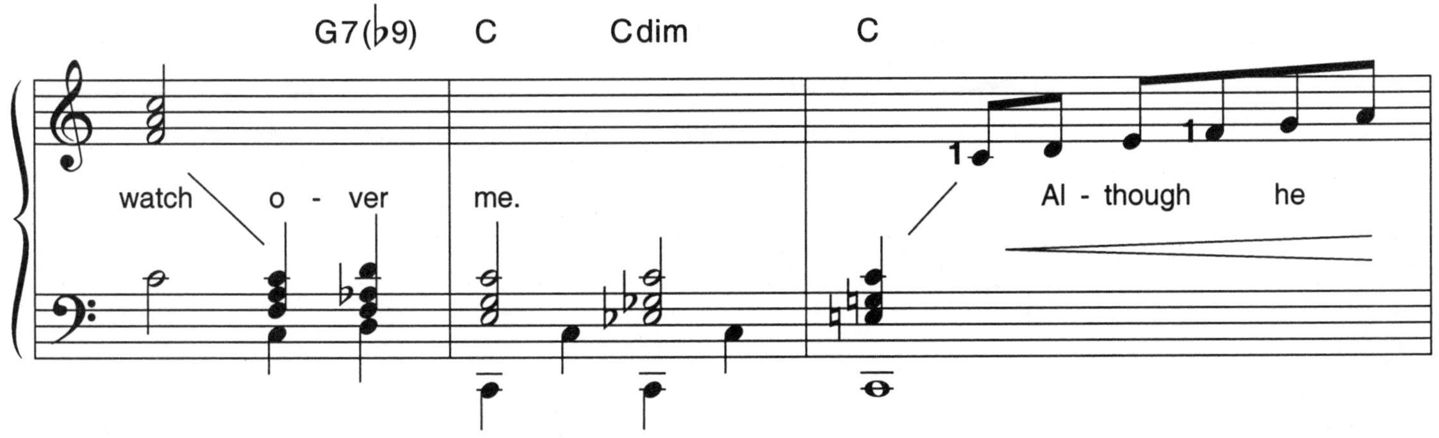
G7(♭9)
C
Cdim
C
watch o - ver
me.
Al - though he

Fdim
F/C
Fdim
F/C
F
Fm
may not be the
man some girls
think of as
mf

C/E
F♯m7(♭5)
B7
E7
hand - some, to
my heart he
car - ries the

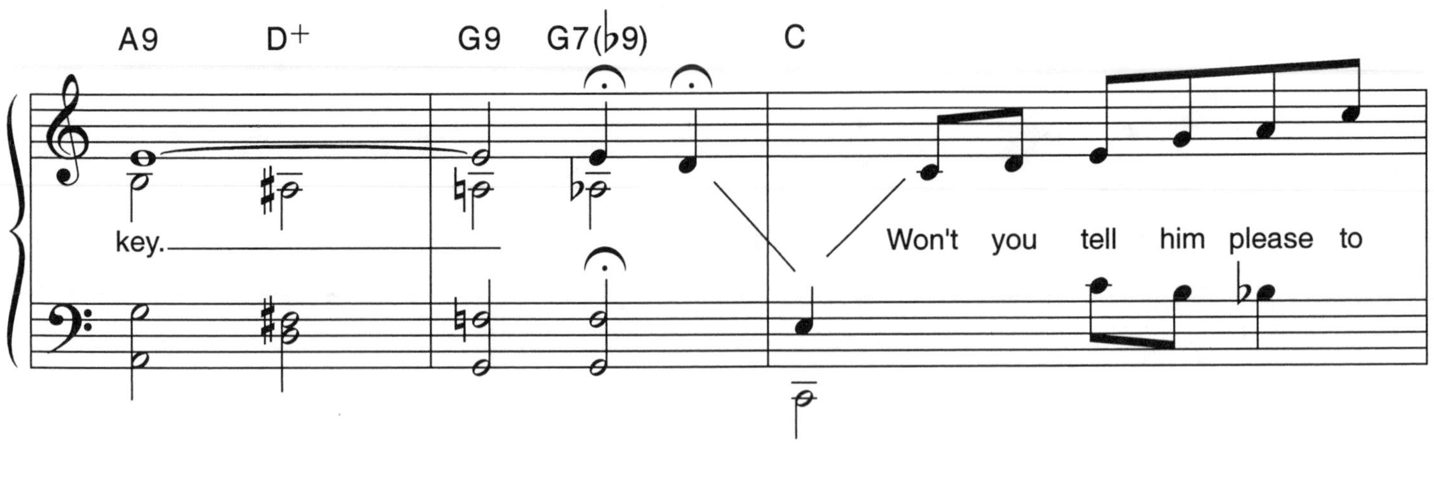
A9
D+
G9
G7(♭9)
C
key.
Won't you tell him please to

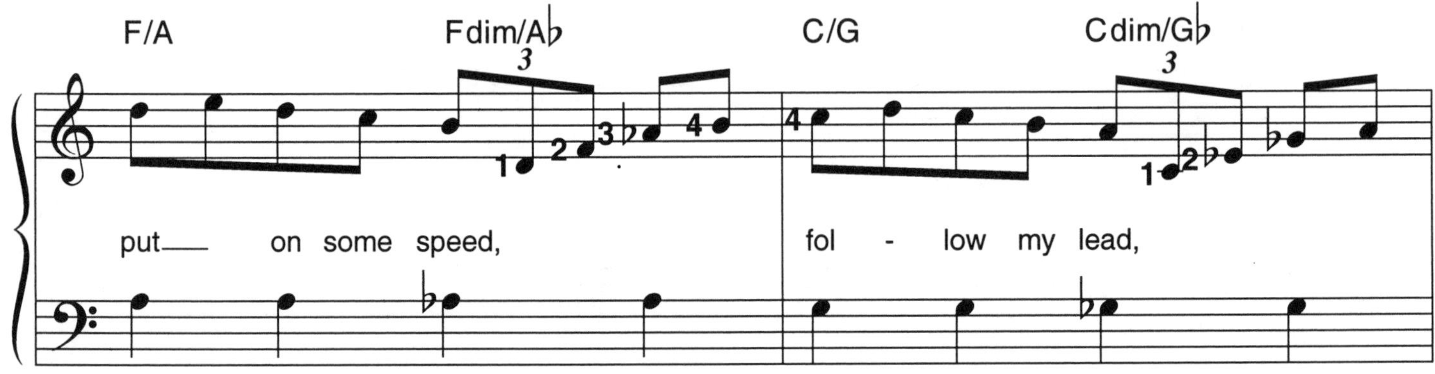
F/A
Fdim/A♭
C/G
Cdim/G♭
put on some speed,
fol - low my lead,

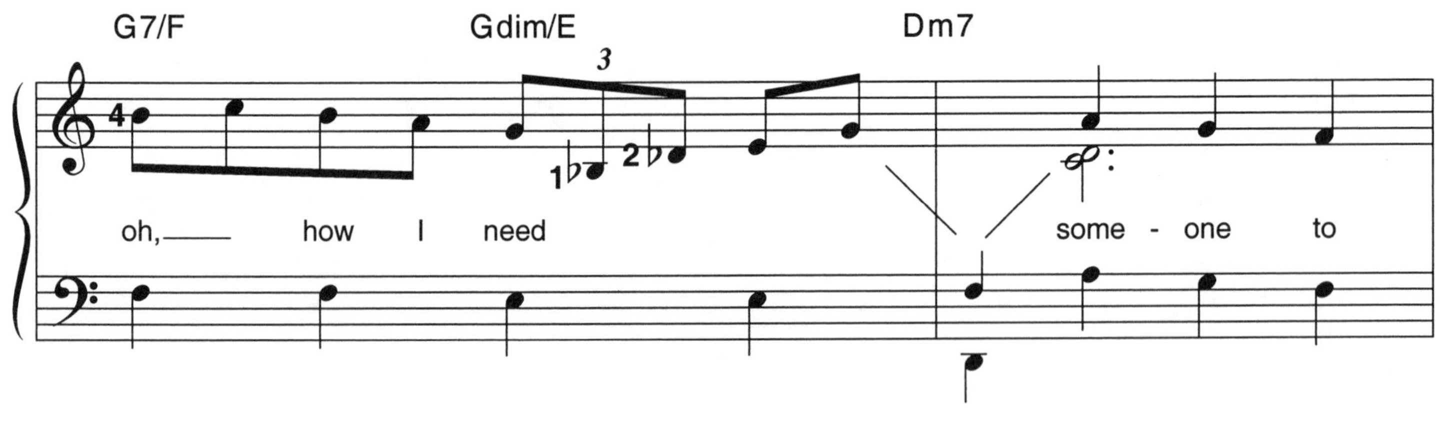
G7/F
Gdim/E
Dm7
oh, how I need
some - one to

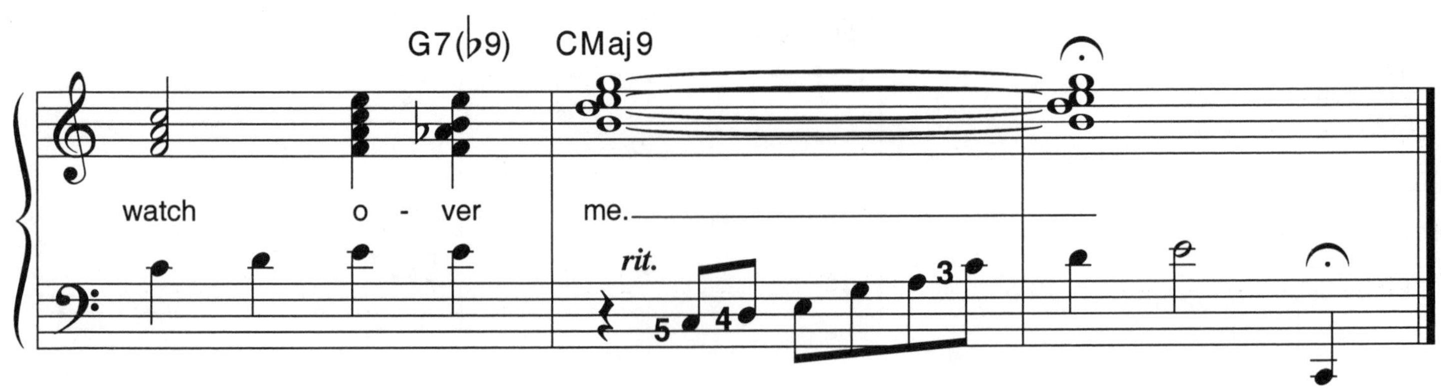
G7(♭9)
CMaj9
watch o - ver
me.
rit.

At Last

Lyric by
MACK GORDON

Music by
HARRY WARREN
Arranged by Richard Bradley

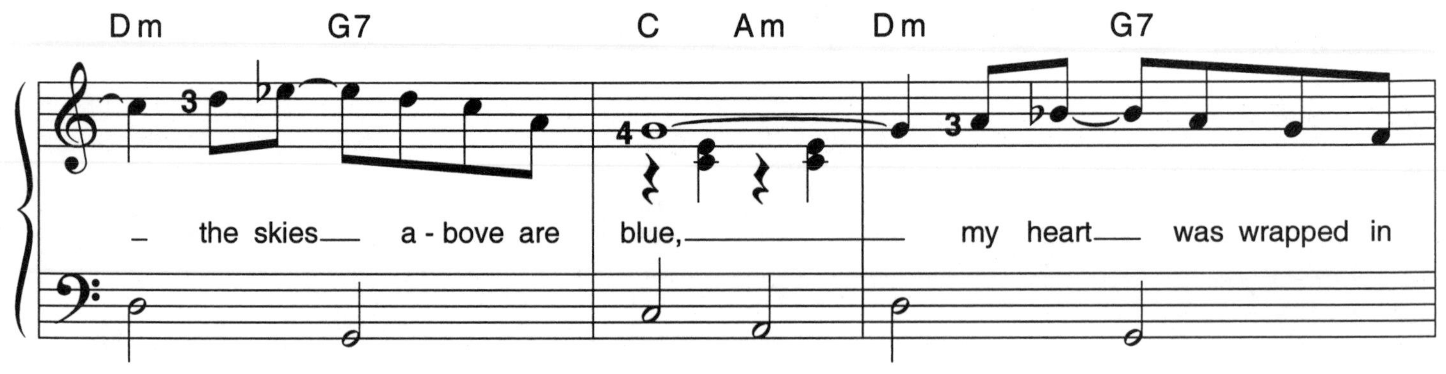
Dm G7 C Am Dm G7
– the skies – a - bove are blue, – my heart – was wrapped in

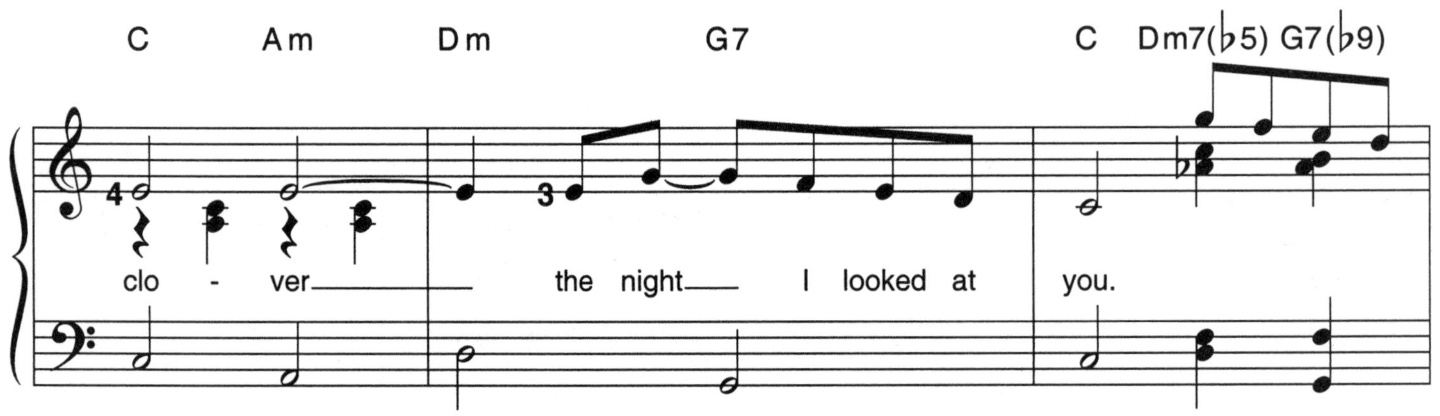
C Am Dm G7 C Dm7(♭5) G7(♭9)
clo - ver – the night – I looked at you.

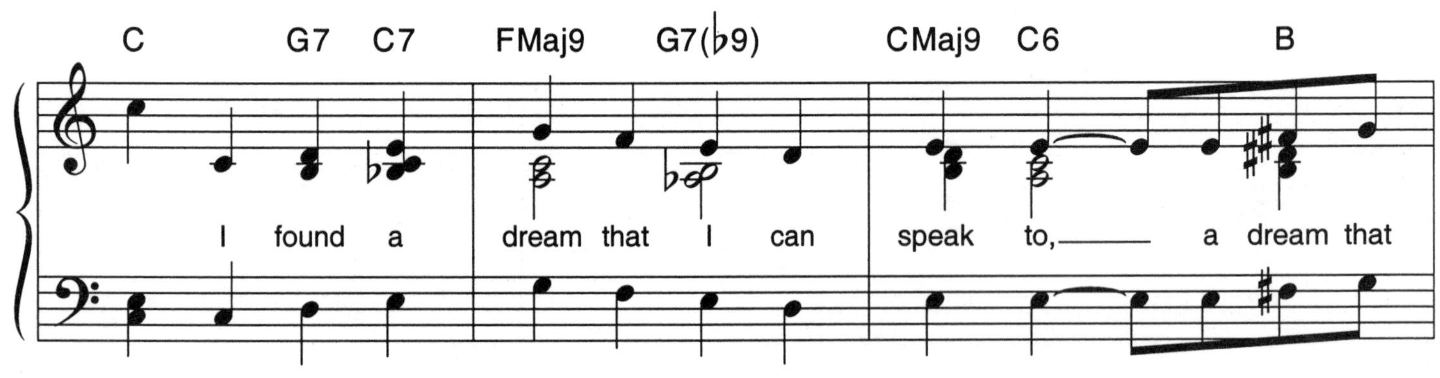
C G7 C7 FMaj9 G7(♭9) CMaj9 C6 B
I found a dream that I can speak to, – a dream that

Am9 B7(♭9) Em N.C. Am7(♭5) D7
I can call my own, – I found a thrill to press my

GMaj7
C
Am7
D7(♭9)
G6
G7(♯5)
cheek to, a thrill I've nev - er known. You

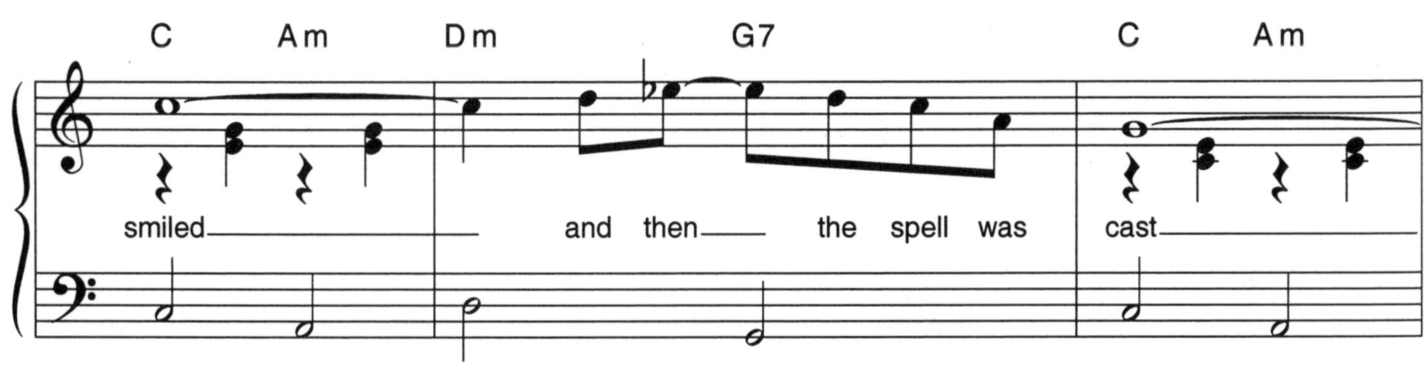
C
Am
Dm
G7
C
Am
smiled and then the spell was cast

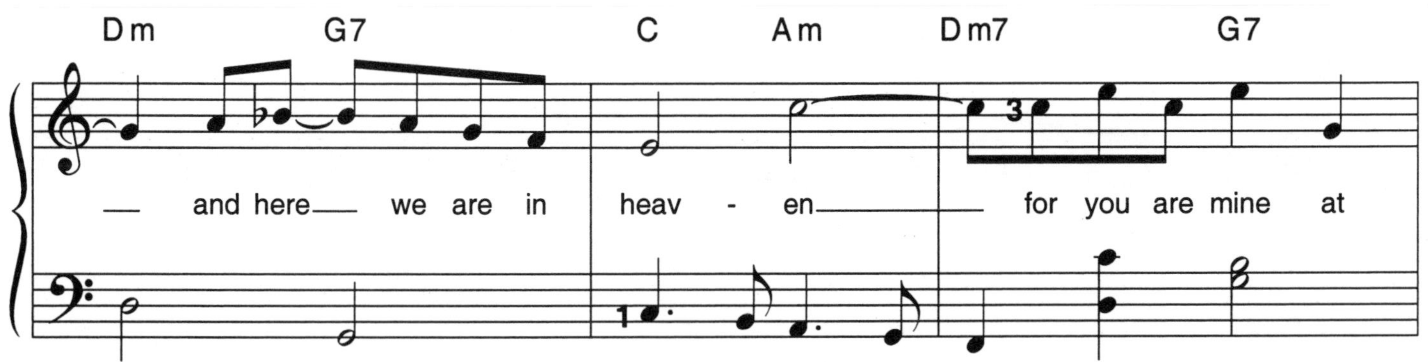
Dm
G7
C
Am
Dm7
G7
and here we are in heav - en for you are mine at

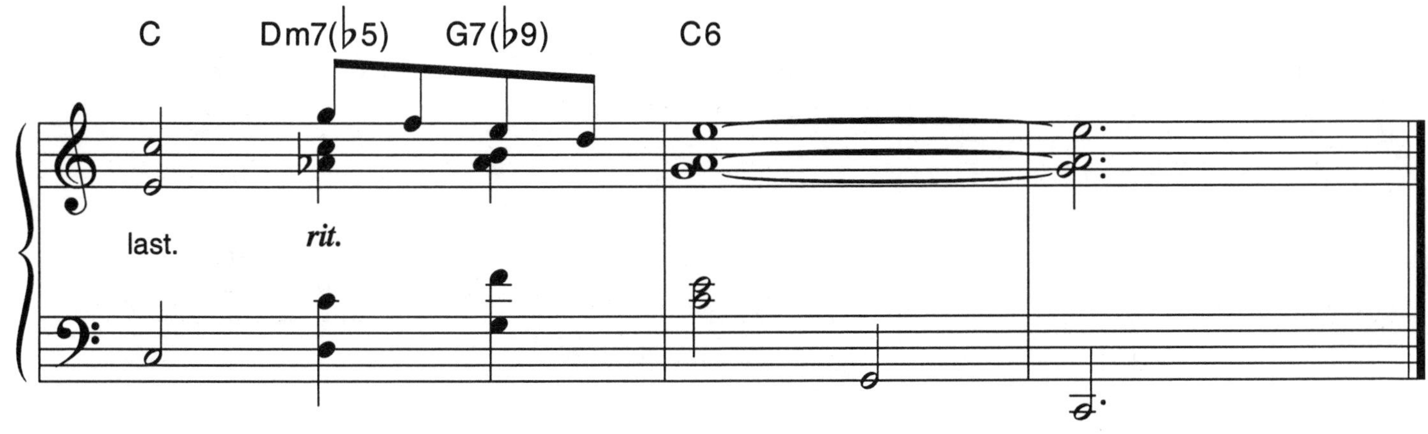
C
Dm7(♭5)
G7(♭9)
C6
last.
rit.

I've Gotta Be Me

From the Broadway Musical *Golden Rainbow*

Music and Lyrics by
WALTER MARKS
Arranged by Richard Bradley

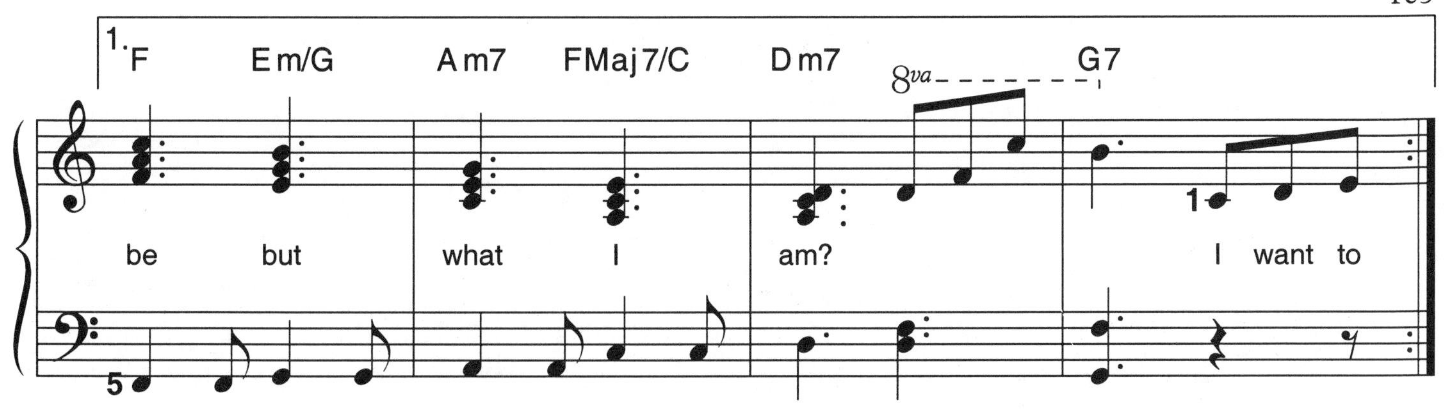
1.
F
Em/G
Am7
FMaj7/C
Dm7
8va
G7
be but what I am? I want to

2.
F
Em
Dm
G9
CMaj7
8va
see makes me what I am!

C6
N.C.
Bm7sus4
E7
(8va)
That far a - way prize, a world of suc -
mf

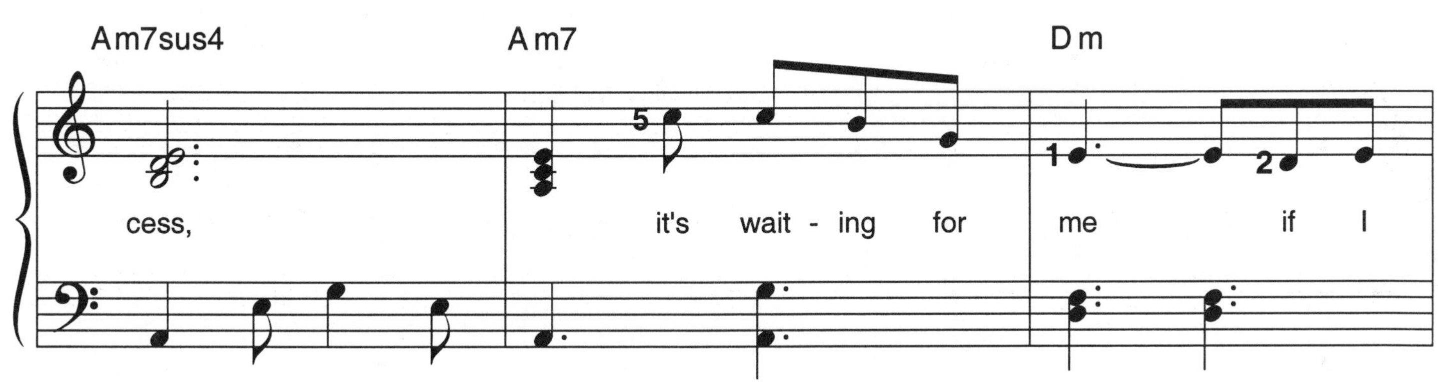
Am7sus4
Am7
Dm
cess, it's wait - ing for me if I

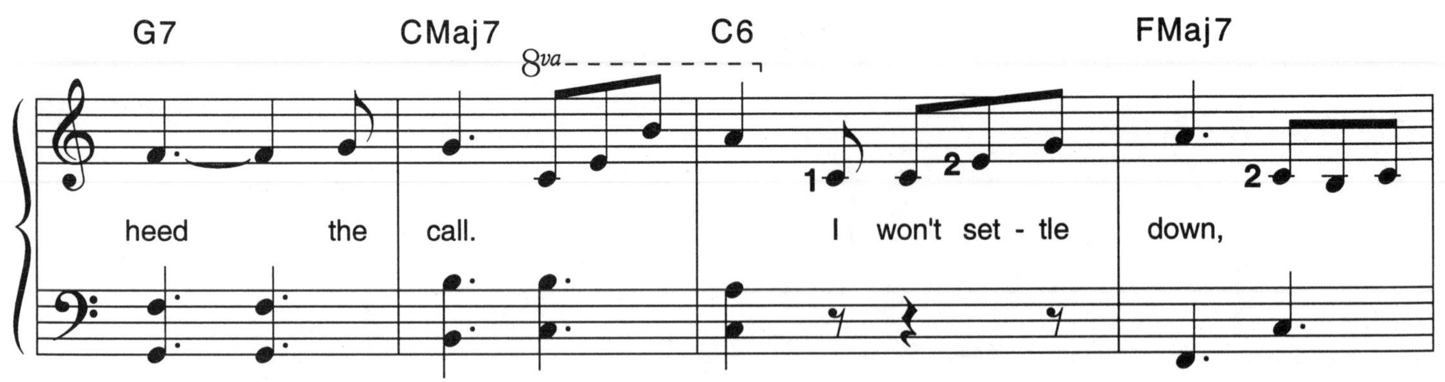
G7
CMaj7
8va
C6
FMaj7
1
2
2
heed the call. I won't set - tle down,

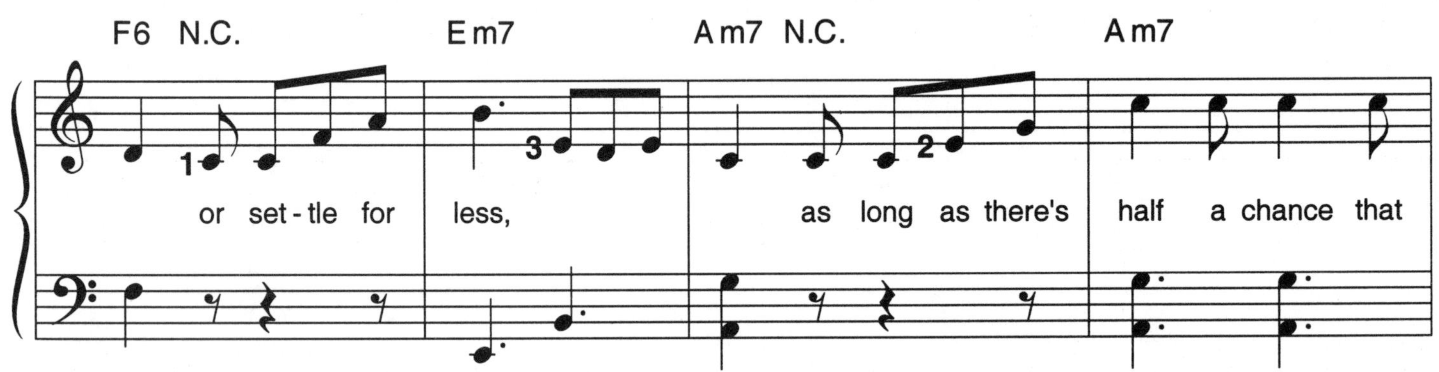
F6 N.C.
Em7
Am7 N.C.
Am7
1
3
2
or set - tle for less, as long as there's half a chance that

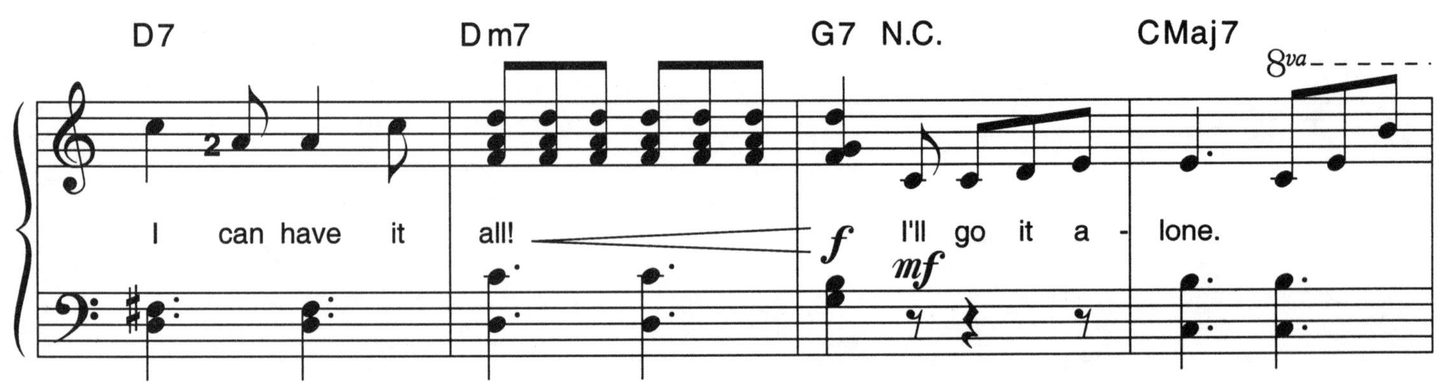
D7
Dm7
G7 N.C.
CMaj7
8va
2
I can have it all! I'll go it a - lone.
f
mf

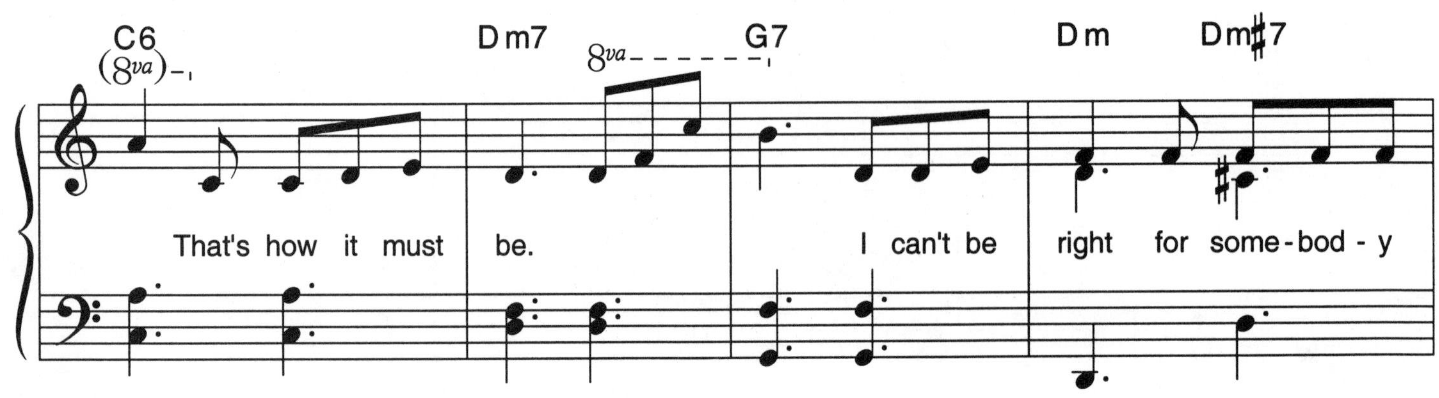
C6
(8va)
Dm7
8va
G7
Dm
Dm♯7
That's how it must be. I can't be right for some - bod - y

Verse 2:
I want to live! Not merely survive!
And I won't give up this dream of life
That keeps me alive!
I've gotta be me! I've gotta be me!
The dream that I see makes me what I am!

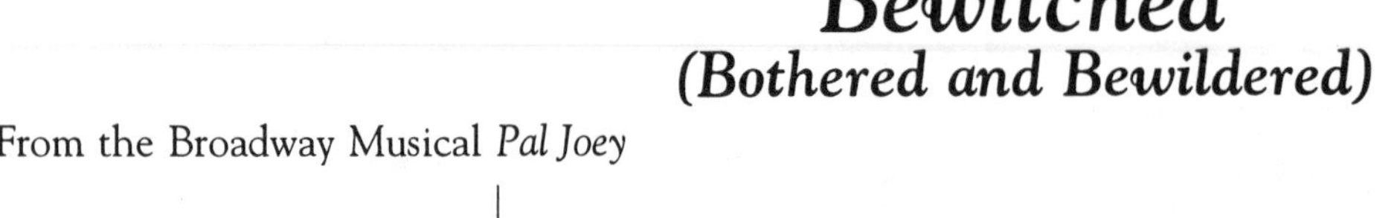

Bewitched
(Bothered and Bewildered)

From the Broadway Musical *Pal Joey*

Words by LORENZ HART
Music by RICHARD RODGERS
Arranged by Richard Bradley

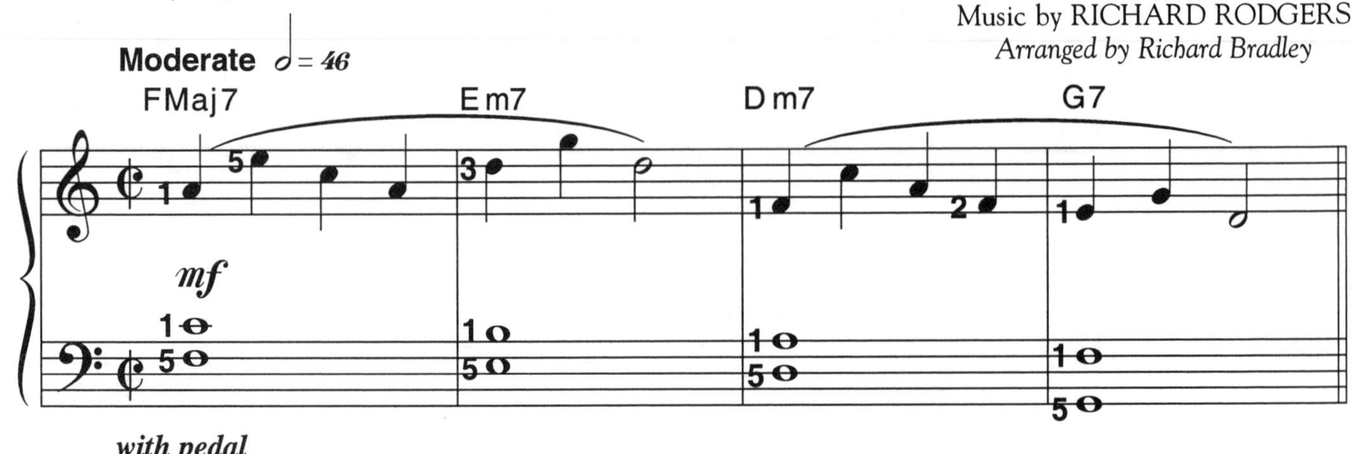

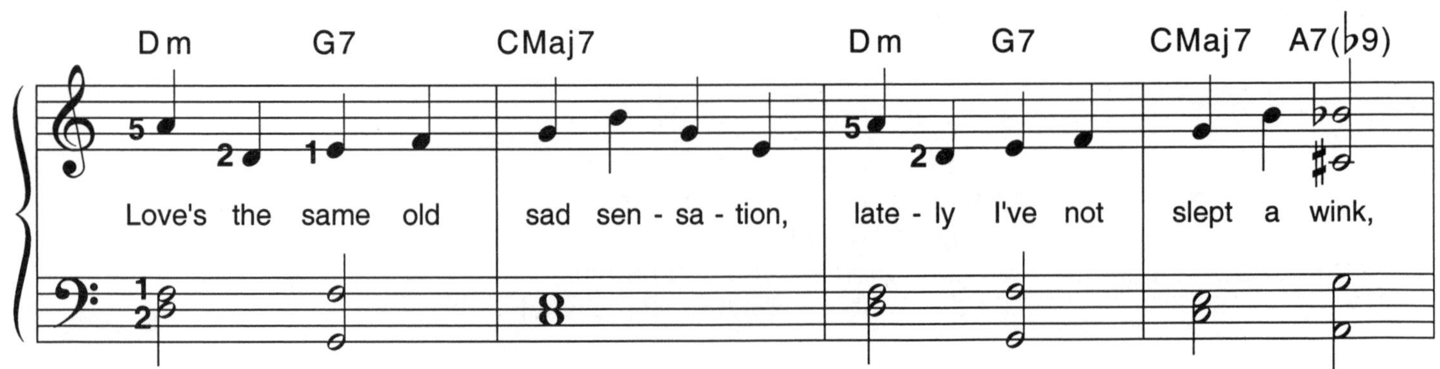

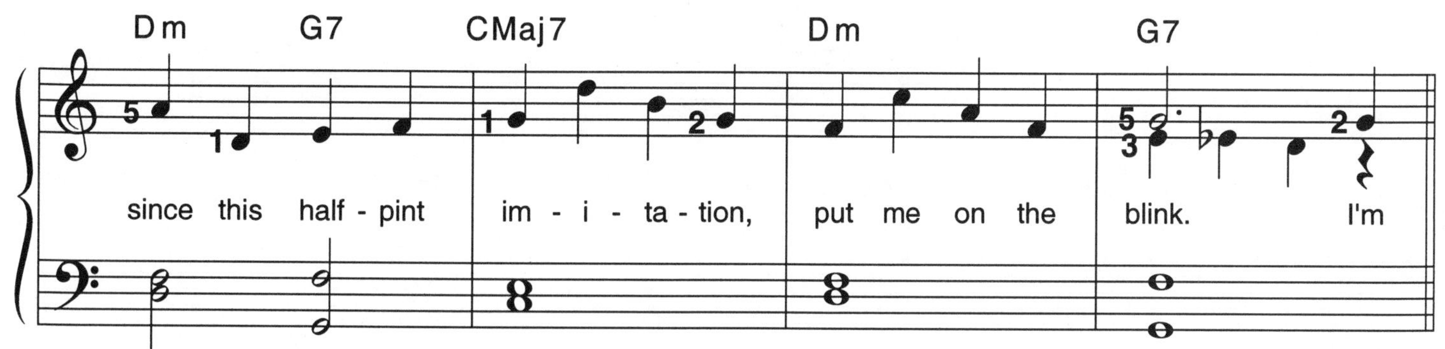
Dm G7 CMaj7 Dm G7
since this half - pint im - i - ta - tion, put me on the blink. I'm

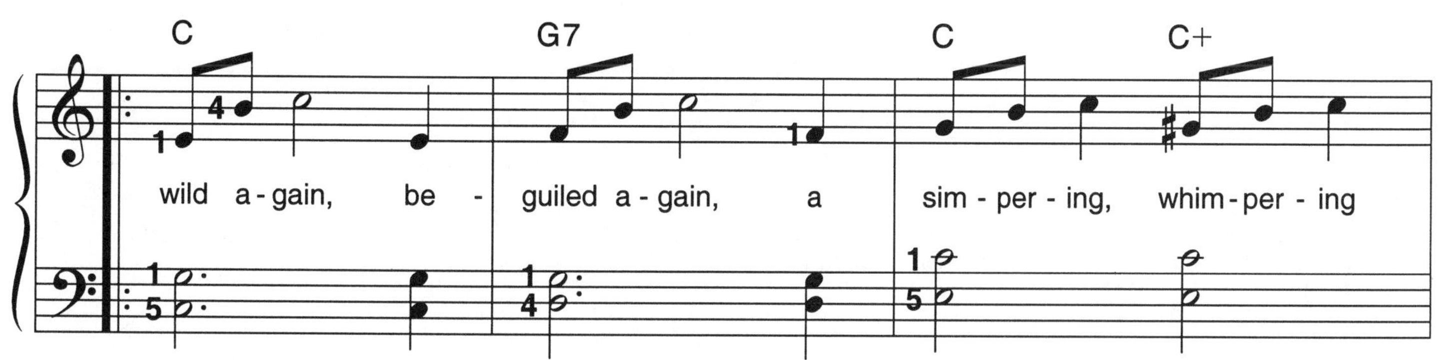
C G7 C C+
wild a - gain, be - guiled a - gain, a sim - per - ing, whim - per - ing

F Fdim C D7 G7 A7
child a - gain, be - witched, both - ered and be - wild - ered am

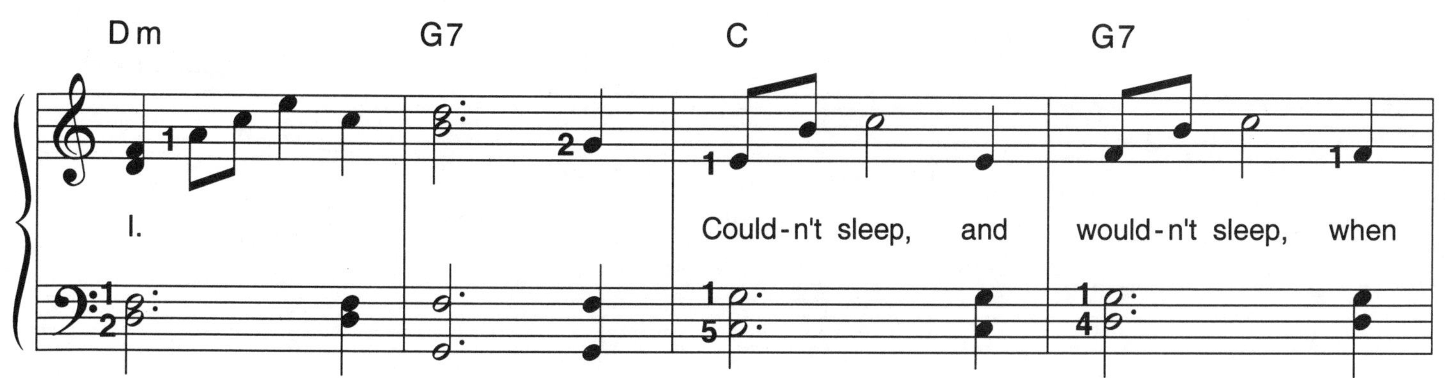
Dm G7 C G7
I. Could - n't sleep, and would - n't sleep, when

C C+ F Fdim C D7
love came and told me I should-n't sleep, be - witched, both-ered and be -

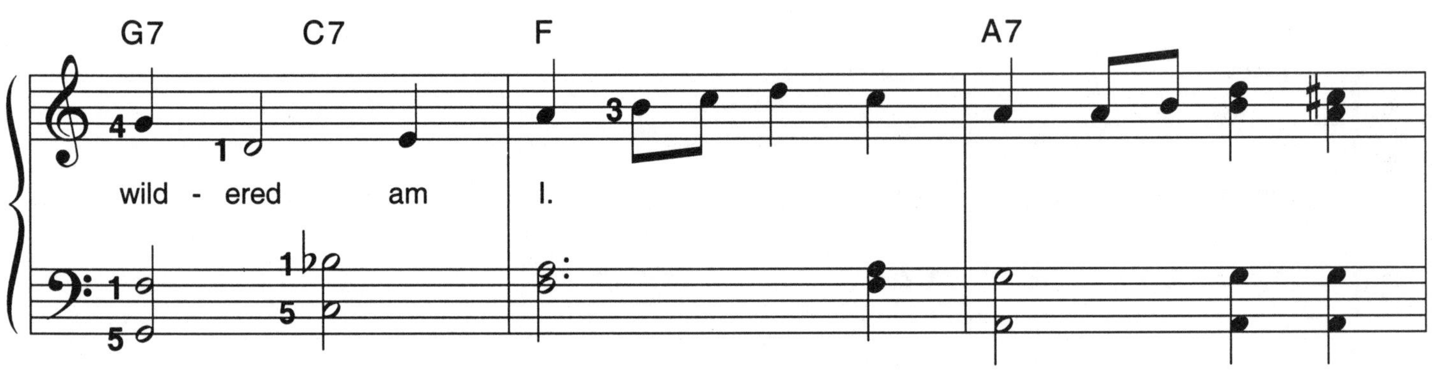
G7 C7 F A7
wild - ered am I.

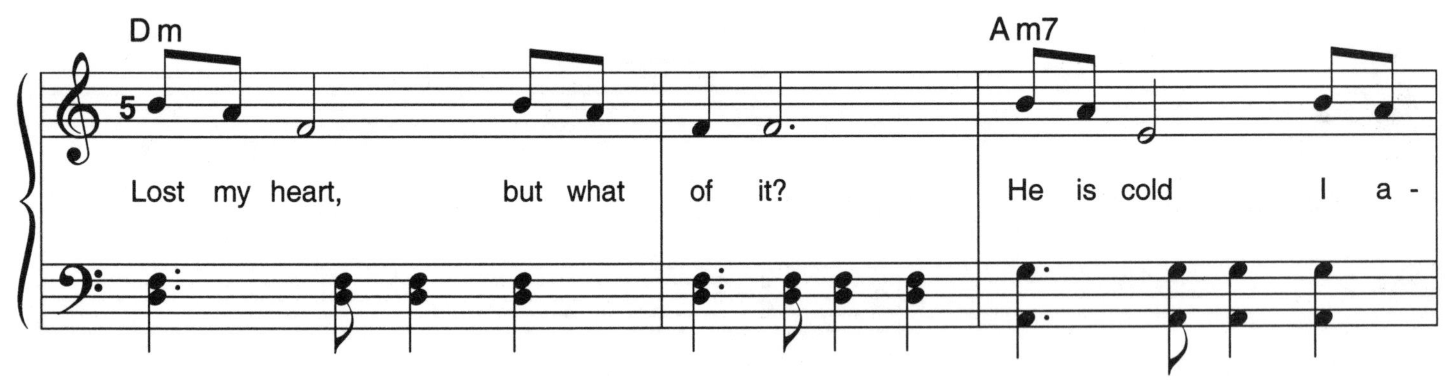
Dm Am7
Lost my heart, but what of it? He is cold I a -

Dm G7 Dm G7
gree. He can laugh, but I love it, al-though the

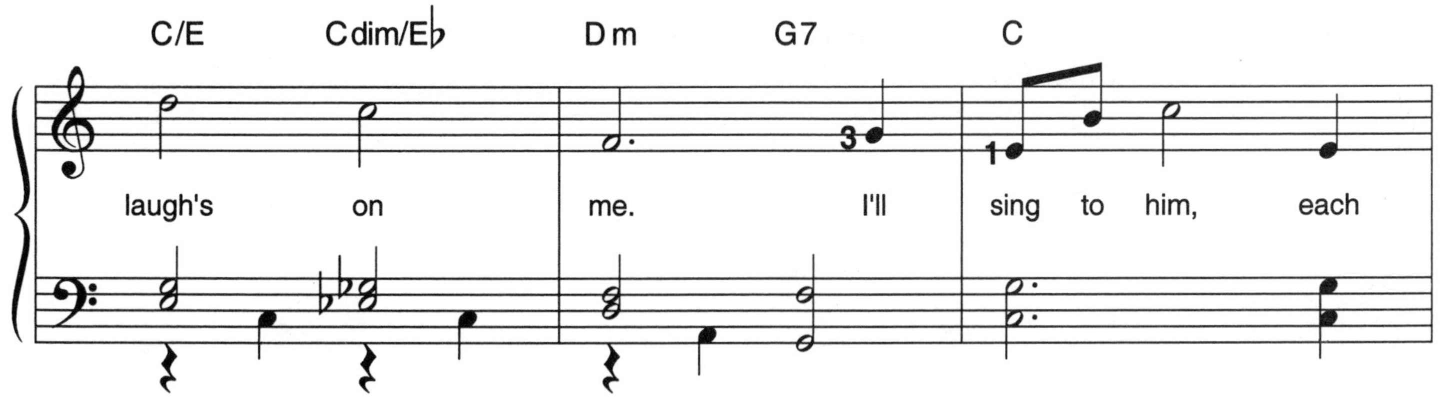
C/E
Cdim/E♭
Dm
G7
C
laugh's on me. I'll sing to him, each

G7
C
C+
F
Fdim
spring to him, and long for the day when I'll cling to him, be -

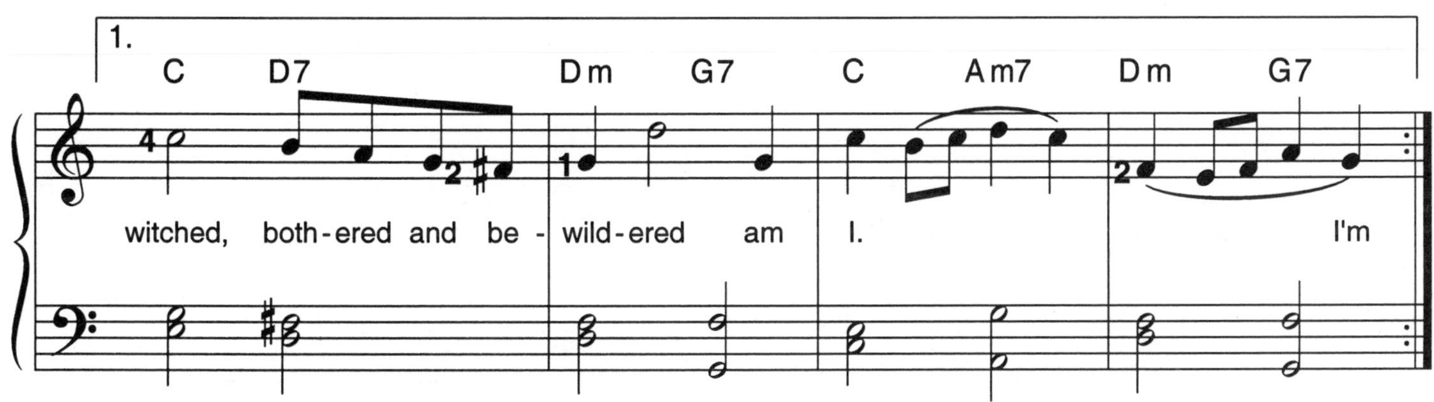
1.
C
D7
Dm
G7
C
Am7
Dm
G7
witched, both-ered and be - wild-ered am I. I'm

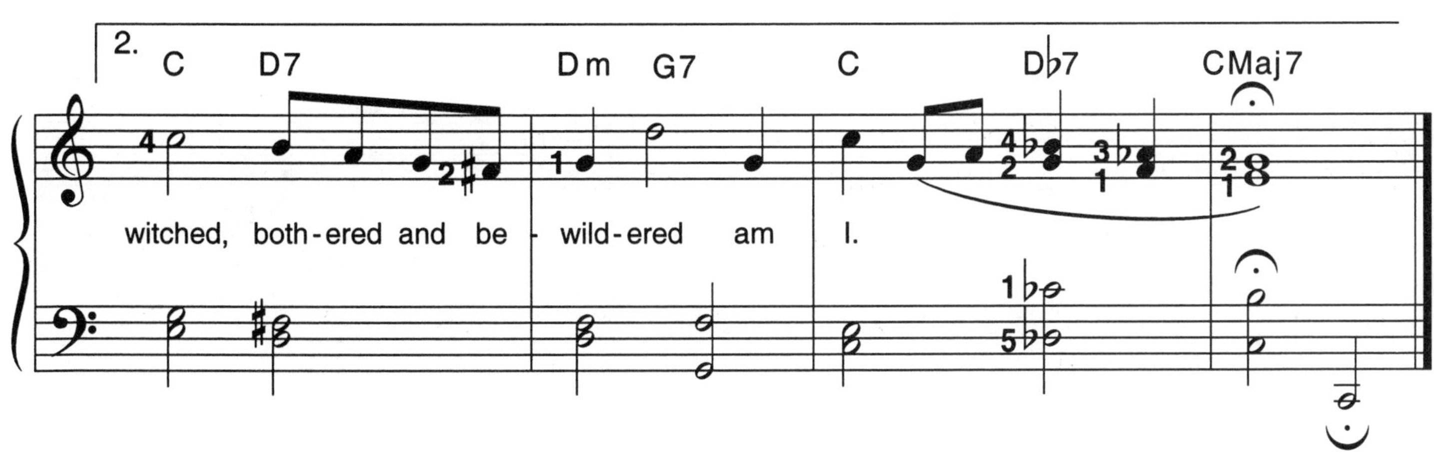
2.
C
D7
Dm
G7
C
D♭7
CMaj7
witched, both-ered and be - wild-ered am I.

The Man I Love

From the Broadway Musical *Strike Up the Band*

Words by IRA GERSHWIN
Muisc by GEORGE GERSHWIN
Arranged by Richard Bradley

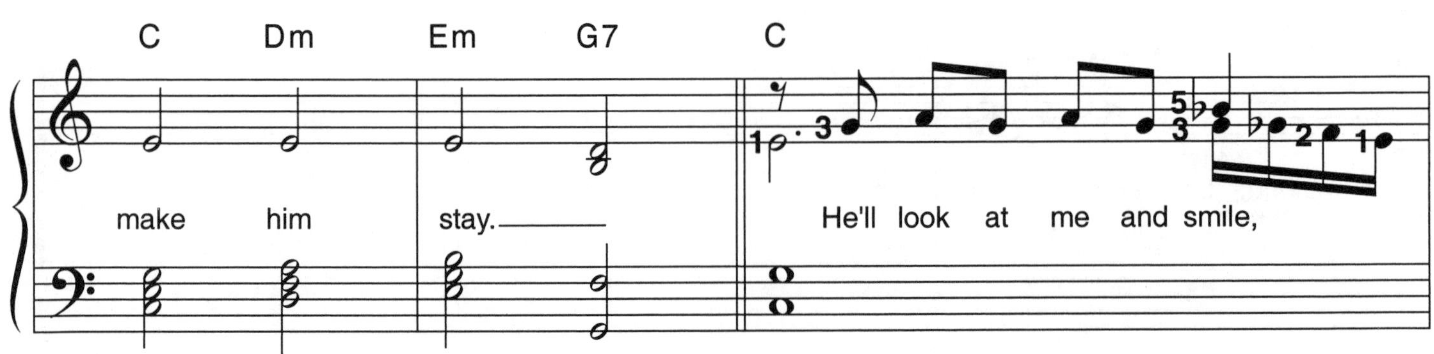

Cm
Em7(♭5)/B♭
I'll un - der - stand,
and in a lit - tle while
A7
Dm7(♭5)/A♭
he'll take my hand;
and though it seems ab - surd,
G7
C
Dm
C
Bm7
E7
I know we both won't
say a
word.
Am7
C/E
Cdim/E♭
Dm7
C
Bm7
May - be I shall meet him
Sun - day, may - be
Mon - day, may - be
mf
E7
Am7
C/E
Cdim/E♭
Dm7
C
C♯dim
not.
Still I'm sure to meet him
one day, may - be
Tues - day will be

Dm7
G7
C
my good news day.
f
He'll build a lit - tle home,
3
Cm
Em7(♭5)/B♭
just meant for two,
from which I'll nev - er roam,
A7
Dm7(♭5)/A♭
Who would, would you?
And so all else a - bove.
G7
C
Dm
Em
Dm
I'm wait - ing for the
man I
love.
D♭Maj7
CMaj7
R.H.
L.H.
mf

Strike Up the Band

From the Broadway Musical *Strike Up the Band*

Words by IRA GERSHWIN
Music by GEORGE GERSHWIN
Arranged by Richard Bradley

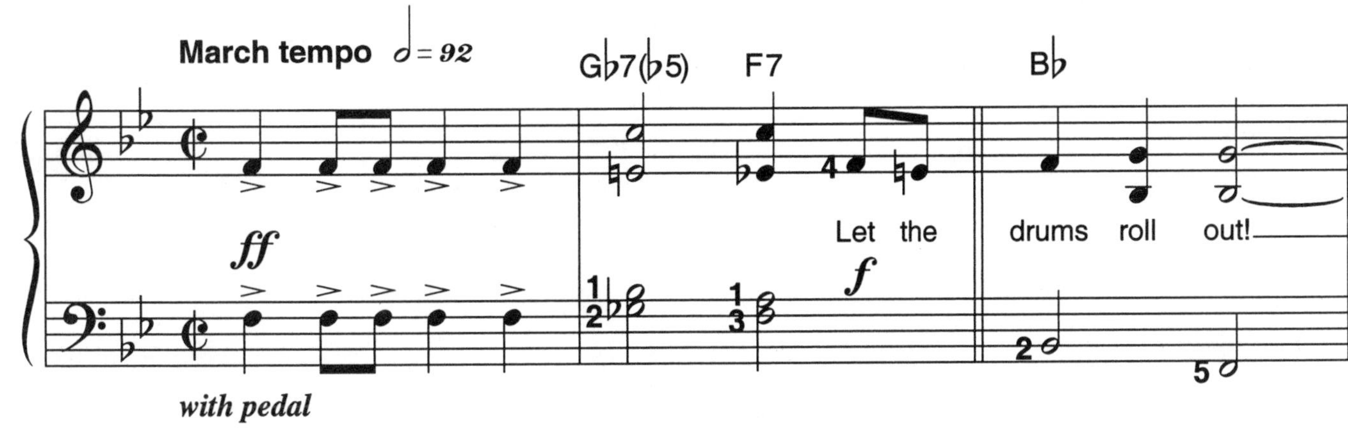

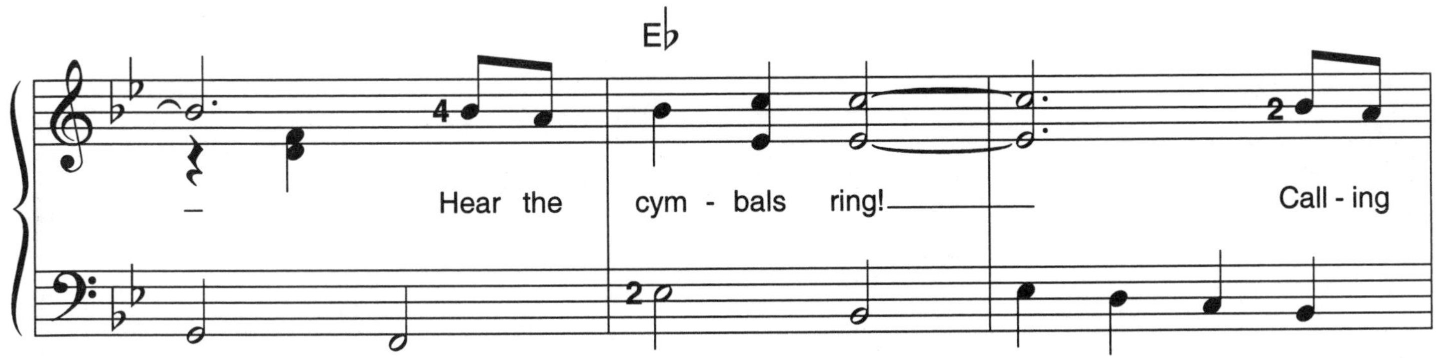

Edim
B♭
one and all
to the
mar - tial swing

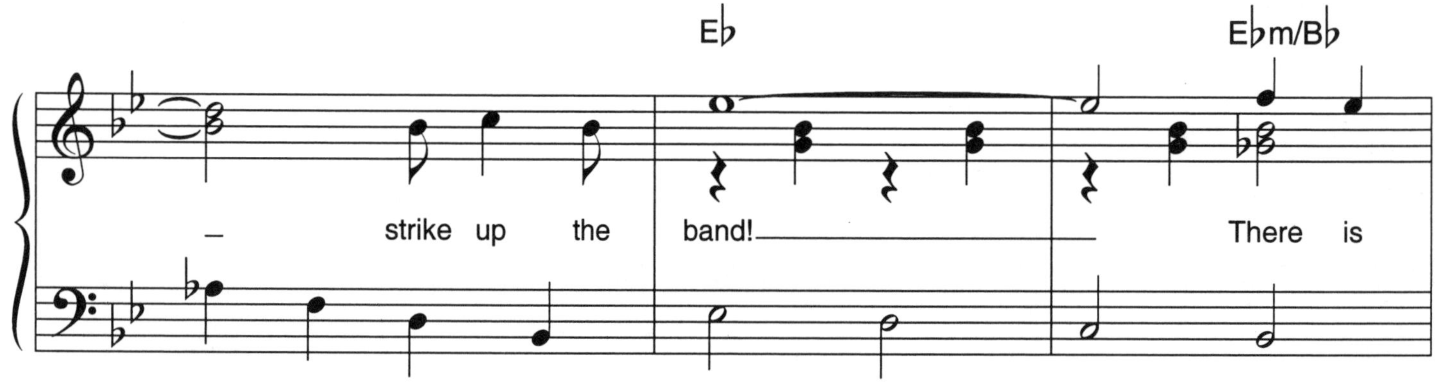
E♭
E♭m/B♭
– strike up the
band!
There is

B♭
Am
work to be done, to be
done! There's a
war to be won, to be

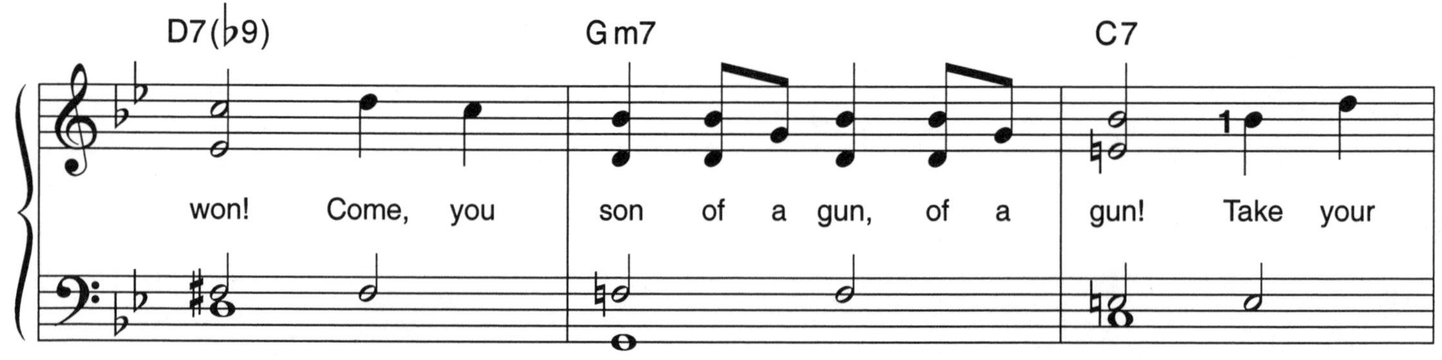
D7(♭9)
Gm7
C7
won! Come, you
son of a gun, of a
gun! Take your

F7
B♭
stand!
Fall in
line, yea bo!

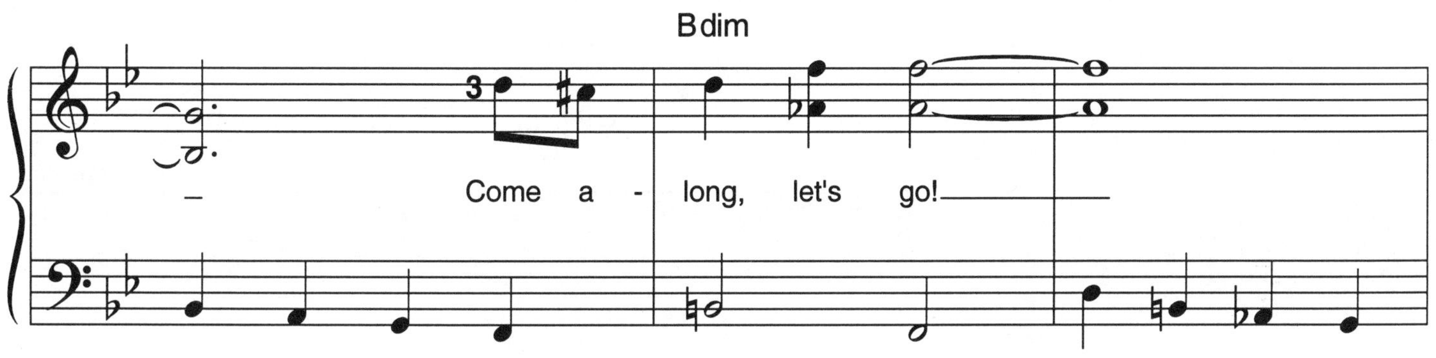
B dim
Come a - long, let's go!

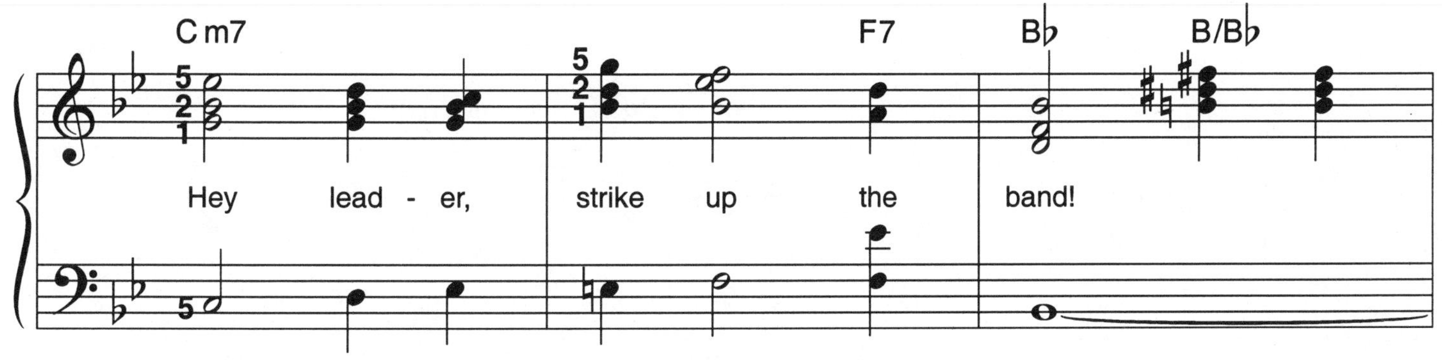
C m7
F7
B♭
B/B♭
Hey lead - er, strike up the band!

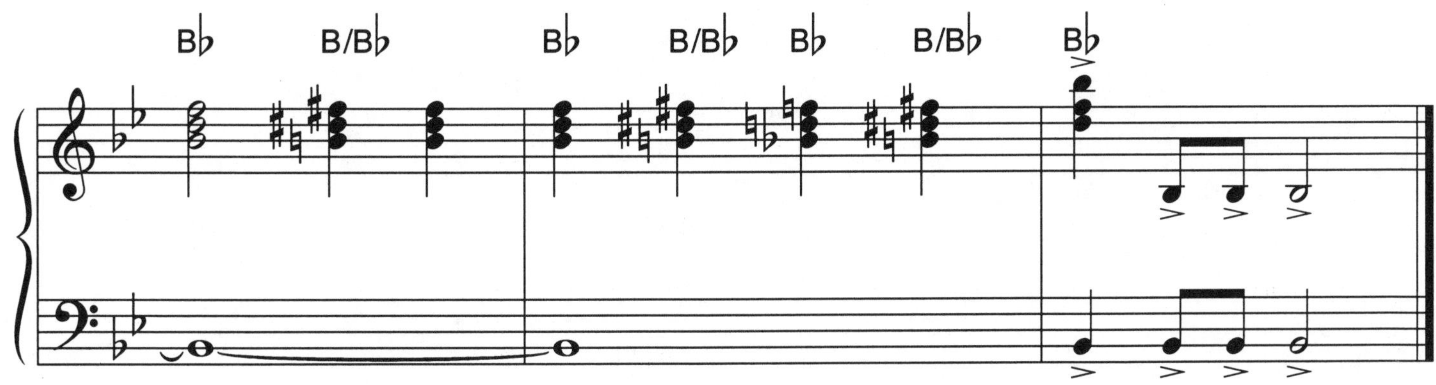
B♭
B/B♭
B♭
B/B♭
B♭
B/B♭
B♭

I Got Rhythm

From the Broadway Musicals *Girl Crazy* and *Crazy For You*

Words by IRA GERSHWIN
Music by GEORGE GERSHWIN
Arranged by Richard Bradley

D7 Am7/E Fm6 D9/F♯ G G♭+ G9/F G7/D
Old Man Troub - le, I don't mind him,

C Dm7 Cdim/E♭ C9/E C7(♭5)/G♭ F7
8va
you won't find him f hang-in' round my door.

B♭ B♭6/D Cm7/E♭ F7 B♭6/9/D Edim7/D♭ Cm7 F7
mf
I got star - light, I got sweet dreams,

B♭ B♭6/D Cm7/E♭ F7 B♭ Fm7/A♭ G7
I got my man who could ask for an - y-thing more? Who could

C9
F7
B♭6
B♭
B♭6
Cm7
F7
ask for an-y-thing more?

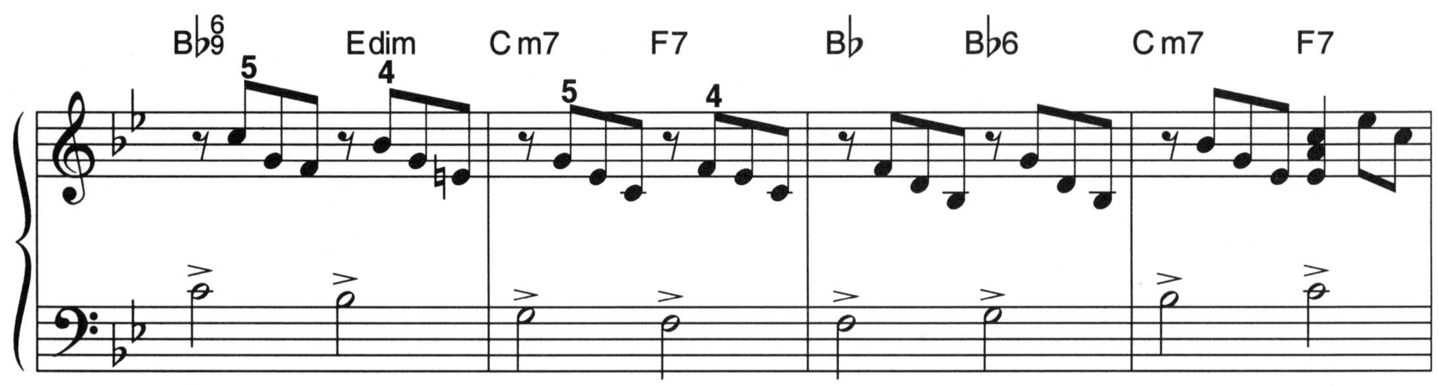
B♭6/9
Edim
Cm7
F7
B♭
B♭6
Cm7
F7

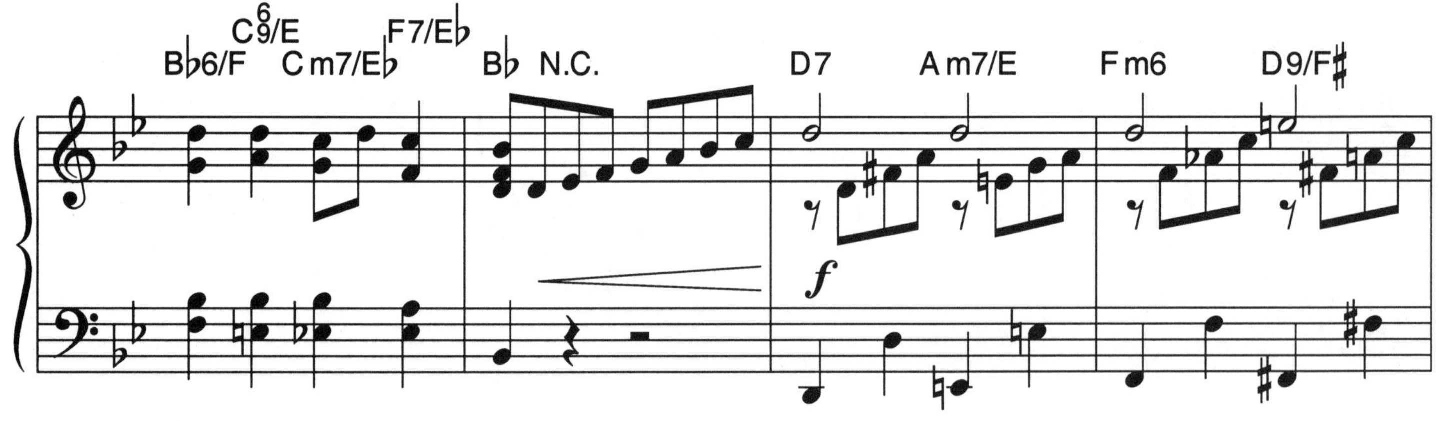
B♭6/F
C6/9/E
Cm7/E♭
F7/E♭
B♭ N.C.
D7
Am7/E
Fm6
D9/F♯

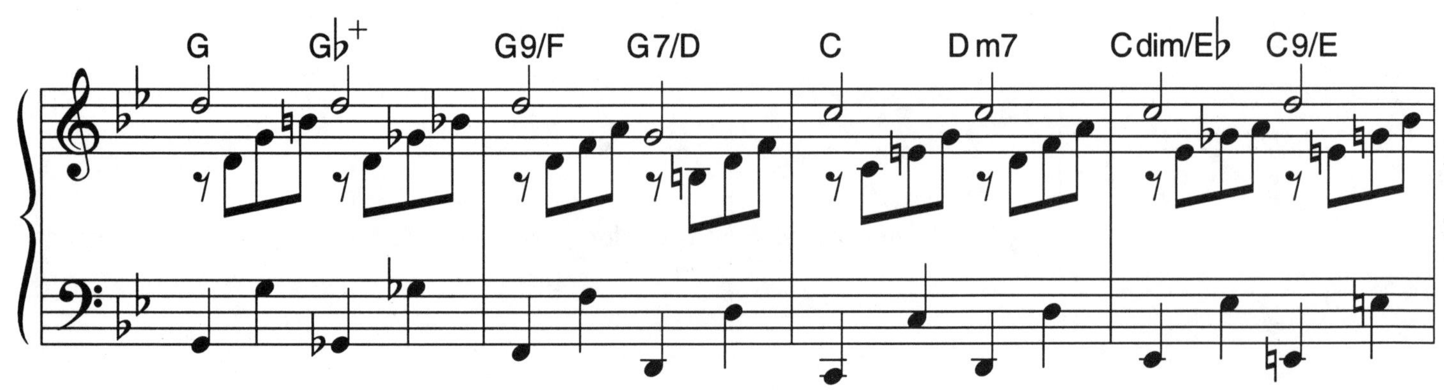
G
G♭+
G9/F
G7/D
C
Dm7
Cdim/E♭
C9/E

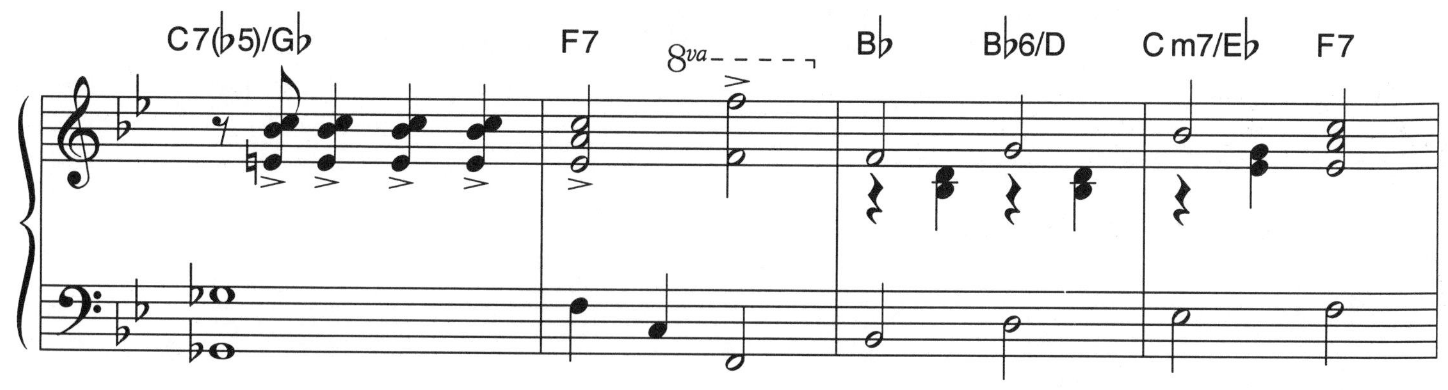
C7(♭5)/G♭
F7
8va
B♭
B♭6/D
Cm7/E♭
F7

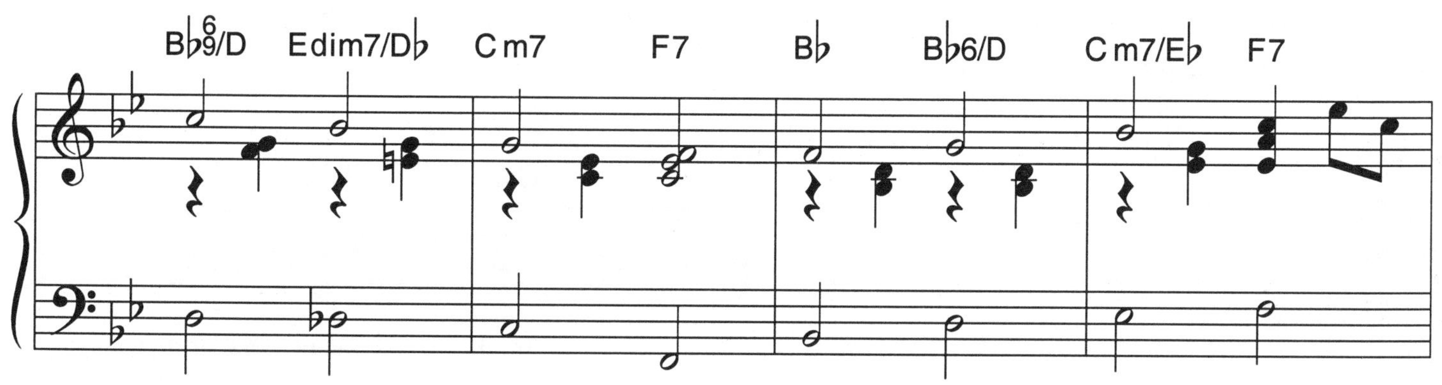
B♭6/9/D
Edim7/D♭
Cm7
F7
B♭
B♭6/D
Cm7/E♭
F7

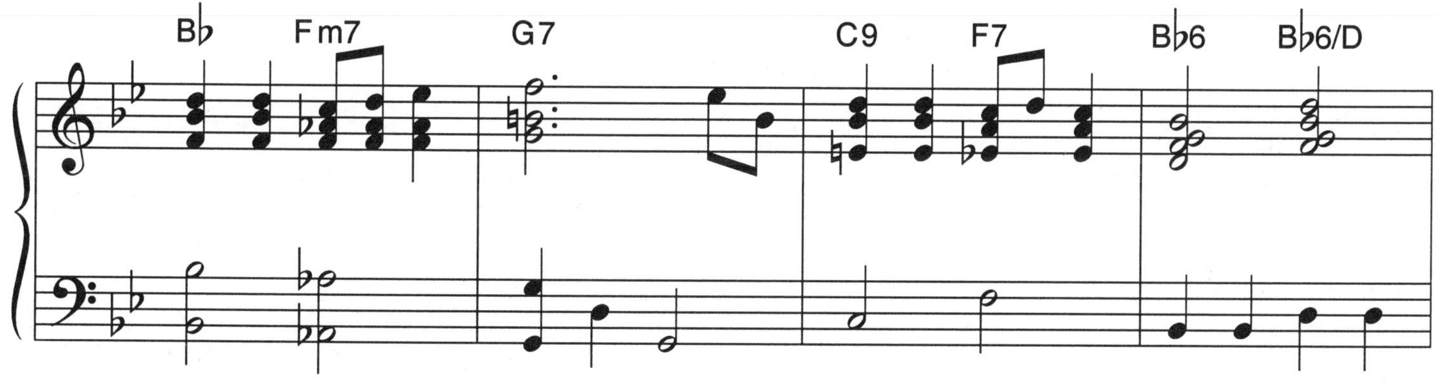
B♭
Fm7
G7
C9
F7
B♭6
B♭6/D

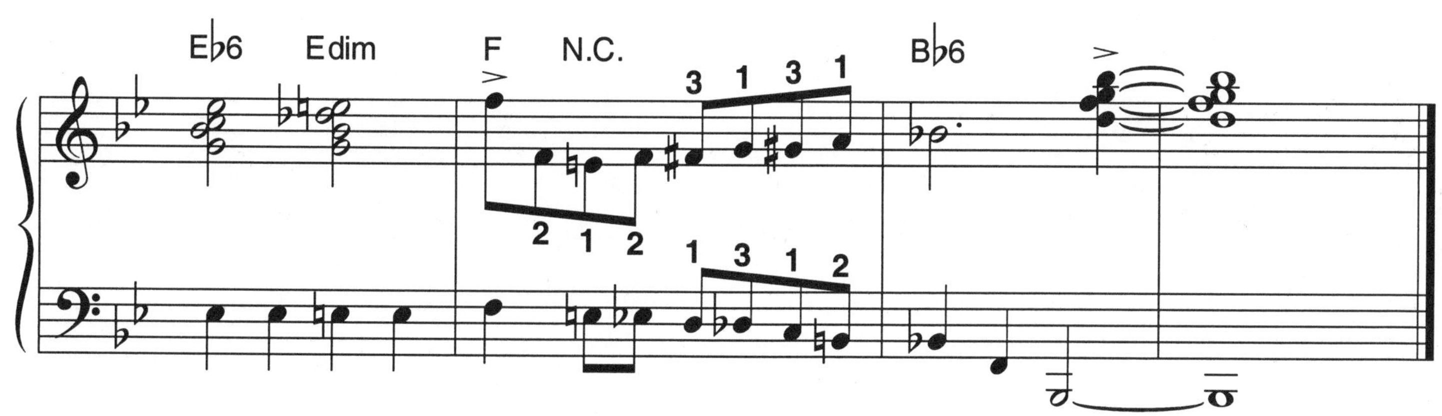
E♭6
Edim
F
N.C.
B♭6

Almost Like Being In Love

From the Broadway Musical *Brigadoon*

Lyrics by ALAN J. LERNER
Music by FREDERICK LOEWE
Arranged by Richard Bradley

Cm7
F9
B♭
B♭7 B♭7(♯5)
al - most like be - ing in love. There's a

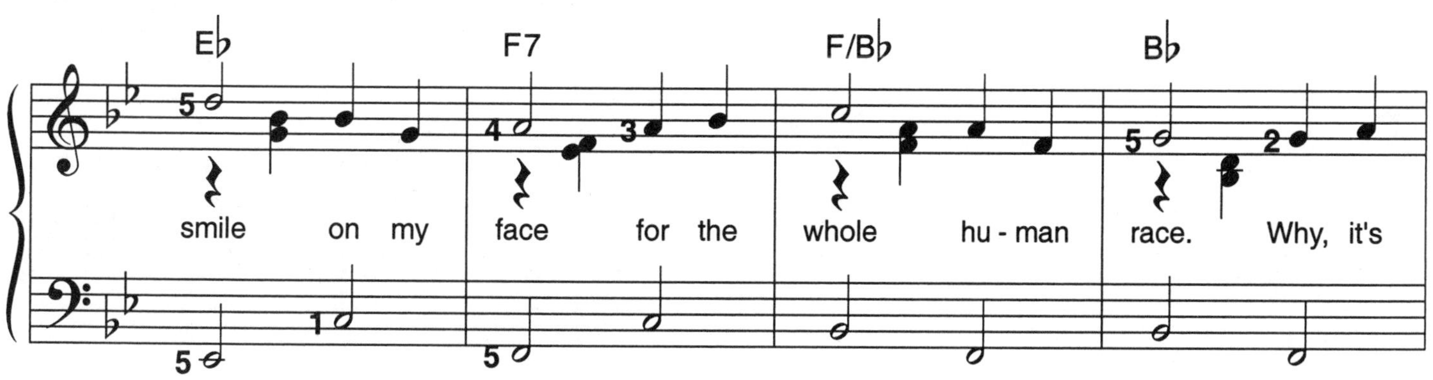
E♭
F7
F/B♭
B♭
smile on my face for the whole hu - man race. Why, it's

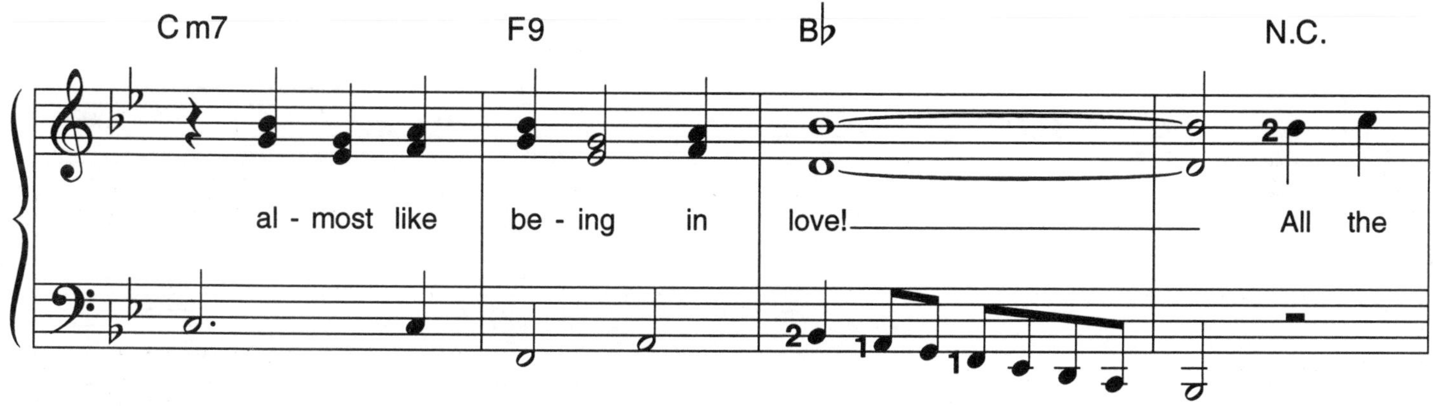
Cm7
F9
B♭
N.C.
al - most like be - ing in love! All the

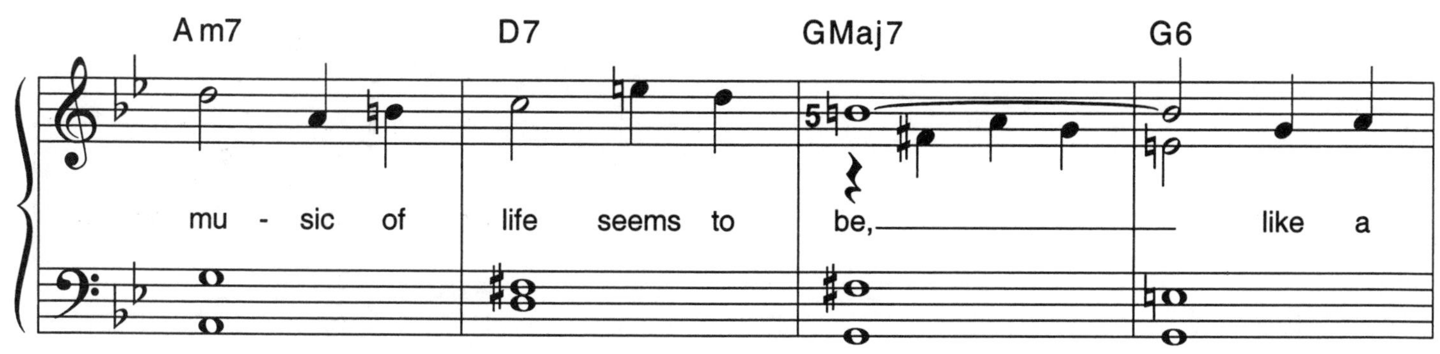
Am7
D7
GMaj7
G6
mu - sic of life seems to be, like a

E♭
Am7(♭5)
D
B♭
D7/A
G♯dim
bell that is ring - ing for me. And from the

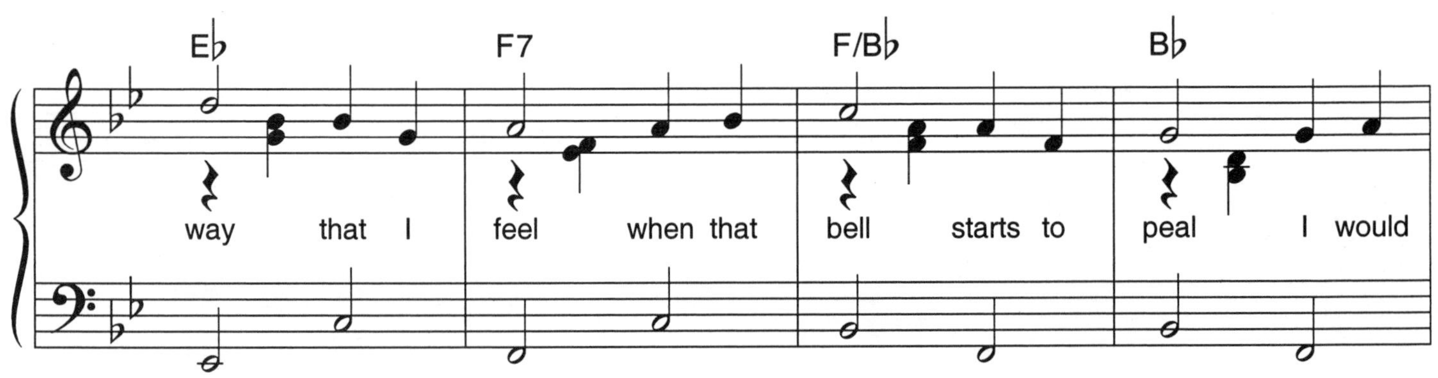
E♭
F7
F/B♭
B♭
way that I feel when that bell starts to peal I would

Cm7
C♯dim
B♭/D
C7/E
swear I was fall - ing, I could swear I was fall - ing, It's

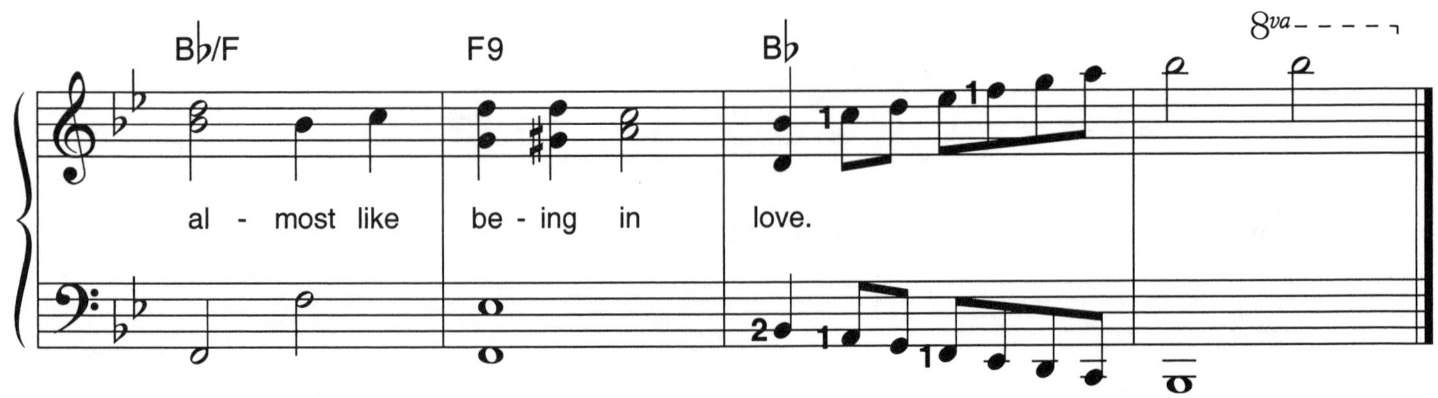
B♭/F
F9
B♭
8va
al - most like be - ing in love.

Heart

From the Broadway Musical *Damn Yankees*

Words and Music by
RICHARD ADLER and JERRY ROSS
Arranged by Richard Bradley

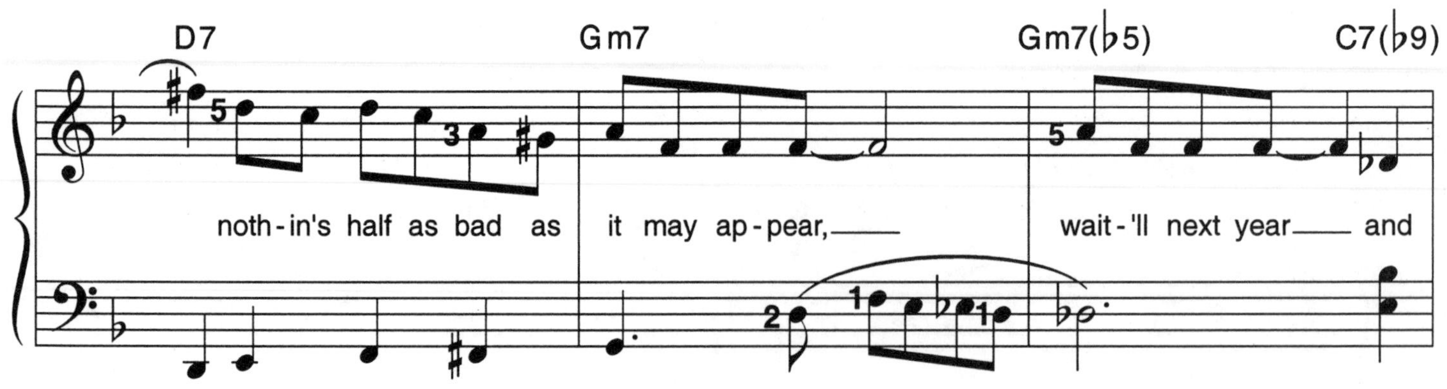
D7
Gm7
Gm7(♭5)
C7(♭9)
noth-in's half as bad as it may ap-pear, wait-'ll next year and

F
B♭9
F N.C.
F7
hope. When your luck is bat-tin' ze-ro,

N.C.
B♭
N.C.
get your chin up off the floor; Mis-ter, you can be a

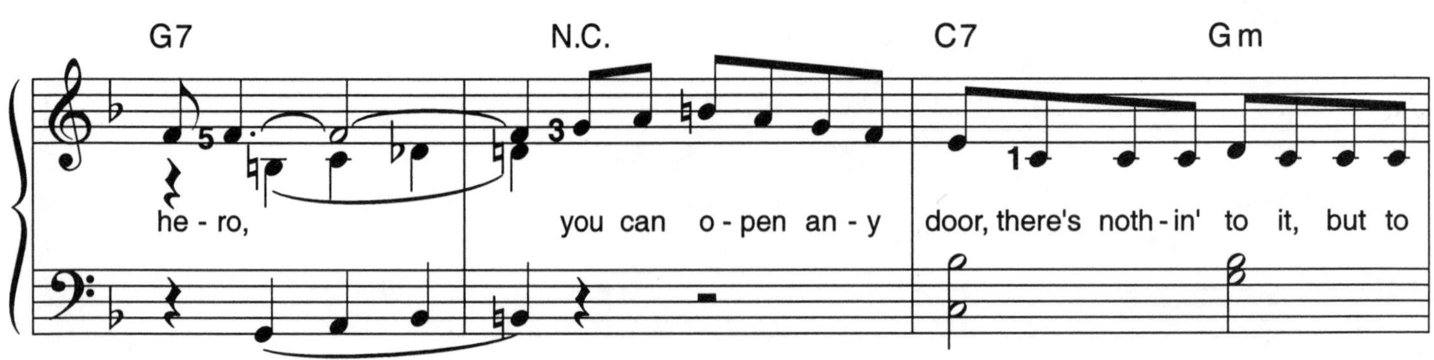
G7
N.C.
C7
Gm
he-ro, you can o-pen an-y door, there's noth-in' to it, but to

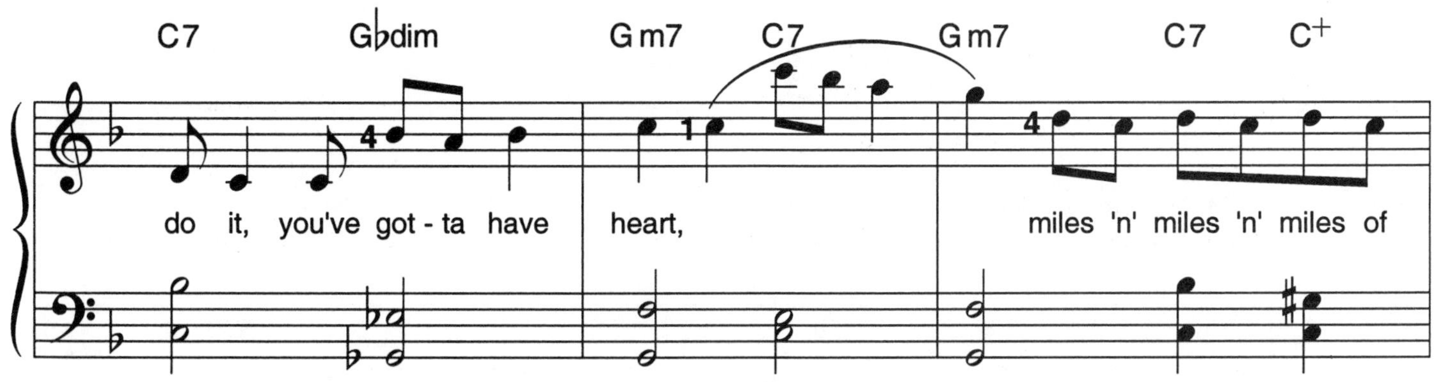
C7 G♭dim Gm7 C7 Gm7 C7 C+
do it, you've got - ta have heart, miles 'n' miles 'n' miles of

F D7 Gm7
heart. Oh, it's fine to be a gen - ius of course, but

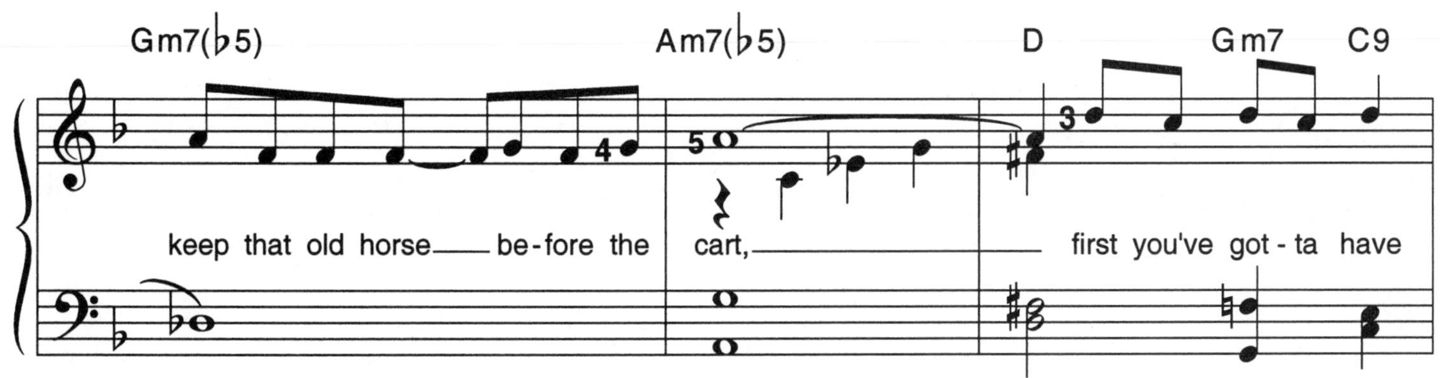
Gm7(♭5) Am7(♭5) D Gm7 C9
keep that old horse be - fore the cart, first you've got - ta have

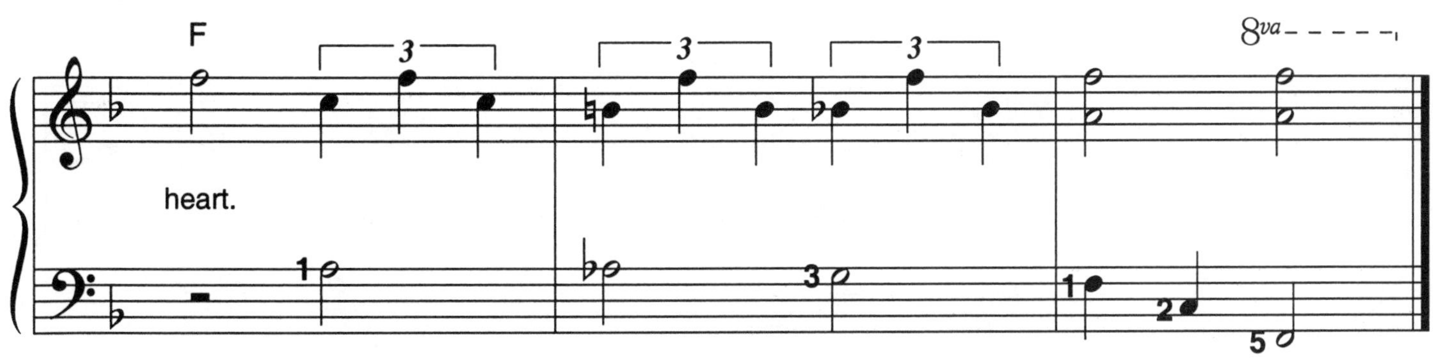
F
8va
heart.

Tara Theme

From the Motion Picture *Gone With the Wind*

Music by
MAX STEINER
Arranged by Richard Bradley

Moderate ♩ = 86

FMaj7 Gm7 C7

mf

with pedal

FMaj7 B♭ B♭+ B♭6 B♭ 1. FMaj7

Gm7 C7 2. FMaj7 Gm7 C7 F

B♭Maj7 Am7

mf

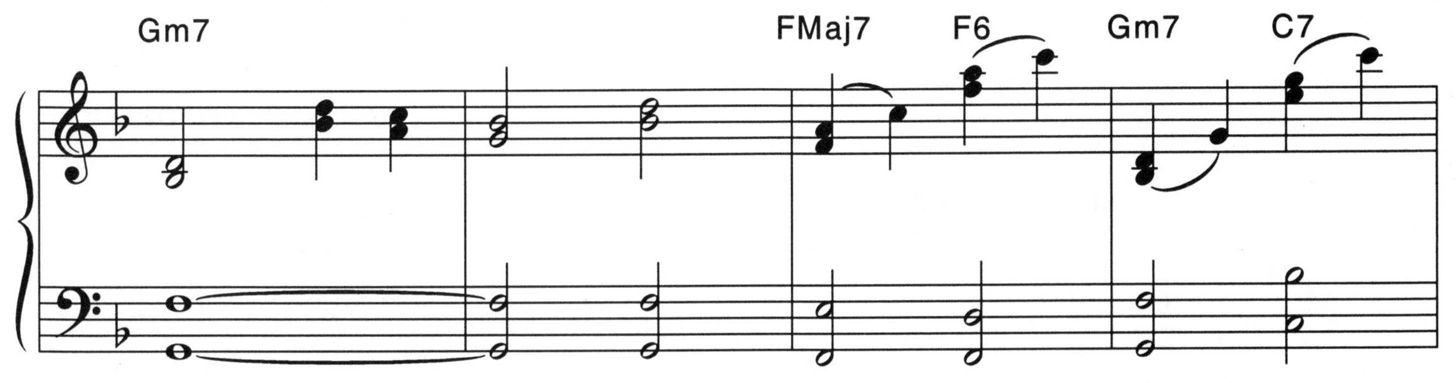
Gm7
FMaj7
F6
Gm7
C7

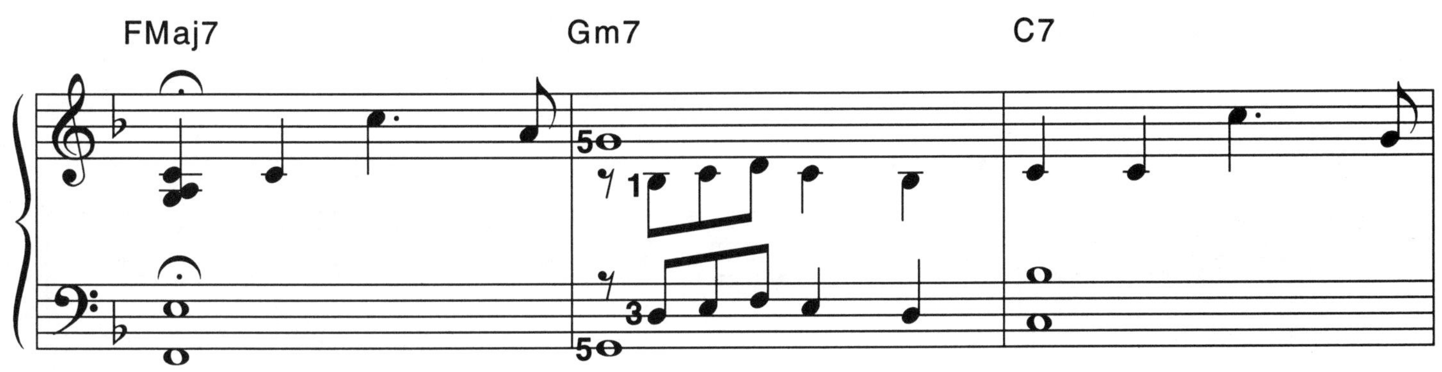
FMaj7
Gm7
C7

FMaj7
B♭
B♭+
B♭6
B♭

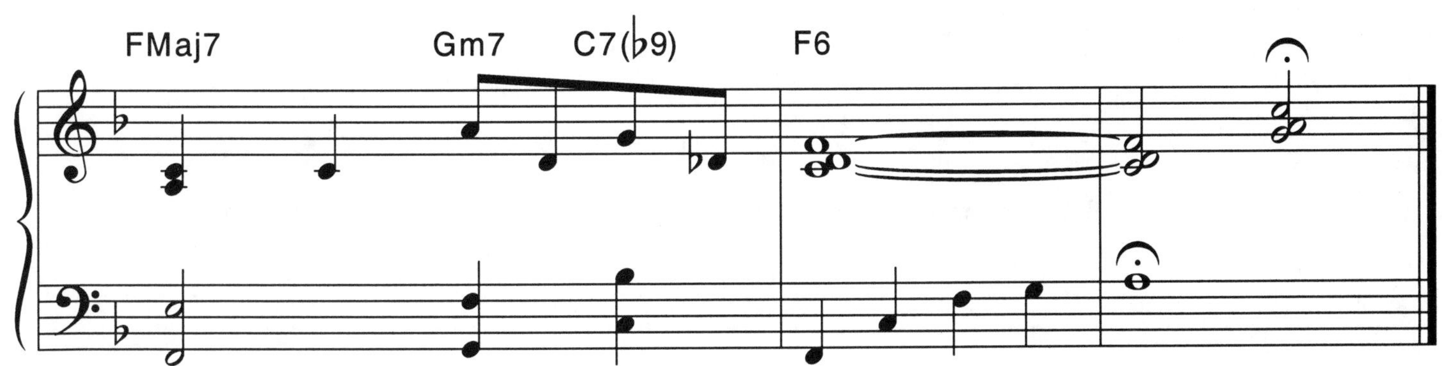
FMaj7
Gm7
C7(♭9)
F6

Real Live Girl

From the Broadway Musical *Little Me*

Music by CY COLEMAN
Lyrics by CAROLYN LEIGH
Arranged by Richard Bradley

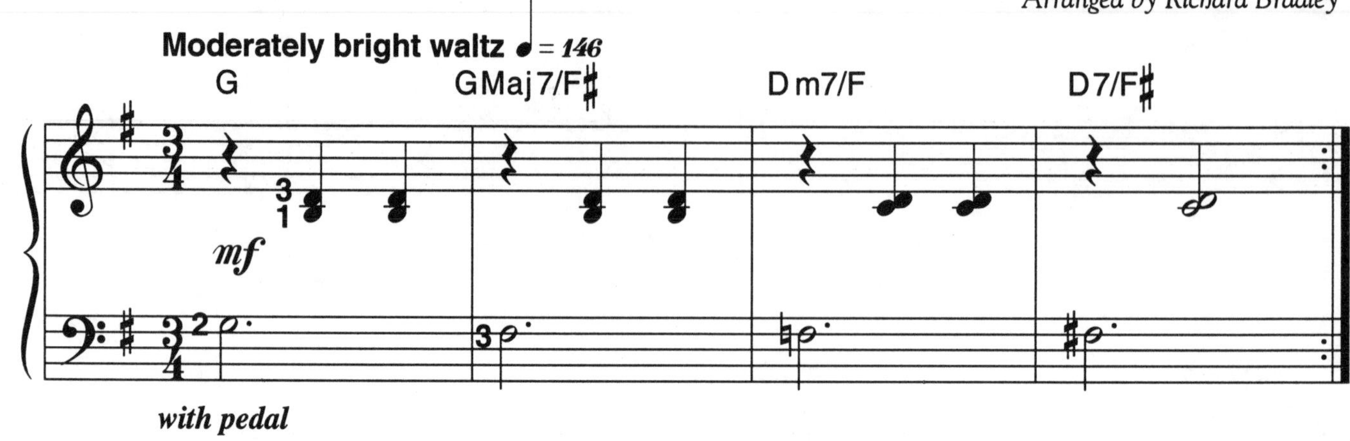

G
GMaj7/F♯
G6/E
G/D
real
live
girl.

G7
G7(♯5)
Par - don me
if your af -
fec - tion - ate
squeeze

C6
F11
fogs up my
gog - gles and
buck - les my
knees.

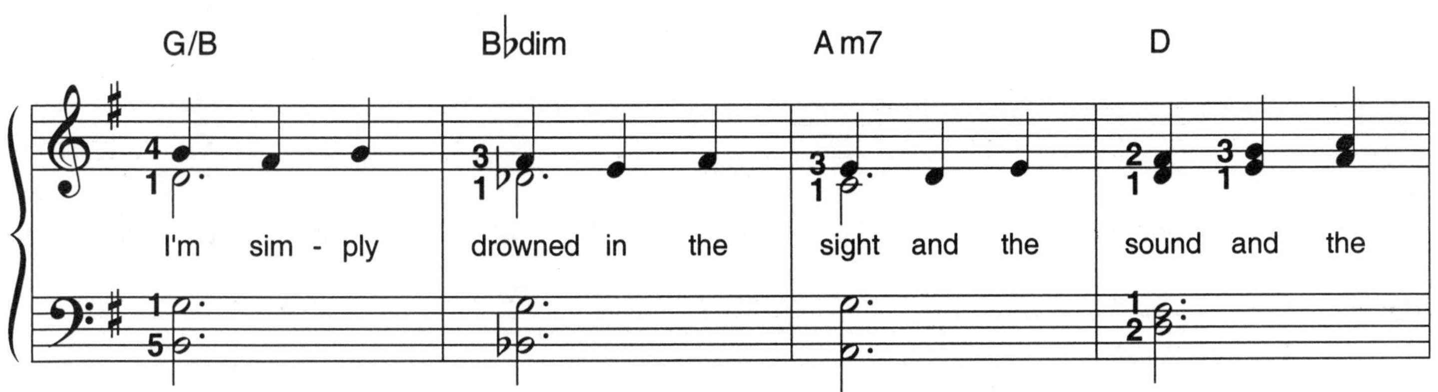
G/B
B♭dim
Am7
D
I'm sim - ply
drowned in the
sight and the
sound and the

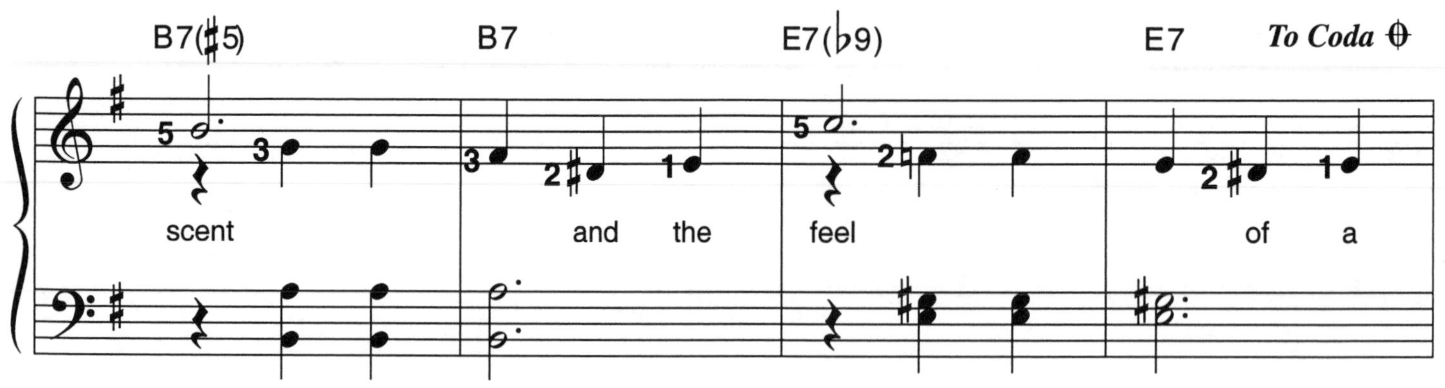
B7(♯5)
B7
E7(♭9)
E7
To Coda
scent
and the
feel
of a

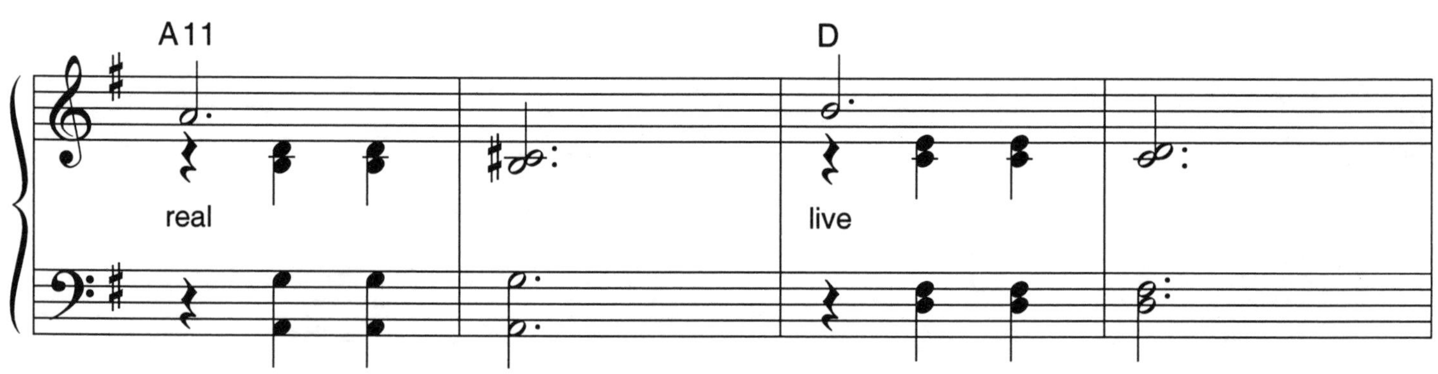
A11
D
real
live

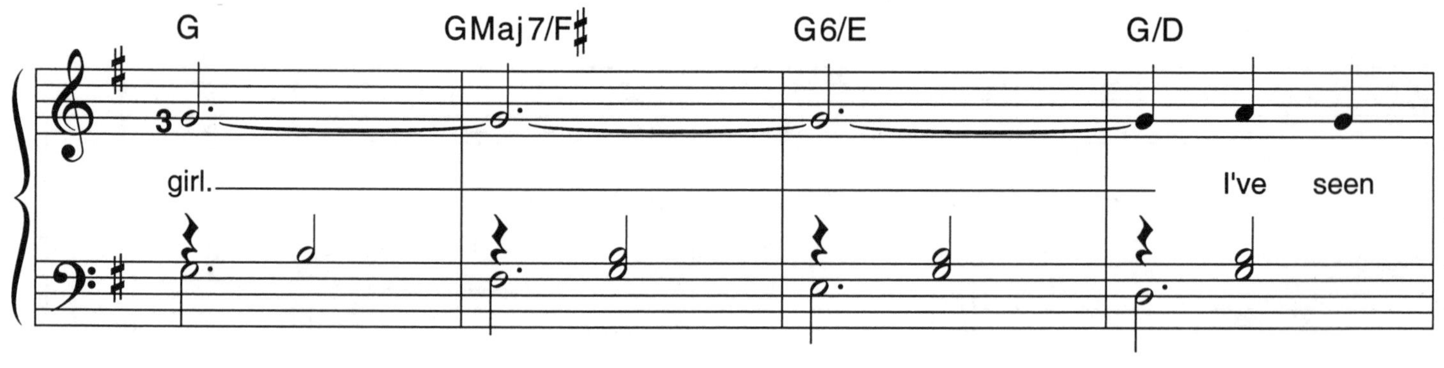
G
GMaj7/F♯
G6/E
G/D
girl.
I've seen

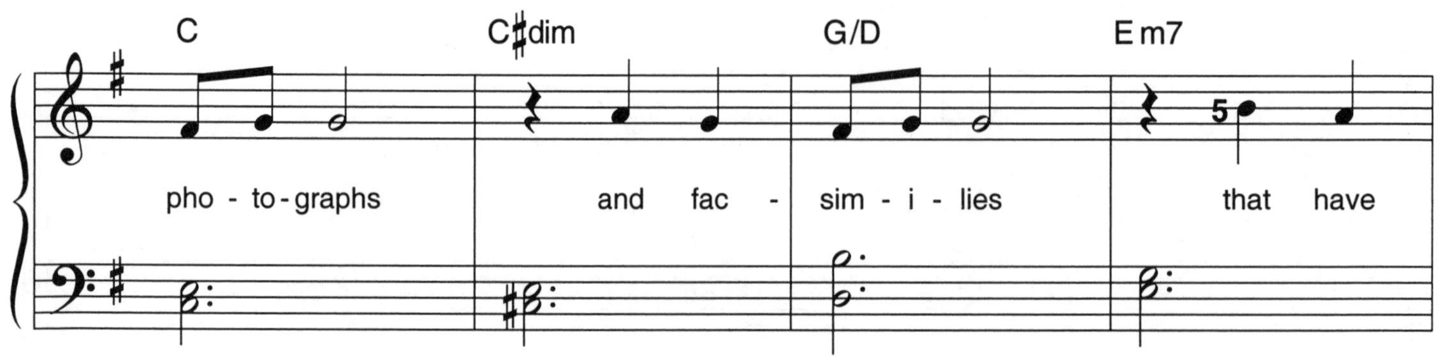
C
C♯dim
G/D
Em7
pho - to-graphs
and fac -
sim - i - lies
that have

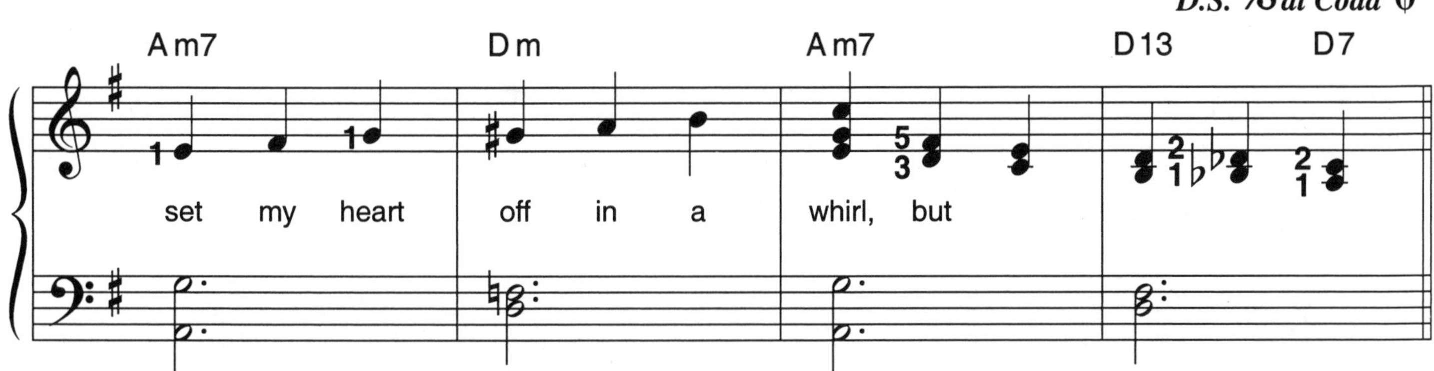

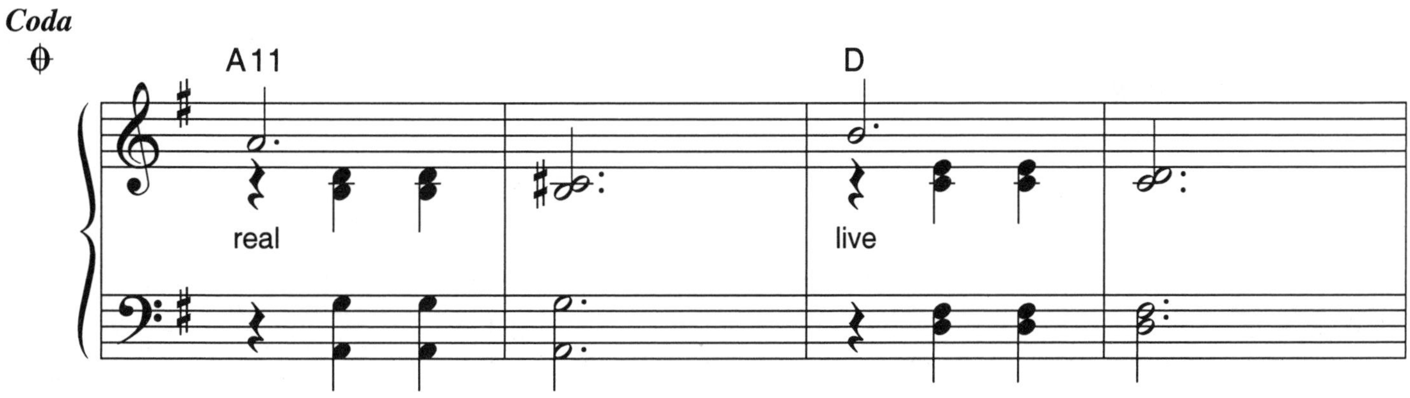

Verse 2:
Nothing can beat getting swept off your feet by a real live girl.
Dreams in your bunk don't compare with a hunk of a real live girl.
Speaking of miracles, this must be it,
Just when I started to learn how to knit.
I'm all in stitches from finding what riches a waltz can reveal
With a real live girl.

Friendly Persuasion
(Thee I Love)

From the Motion Picture *Friendly Persuasion*

Lyrics by PAUL FRANCIS WEBSTER
Music by DIMITRI TIOMKIN
Arranged by Richard Bradley

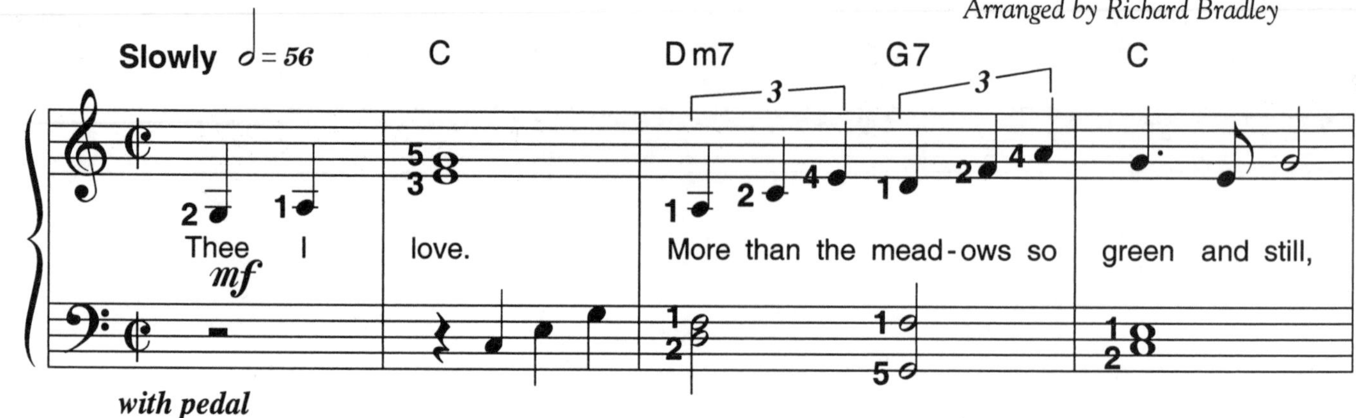

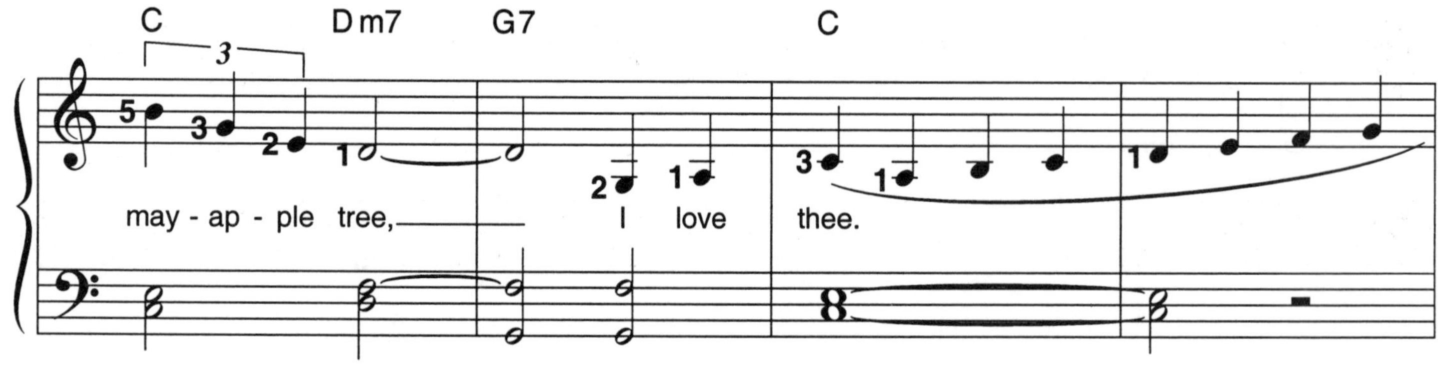

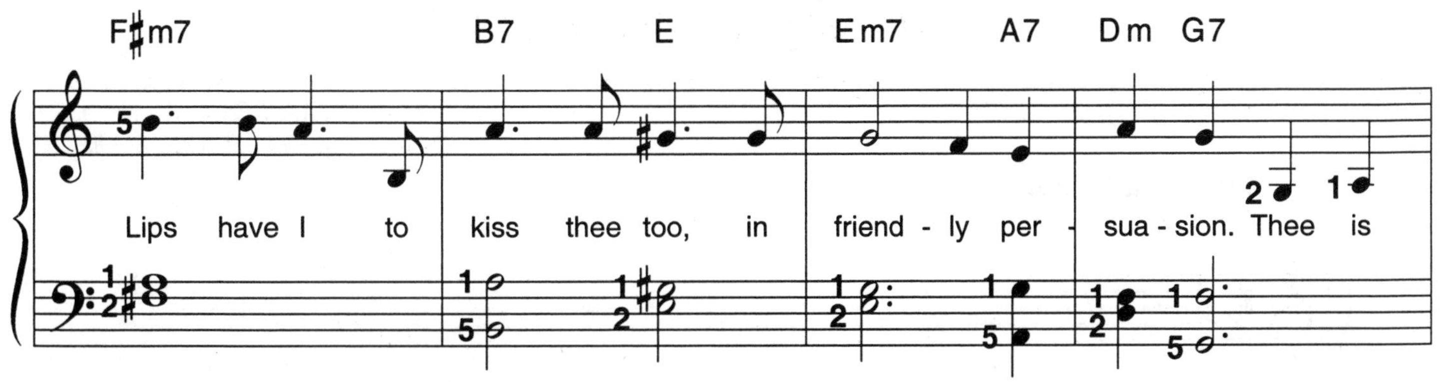
F♯m7
B7
E
Em7
A7
Dm
G7
Lips have I to kiss thee too, in friend - ly per - sua - sion. Thee is

C
Dm7
G7
C
mine, though I don't know man - y words of praise;

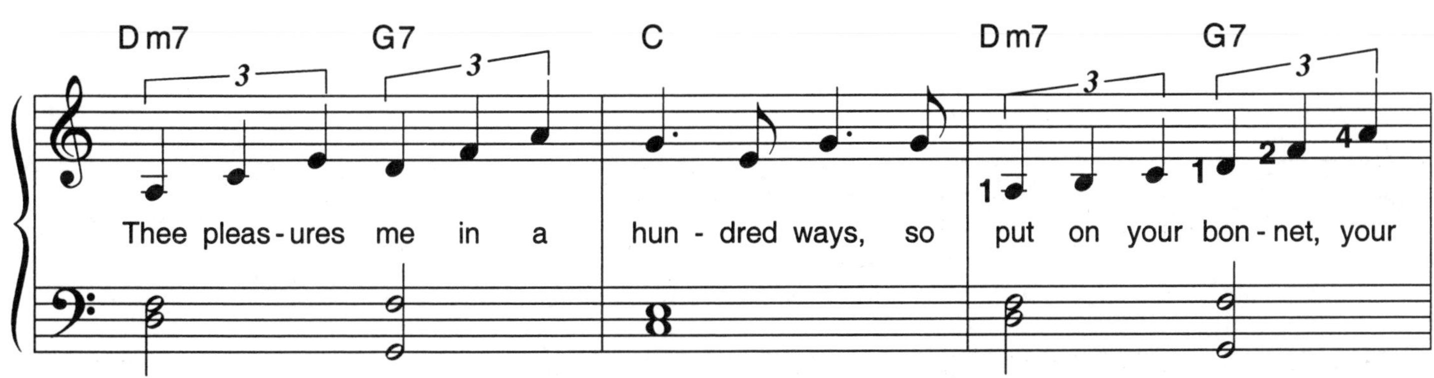
Dm7
G7
C
Dm7
G7
Thee pleas - ures me in a hun - dred ways, so put on your bon - net, your

C
Dm7
G7
C6
cape and your glove and come with me, for thee I love.

The Second Time Around

From the Motion Picture *The Second Time Around*

Words by SAMMY CAHN
Music by JAMES VAN HEUSEN
Arranged by Richard Bradley

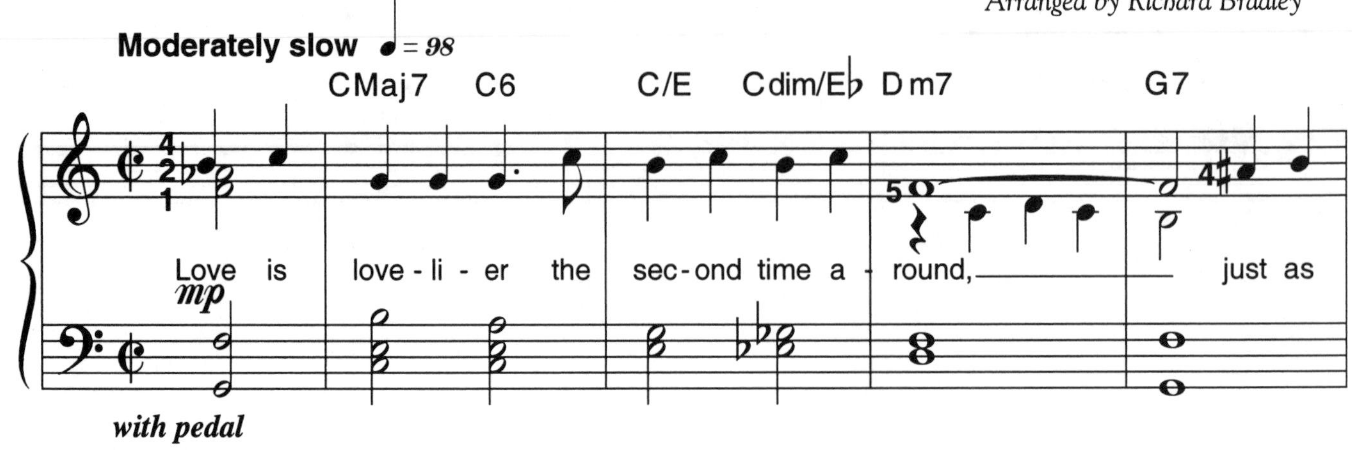

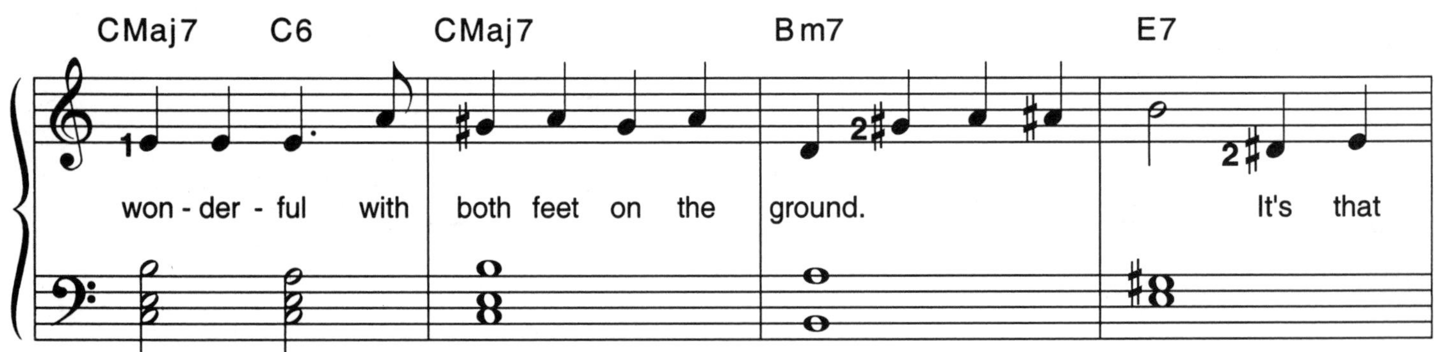

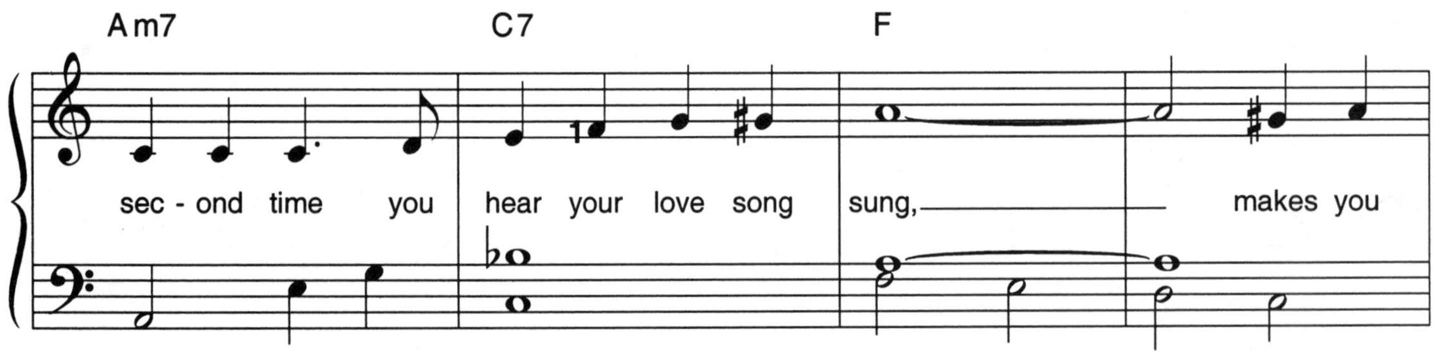

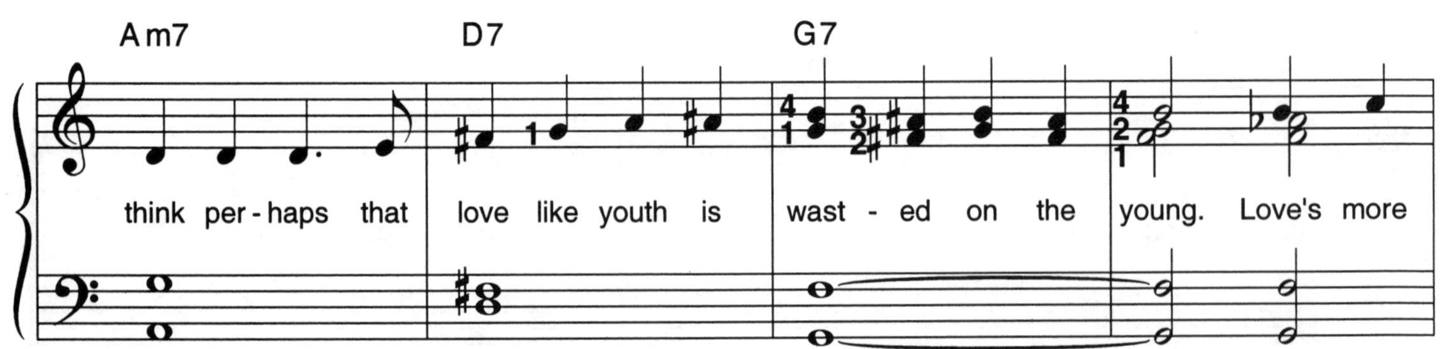

CMaj7 C6 C/E Cdim/E♭ Dm7 G7
com - f'ta - ble the sec - ond time you fall, like a
CMaj7 C6 CMaj7 Bm7 E7
friend - ly home the sec - ond time you call. Who can
Am7 C7 F E♭7 D7 E♭dim
say what led us to this mir - a - cle we found? There are
Dm7 G7 Bm7 E7 A7
those who'll bet love comes but once, and yet, I'm, oh, so
Am7 D7 Dm7 G7 C C6/9
glad we met the sec - ond time a - round.

Embraceable You

From the Broadway Musicals *Girl Crazy* and *Crazy For You*

Words by IRA GERSHWIN
Music by GEORGE GERSHWIN
Arranged by Richard Bradley

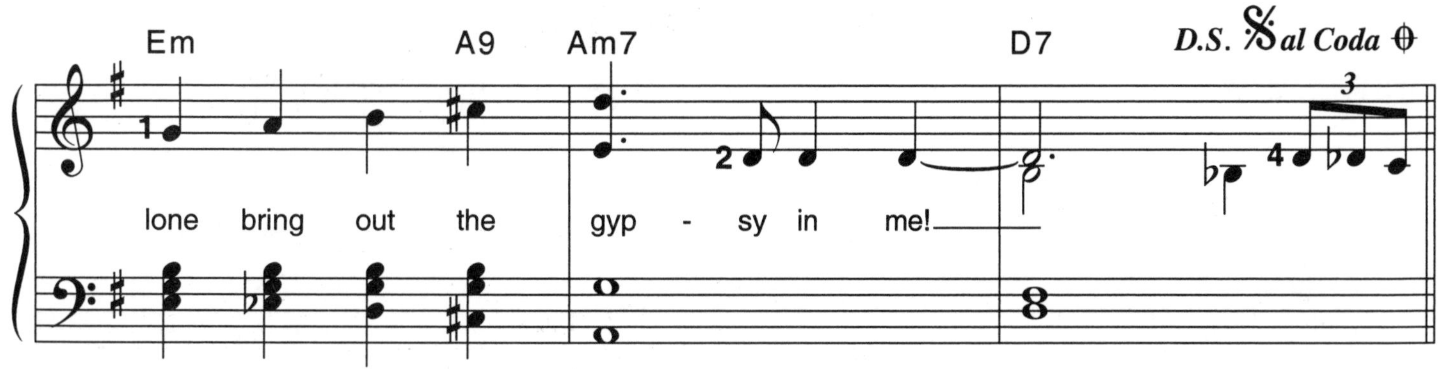
Em
A9
Am7
D7
D.S. 𝄋 al Coda ⊕
lone bring out the gyp - sy in me!

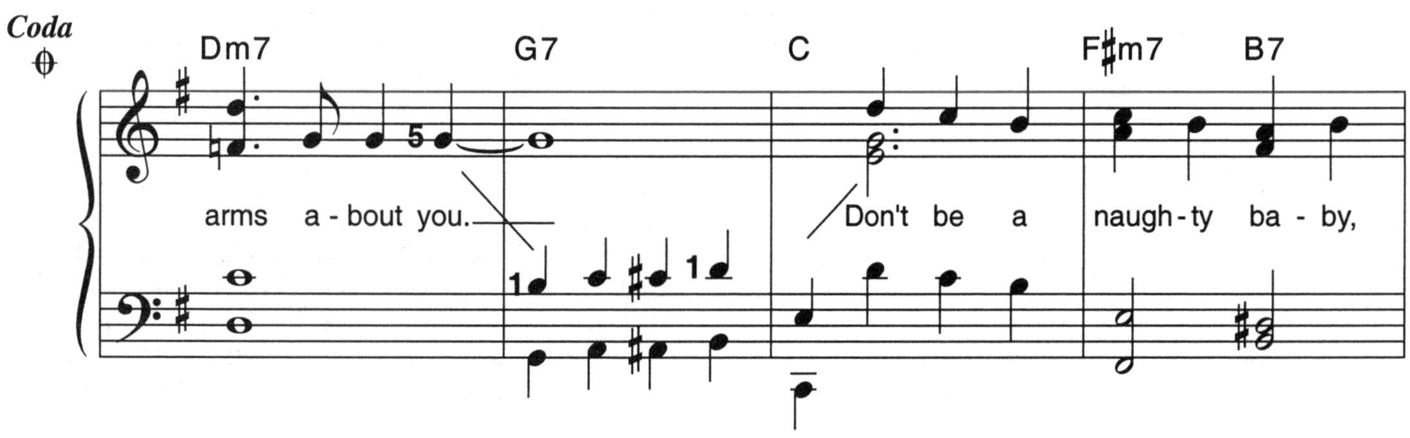
Coda
Dm7
G7
C
F♯m7
B7
arms a - bout you.
Don't be a naugh - ty ba - by,

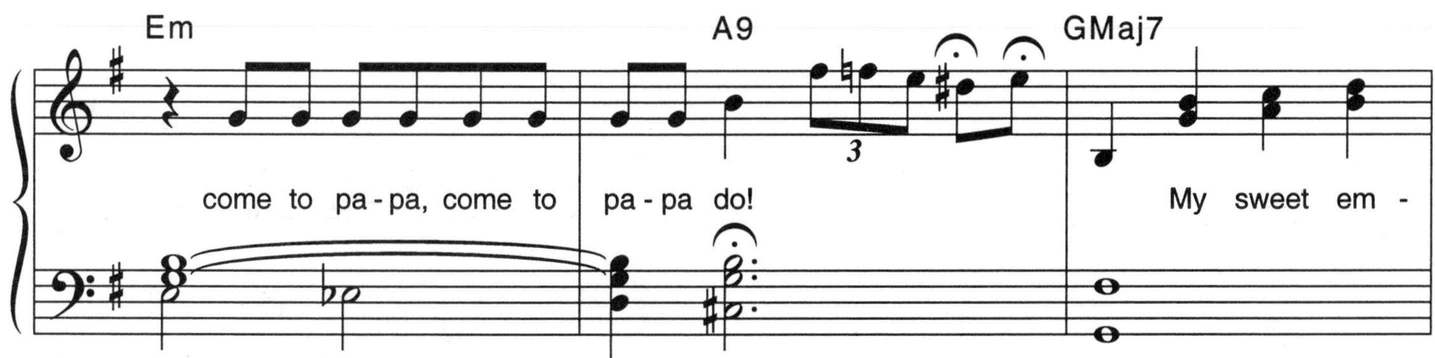
Em
A9
GMaj7
come to pa - pa, come to pa - pa do!
My sweet em -

Am7(♭5)
D7
G
A♭
GMaj9
8va
brace - a - ble you.
8vb

Dear Heart

From the Motion Picture *Dear Heart*

Words by JAY LIVINGSTON and RAY EVANS
Music by HENRY MANCINI
Arranged by Richard Bradley

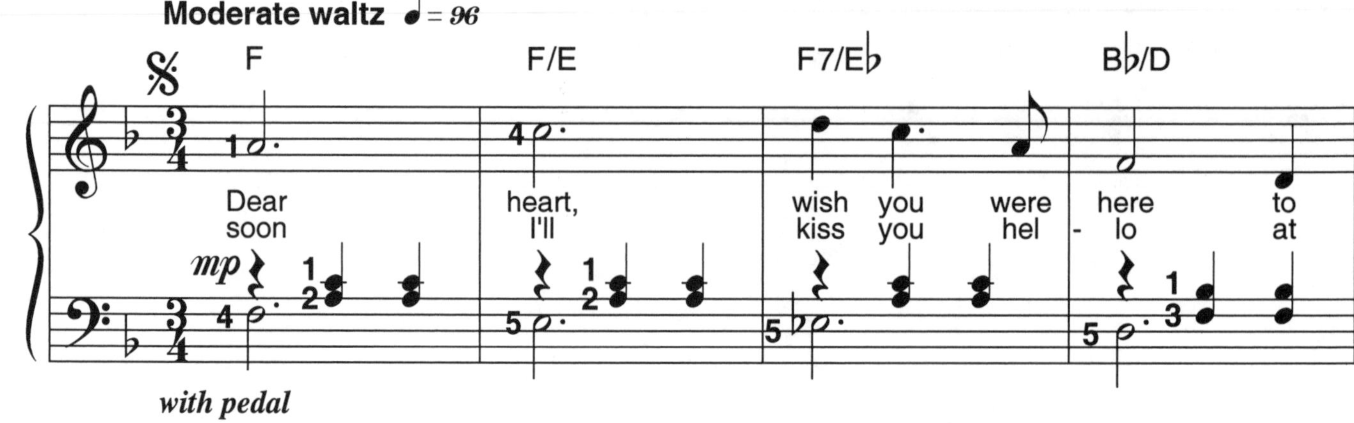

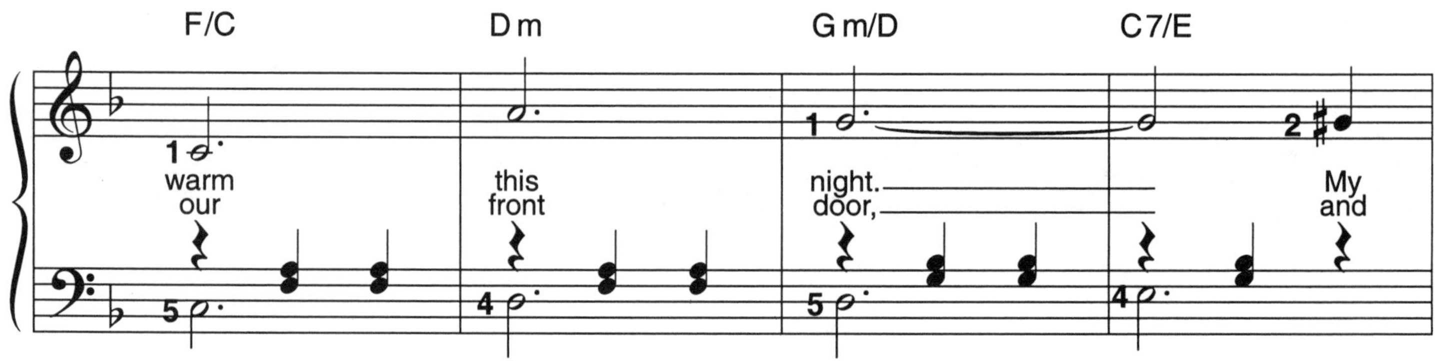

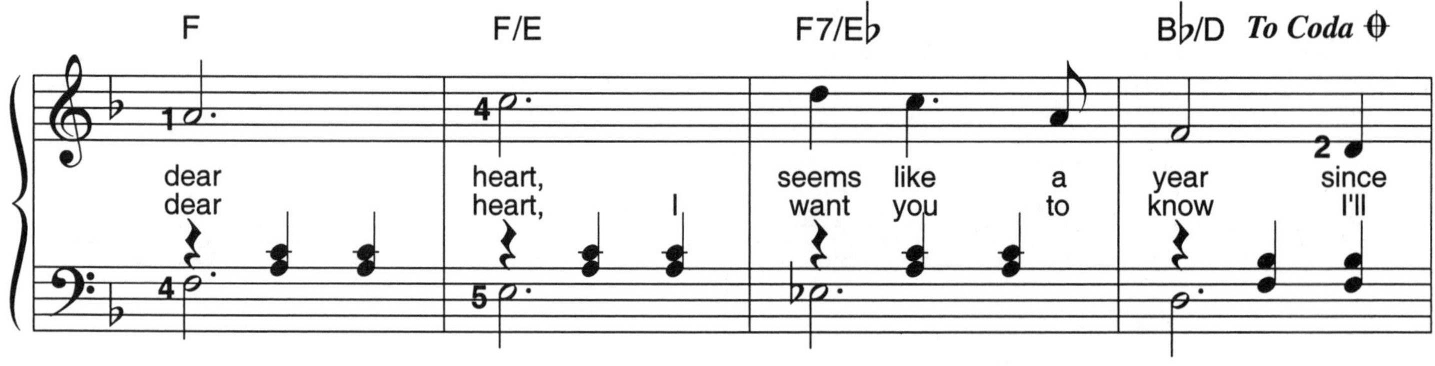

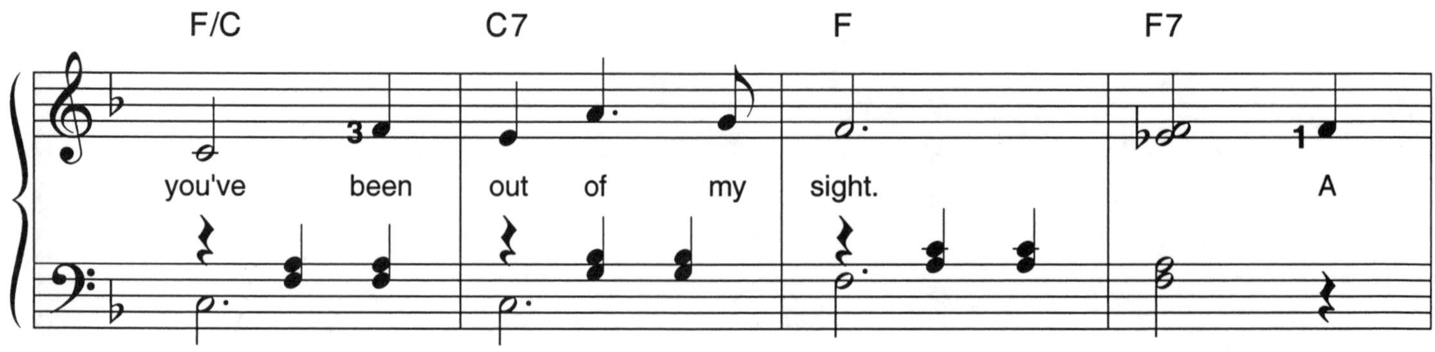

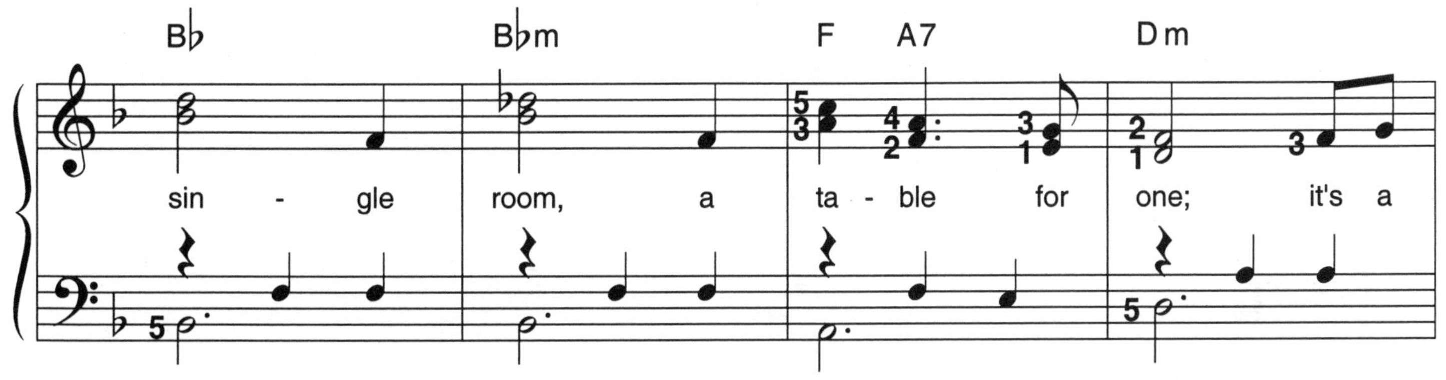
B♭
B♭m
F
A7
Dm
sin - gle
room, a
ta - ble for
one; it's a

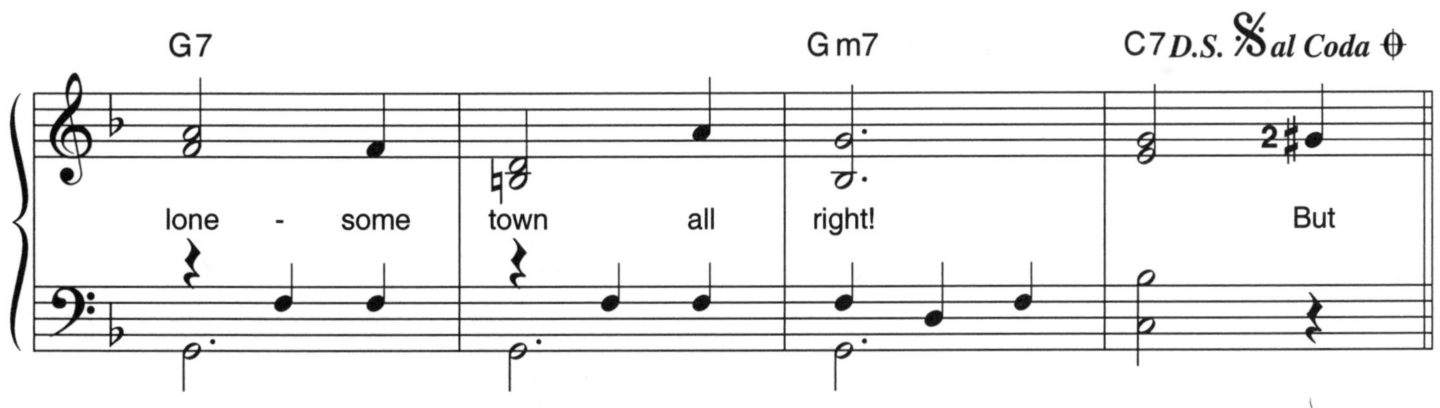
G7
Gm7
C7 D.S. 𝄋 al Coda 𝄌
lone - some
town all
right!
But

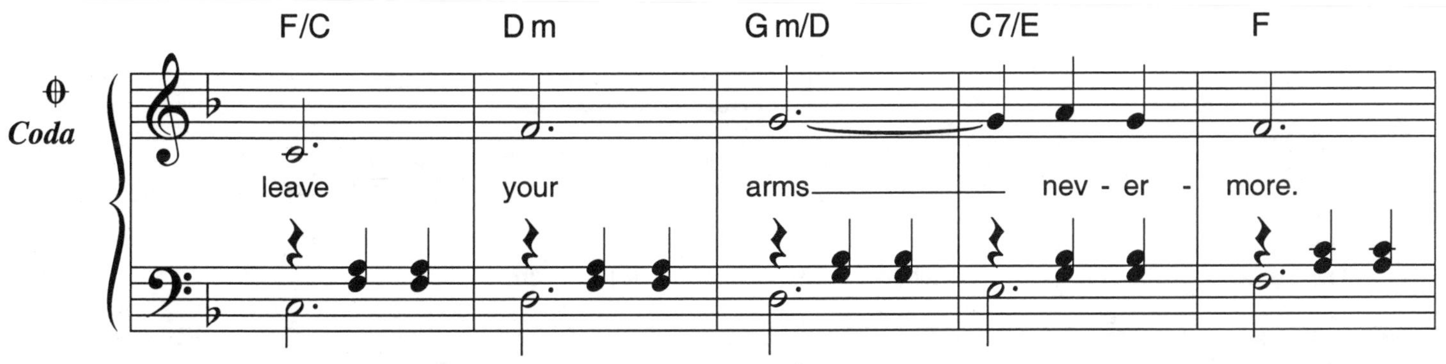
𝄌 Coda
F/C
Dm
Gm/D
C7/E
F
leave
your
arms
nev - er -
more.

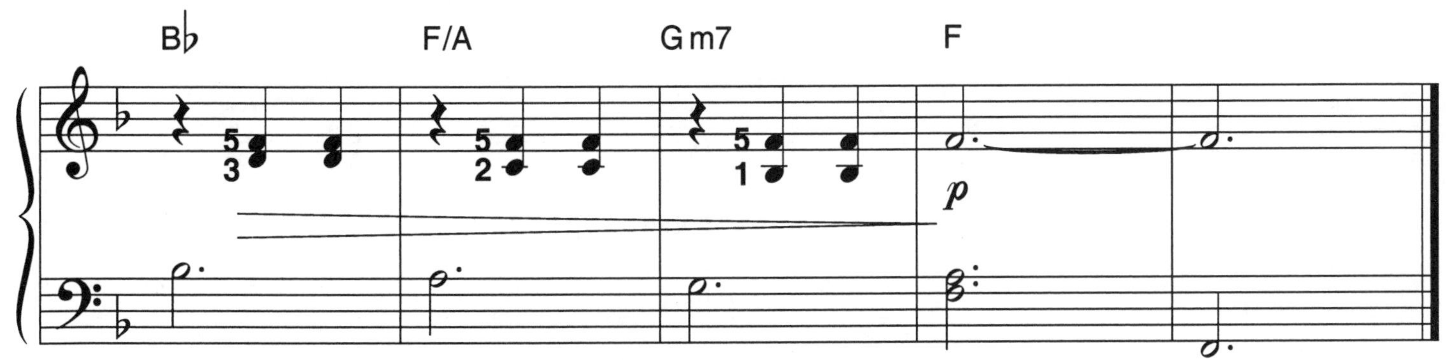
B♭
F/A
Gm7
F
p

Bidin' My Time

From the Broadway Musicals *Girl Crazy* and *Crazy For You*

Words by IRA GERSHWIN
Music by GEORGE GERSHWIN
Arranged by Richard Bradley

C
E7
A
E7
A7
5
1
5
1
time.
Next
year,
next
year,
1
5
2
1

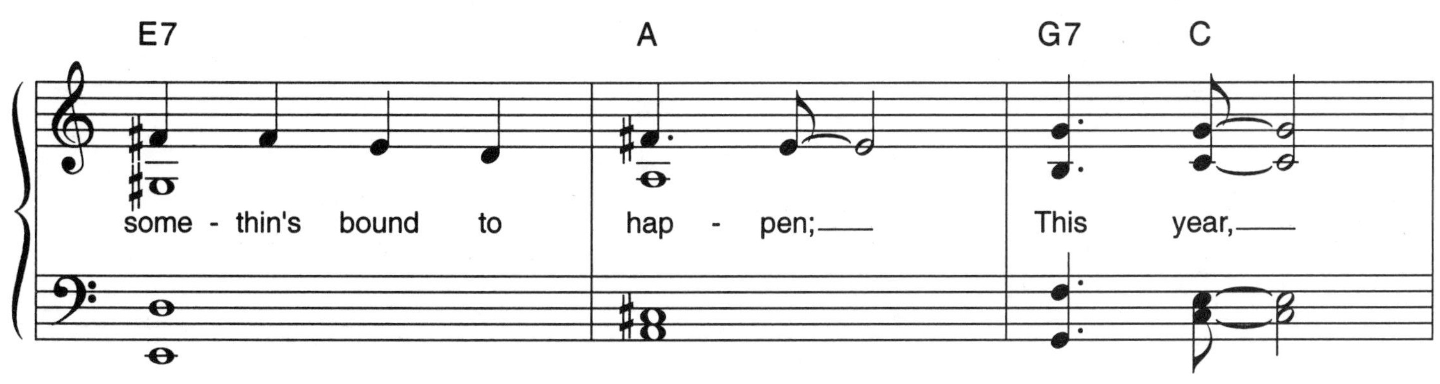
E7
A
G7
C
some - thin's bound to
hap - pen;
This
year,

G7
C
Am7
D7
G7
this
year,
I'll just keep on
nap - pin', and

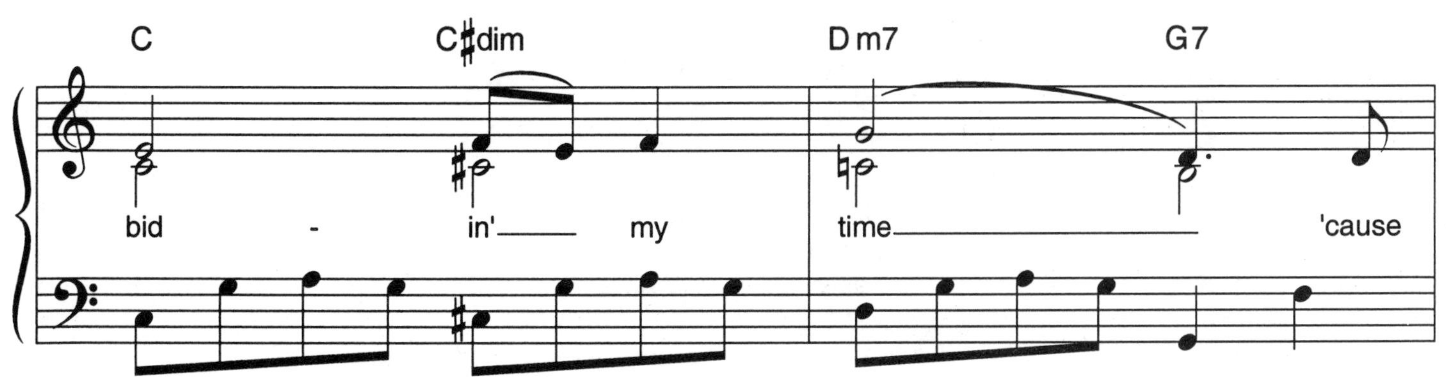
C
C♯dim
Dm7
G7
bid - in' my
time
'cause

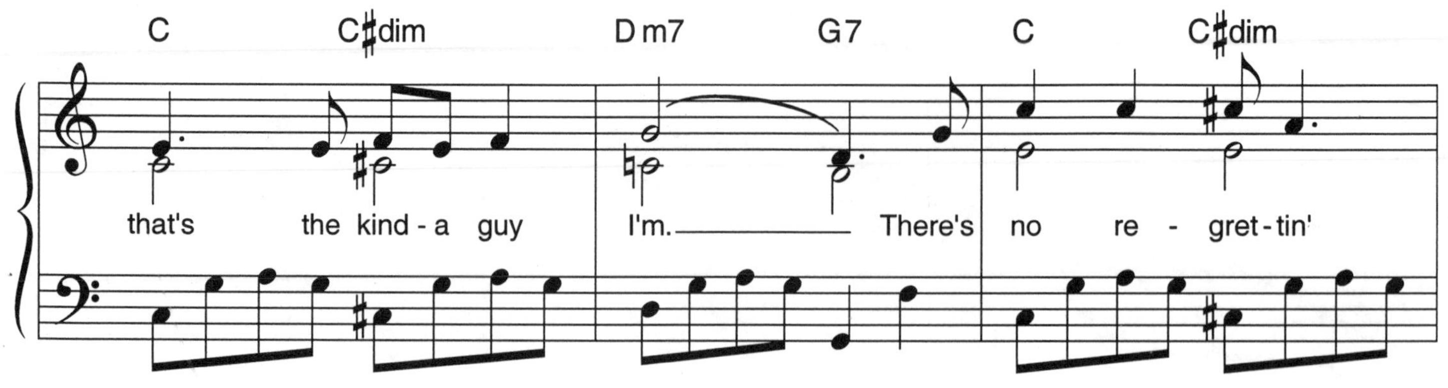

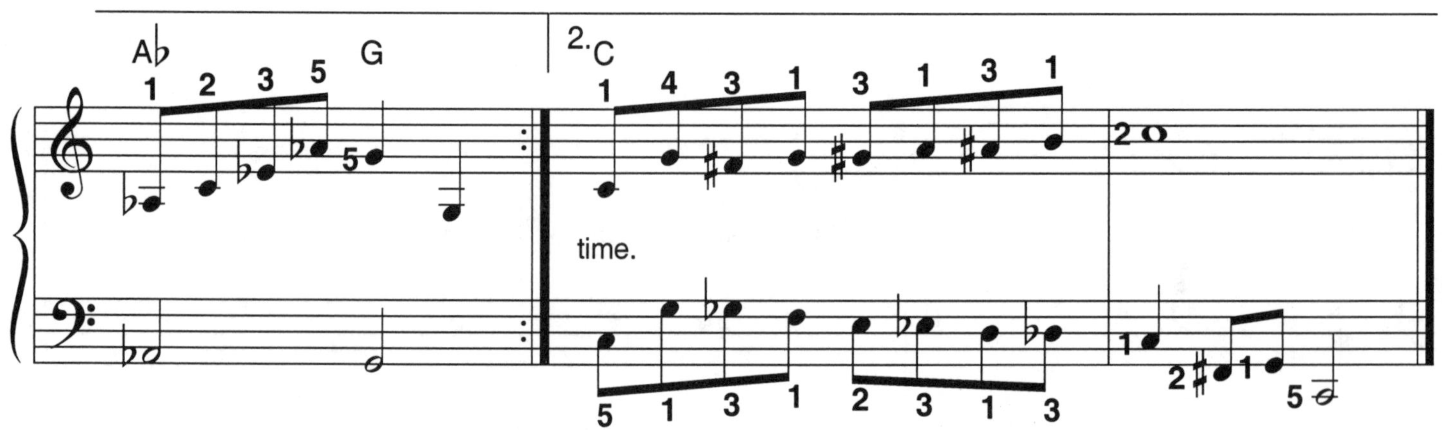

Verse 2:
I'm bidin' my time;
'Cause that's the kinda guy I'm,
Beginin' on a Monday
Right through Sunday,
Bidin' my time.
Give me, give me,
Glass that's bright and twinkles.
Let me, let me,
Dream like Rip Van Winkle.
He bided his time
And that's the winkle guy I'm,
Chasin' way flies,
How the day flies,
Bidin' my time.